TUTTLE
NEW DICTIONARY OF
LOANWORDS IN JAPANESE

TUTTLE

NEW DICTIONARY OF

LOANWORDS IN JAPANESE

TUTTLE
NEW DICTIONARY OF
LOANWORDS IN JAPANESE

A User's Guide
to Gairaigo

TAEKO KAMIYA

CHARLES E. TUTTLE COMPANY
Rutland, Vermont & Tokyo, Japan

Published by the Charles E. Tuttle Company, Inc.
of Rutland, Vermont & Tokyo, Japan
with editorial offices at
2-6 Suido 1-chome, Bunkyo-ku, Tokyo 112

© 1994 by Charles E. Tuttle Publishing Co., Inc.

LCC Card No. 93-60036
ISBN 0-8048-1888-6

First edition, 1994

Printed in Japan

Contents

Foreword vii

Pronunciation ix

Reading Loanwords in Katakana.. xv

Writing Loanwords in Katakana xx

Brief Grammar xxvi

Dictionary of Loanwords in Japanese 3

Place Names 376

Foreword

Thousands of words in the Japanese language today are loanwords, which are words derived from other languages. Whenever you read a Japanese newspaper or magazine, whenever you turn on the radio or television, whenever you listen to a political speech or conversation on a train, you will be surprised at how widely these words are used. In fact, they have become an integral part of the Japanese language.

Japanese loanwords are derived not only from English but also from other European languages, such as Portuguese, Dutch, French, German, and so on. The oldest are from Portuguese, e.g. *tabako* (tobacco), and from Dutch, e.g. *garasu* (glass). From the nineteenth century on, especially after World War II, countless English words have been adopted in Japanese, e.g. *rajio* (radio), *meritto* (merit), *ōtomēshon* (automation), etc. From Italian came words related to music and food, e.g. *opera* (opera) and *makaroni* (macaroni). From French came words related to art and fashion such as *dessan* (*dessin*/rough sketch) and *ōtokuchūru* (*haute couture*/high-class dress shop), and from German words related to medical science such as *karute* (*Karte*/medical record) and *horumon* (*Hormon*/hormone).

This dictionary contains approximately 4,000 loanwords strictly selected for their frequency—those used most often in daily conversation, radio, television, newspapers, and magazines. Ample example phrases and sentences are provided to help convey the meanings and usages of the words. It is my wish that this dictionary will be found useful by those studying Japanese.

—Taeko Kamiya

Pronunciation

Vowels

The Japanese language has five vowels: a, i, u, e, and o. They are pronounced as follows:

a	as in father
i	as in eat
u	as in rule
e	as in met
o	as in toe

Long vowels are pronounced twice as long as regular vowels and are marked $\bar{a}$, *ii*, $\bar{u}$, $\bar{e}$ and $\bar{o}$. In this book the double i is used instead of a macron because it is easier to read.

Consonants

Most Japanese consonants are pronounced like English consonants. One exception is the Japanese r, which sounds like a combination of the English r and l. Another exception is the Japanese f, which sounds like something between an f and an h.

The consonants are pronounced as follows:

b	as in bed
d	as in duck
f	between food and hood
g	as in get
h	as in hen
j	as in joy
k	as in kit
m	as in man
n	as in night (but note exception below)
p	as in pen
r	between right and light
s	as in sit
t	as in top
z	as in zoo
ch	as in choice
sh	as in English (unstressed)
ts	as in cats

Semi-vowels

There are two semi-vowels: w and y. They are pronounced as follows:

w	as in waft
y	as in yard

Syllables

With the exception of the consonant n which can stand by itself, each syllable is made up of a single vowel, a consonant followed by a vowel, or a consonant followed by y or h and then a vowel. Each syllable is clearly pronounced; thus *haru* (spring) is ha-ru; *kyaku* (customer) is kya-ku; and *shumi* (hobby) is shu-mi.

In spoken Japanese, however, the i and u vowel sounds are often weak. This is especially true between two voiceless consonants (k, s, t, p, or h). Thus words like *suki* (like) and *shita* (under) may sound like "ski" and "shta." Also, u at the end of a word following a voiceless consonant is weakened, as in *desu* (am, is, are), which may sound like "des."

When the single consonant n is followed by a vowel or a y within a word, an apostrophe is used to show the break between syllables. Examples of this include *kin'en* (nonsmoking), *man'in* (no vacancy), and *hon'ya* (bookstore).

Double consonants (kk, pp, ss, tt) are pronounced as follows: *Nikkō* (Nikko) like the k sound in "bookkeeper"; *rippa* (fine) like the p sound in "top part"; *issō* (more) like the s sound in "less sleep"; *kitte* (stamp) like the t sound in "hot tub." The double consonants dd, ff, gg and jj are used only in loanwords such as *beddo* (bed), *sutaffu* (staff), *biggu* (big), and *bajji* (badge), and are pronounced similarly to the original pronunciation.

The following is a table showing all Japanese sounds, including those used only in loanwords. They are represented both in Roman letters and katakana, a Japanese script which is primarily used for writing loanwords and foreign names.

Japanese Sounds

ア	イ	ウ	エ	オ
a	i	u	e	o
カ	キ	ク	ケ	コ
ka	ki	ku	ke	ko
クァ	クィ		クェ	クォ
kwa*	kwi*		kwe*	kwo*

ガ	ギ	グ	ゲ	ゴ
ga	gi	gu	ge	go
グァ				
gwa*				
サ	シ	ス	セ	ソ
sa	shi	su	se	so
ザ	ジ	ズ	ゼ	ゾ
za	ji	zu	ze	zo
タ	チ	ツ	テ	ト
ta	chi	tsu	te	to
ツァ	ティ	トゥ	ツェ	ツォ
tsa*	ti*	tu*	tse*	tso*
	ツィ	テュ		
	tsi*	tyu*		
ダ	ディ	ドゥ	デ	ド
da	di*	du*	de	do
		デュ		
		dyu*		
ナ	ニ	ヌ	ネ	ノ
na	ni	nu	ne	no
ハ	ヒ	フ	ヘ	ホ
ha	hi	fu	he	ho
バ	ビ	ブ	ベ	ボ
ba	bi	bu	be	bo
ヴァ	ヴィ	ヴ	ヴェ	ヴォ
va*	vi*	vu*	ve*	vo*

パ pa	ピ pi	プ pu	ペ pe	ポ po
ファ fa*	フィ fi*		フェ fe*	フォ fo*
マ ma	ミ mi	ム mu	メ me	モ mo
ヤ ya		ユ yu	イェ ye*	ヨ yo
ラ ra	リ ri	ル ru	レ re	ロ ro
ワ wa	ウィ wi*		ウェ we*	ウォ wo*
ン n				
キャ kya		キュ kyu		キョ kyo
ギャ gya		ギュ gyu		ギョ gyo
シャ sha		シュ shu	シェ she*	ショ sho
ジャ ja		ジュ ju	ジェ je*	ジョ jo
チャ cha		チュ chu	チェ che*	チョ cho
ニャ nya		ニュ nyu		ニョ nyo

ヒャ	ヒュ	ヒョ
hya	hyu	hyo
	フュ	
	fyu*	
ビャ	ビュ	ビョ
bya	byu	byo
	ヴュ	
	vyu*	
ピャ	ピュ	ピョ
pya	pyu	pyo
ミャ	ミュ	ミョ
mya	myu	myo
リャ	リュ	リョ
rya	ryu	ryo

Sounds used only in loanwords.

Reading Loanwords in Katakana

Forming Loanwords

Most loanwords are pronounced similarly to their pronunciation in the original language. However, some adjustments have to be made to conform to the Japanese phonetic system.

1. Vowels are inserted between consonants and added to the end of foreign words when the final sound is any consonant except n.

present	*purezento*	プレゼント
Christmas	*Kurisumasu*	クリスマス
strike	*sutoraiki*	ストライキ
calcium	*karushiumu*	カルシウム

2. The l, th, v, q, and x sounds which do not exist in Japanese are expressed as follows:

light	*raito*	ライト
hotel	*hoteru*	ホテル
thermometer	*sāmomētā*	サーモメーター
Smith	*Sumisu*	スミス

violin	*baiorin*	バイオリン
live	*raibu*	ライブ
quiz	*kuizu*	クイズ
quick	*kuikku*	クイック
taxi	*takushii*	タクシー
mixer	*mikisā*	ミキサー

3. The hard and soft c are expressed as either s or k.

cent	*sento*	セント
census	*sensasu*	センサス
cake	*kēki*	ケーキ
cookie	*kukkii*	クッキー

4. The er, or, and ar sounds are expressed as long vowel sounds. In some cases, however, the long sound can be omitted.

computer	*konpyūtā* or	コンピューター or
	konpyūta	コンピュータ
elevator	*erebētā* or	エレベーター or
	erebēta	エレベータ
guitar	*gitā*	ギター

5. A vowel sometimes can be used instead of a long sound mark.

ballet	*barē* or *baree*	バレー, バレエ
bowling	*bōringu* or	ボーリング or
	bouringu	ボウリング

6. The u, n, and double consonants are sometimes omitted, even when they exist in the original language.

sandwich	*sandoitchi* (not *sandouitchi*)	サンドイッチ
switch	*suitchi* (not *suuitchi*)	スイッチ
inning	*iningu* (not *inningu*)	イニング
accessory	*akusesarii* (not *akusessari*)	アクセサリー
Philippines	*Firipin* (not *Firippin*)	フィリピン

Some special sounds have been developed that are actually non-traditional ways of pronouncing loanwords. In most cases these are closer in pronunciation to the language they came from (see the asterisks (*) in the table pages xi–xiv). The following are some examples. Note that the traditional pronunciations are also used as alternatives for some words.

jet	*jetto*	ジェット
condition	*kondishon*	コンディション
check	*chekku*	チェック
finger	*fingā*	フィンガー
sheriff	*sherifu*	シェリフ
tea	*tii*	ティー
Mozart	*Mōtsaruto*	モーツァルト
artist	*āchisuto* or *ātisuto*	アーチスト or アーティスト
education	*ejukēshon* or *edyukēshon*	エジュケーション or エデュケーション
Hindu	*Hinzū* or *Hindū*	ヒンズー or ヒンドゥー

veil	*bēru* or *vēru*	ベール or ヴェール
interview	*intabyū* or	インタビュー or
	intavyū	インタヴュー
fan	*fuan* or *fan*	フアン or ファン
fuse	*hyūzu* or *fyūzu*	ヒューズ or
		フューズ
two	*tsū* or *tū*	ツー or トゥー
yes	*iesu* or *yesu*	イエス or イェス

There are a great number of Japanized loanwords that have been changed in some way during the adoption process. Long loanwords are often abbreviated. Some words are used differently from their original meanings, and others have been coined in Japan.

1) Abbreviated loanwords

building	*biru*	ビル
television	*terebi*	テレビ
apartment	*apāto*	アパート
platform	*hōmu*	ホーム
mass communi- cation/media	*masu komi*	マスコミ
general strike	*zene suto*	ゼネスト
arbeit	*baito*	バイト
(German: part-time job)		

2) Loanwords with altered meanings or those coined in Japan

imēji appu	イメージ アップ	image up (to improve one's image)
manē biru	マネービル	money building (making money)
rifōmu	リフォーム	reform (to alter

xviii

		clothes or a house)
iijiiōdā	イージー オーダー	easy order (semi-custom-made)
gōruden awā	ゴールデンア ワー	golden hour (prime time)
nō meiku	ノーメイク	no make (without make-up)

...

Writing Loanwords in Katakana

1. The sound she can be written シェ or セ.

shaker	*shēkā*	シェーカー
milk shake	*miruku sēki*	ミルクセーキ
shepherd	*shepādo* or *sepādo*	シェパード or セパード

Je can be written ジェ or ゼ.

jelly	*jerii* or *zerii*	ジェリー or ゼリー

2. Ti can be written ティ, チ, or テ.

party	*pātii*	パーティー
etiquette	*echiketto*	エチケット
sticker	*sutekkā*	ステッカー
steam	*suchiimu* or *sutiimu*	スチーム or スティーム

Di can be written ジ, デ, or ディ.

dilemma	*jirenma* or	ジレンマ or
	direnma	ディレンマ
design	*dezain*	デザイン

3. Fa, fi, fe and fo can be written ハ, ファ or フア, ヒ, フィ or フイ, ヘ, フェ, or フエ, and ホ, フォ or フオ.

Eiffel	*Efferu*	エッフェル
cellophane	*serohan* or	セロハン or
	serofan	セロファン
morphine	*moruhine* or	モルヒネ or
	morufin	モルフィン
telephone	*terehon* or	テレホン or
	terefon	テレフォン
film	*firumu* or	フィルム or
	fuirumu	フイルム
felt	*feruto* or	フェルト or
	fueruto	フエルト

4. Dyu or ju can be written ジュ or デュ.

education	*ejukēshon* or	エジュケーション
	edyukēshon	or エデュケーショ
		ン

5. Ye can be written イエ or イェ.

yes	*iesu* or *yesu*	イエス or イェス
yellow	*ierō* or *yerō*	イエロー or イェ
		ロー

6. Wi, we and wo can be written ウイ or ウィ, ウ エ or ウェ, and ウオ or ウォ.

week	*uiiku* or *wiiku*	ウイーク or ウィーク
waiter	*uētā* or *weitā*	ウエーター or ウェイター
water	*uōtā* or *wōtā*	ウオーター or ウォーター

7. Kwa, kwi, kwe and kwo can be written カ, クア or クァ, キ, クイ or クィ, ケ, クエ or クェ, and コ, クオ or クォ.

quartet	*karutetto,* *kuarutetto,* or *kwarutetto*	カルテット or クアルテット or クァルテット
quintet	*kuintetto* or *kwintetto*	クインテット or クィンテット
question	*kuesuchon* or *kwesuchon*	クエスチョン or クェスチョン
quarterly	*kuōtarii* or *kwōtarii*	クオータリー or クォータリー
quilting	*kirutingu*	キルティング
equal	*ikōru*	イコール

8. Gwa can be written グア, グァ or ガ.

| Guatemala | *Guatemara,* *Gwatemara,* or *Gatemara* | グアテマラ or グァテマラ or ガテマラ |

9. Tsi can be written チ or ツィ.

| Tiziano | *Tichiāno* or *Titsiāno* | ティチアーノ or ティツィアーノ |

10. Tu can be written ツ, トゥ or ト.

| two | *tsū* or *tū* | ツー or トゥー |
| Khachaturyan | *Hachatorian* or *Hachaturian* | ハチャトリアン or ハチャトゥリアン |

Du can be written ズ, ドゥ or ド.

| Hindu | *Hinzū* or *Hindū* | ヒンズー or ヒンドゥー |
| Debussy | *Dobyusshii* | ドビュッシー |

11. Va, vi, vu, ve and vo can be written バ or ヴァ, ビ or ヴィ, ブ or ヴ, ベ or ヴェ, and ボ or ヴォ.

violin	*baiorin* or *vaiorin*	バイオリン or ヴァイオリン
vivid	*bibiddo* or *vividdo*	ビビッド or ヴィヴィッド
eve	*ibu* or *ivu*	イブ or イヴ
veil	*bēru* or *vēru*	ベール or ヴェール
vocal	*bōkaru* or *vōkaru*	ボーカル or ヴォーカル

12. Tyu can be written チュ or テュ.

| tuba | *chūba* or *tyūba* | チューバ or テューバ |

13. Fyu can be written ヒュ or フュ.

| fuse | *hyūzu* or *fyūzu* | ヒューズ or フューズ |

14. Vyu can be written ビュ or ヴュ.

interview	*intabyū* or	インタビュー or
	intavyū	インタヴュー

15. N can be written ン or ム.

symposium	*shinpojiumu* or	シンポジウム or
	shimupojiumu	シムポジウム
comeback	*kamubakku* or	カムバック or
	kanbakku	カンバック

16. Long sounds can be written by adding another vowel.

computer	*konpyūtā* or	コンピューター or
	konpyūta	コンピュータ

17. A after i can be written ア or ヤ.

dial	*daiaru* or	ダイアル or
	daiyaru	ダイヤル
campfire	*kyanpufaiyā* or	キャンプファイ
	kyanpufaia	ヤー or キャンプ
		ファイア

18. The word ending (i)um can be written (イ)ウム or (イ)ニューム.

aluminum	*aruminiumu* or	アルミニウム or
	aruminyūmu	アルミニューム

19. The sound made by the letter X can be written キサ or クサ, キシ or クシ, キス or クス, and キソ or クソ.

exercise	*ekisasaizu* or *ekusasaizu*	エキササイズ or エクササイズ
exhibition	*ekishibishon,* *ekijibishon* or *ekujibishon*	エキシビション or エキジビション or エクジビション
text	*tekisuto* or *tekusuto*	テキスト or テクスト
exotic	*ekizochikku* or *ekuzotikku*	エキゾチック or エクゾティック

Brief Grammar

The following points illustrate some of the important differences between Japanese and English grammar. You are advised to read them in order to familiarize yourself with some of the special features of the Japanese language.

1. In a Japanese sentence the topic or subject comes at the beginning and the verb at the end.

   • *Watashi wa hon o yomimasu.*
     I read a book.

2. Japanese nouns and pronouns generally do not have plural forms. The noun *kodomo* can mean child or children, and the pronoun *kore* can mean this one or these ones. When necessary to be specific, plural suffixes are added.

   kodomo-tachi (children), *kore-ra* (these ones)

   Plural suffixes are added to some personal pronouns.
   watashi-tachi (we), *kare-ra* (they)

3. Articles such as the, a, or an, are not used with nouns. The English words some and any are not translated in many cases.

4. The subject of a sentence, especially if it is a personal pronoun, is often omitted if the meaning of the sentence is clear.

   • *Ikimasu.*
     I'm going.

5. Japanese verbs have two tenses: present and perfective. The same verb form is used for both the present and future tenses.

   • *Kanojo wa ikimasu.*
     She goes/will go.

   The same perfective form is used for the past, present perfect, and past perfect tenses.

   • *Kare wa arukimashita.*
     He walked/has walked/had walked.

6. Japanese verbs have various polite and plain styles. The polite styles are used in everyday conversation among adults who are not close friends. The plain styles are used among friends, family, and others with whom one is familiar. A plain style is also used in writing in newspapers, magazines, and books.

   • *Kare wa Kyōto e ikimashita.*
     He went to Kyoto. (polite)

- *Kare wa Kyōto e itta.*
  He went to Kyoto. (plain)

7. Japanese verbs may be divided into three groups: regular, semi-regular, and irregular. These can be recognized as follows:

a. The dictionary (infinitive) form of a regular verb has a consonant +*u* ending.

   iku (go), *yomu* (read)

b. The dictionary form of a semi-regular verb has a vowel (*e* or *i*) +ru ending (-*eru* or -*iru*).

   taberu (eat), *miru* (see, watch, look)

   Note that some verbs ending with -*eru*/-*iru* are regular verbs.

   kaeru (return), *hashiru* (run)

c. There are only two irregular verbs. Their dictionary forms are *kuru* (come) and *suru* (do). The verb *suru* often combines with nouns to make new verbs.

   shigoto (work)   *shigoto suru* (to work)

   When a foreign loanword is made into a verb in a Japanese sentence, *suru* is added to the infinitive or in some cases the gerund form.

   drive   *doraibu suru* (to drive)
   control   *kontorōru suru* (to control)

parking   *pākingu suru* (to park)
cashing   *kyasshingu suru* (to cash)

8. Auxiliary verbs are added to main verbs to give them additional meanings.

• *Kare wa kuru kamo shiremasen.*
  He might come.
• *Kanojo wa kuruma o kawanakereba narimasen.*
  She must buy a car.

9. The Japanese copulas *desu* (polite form) and *da* (plain form) are equivalent to the English am, is, or are. Both are used as follows:

a. The A is B construction

• *Kare wa isha desu/da.*
  He is a doctor.

b. As a substitute for other verbs

• *Watashi wa tenpura desu/da.*
  I'll have tenpura.

10. Nouns are modified as follows:

a. Placing an adjective (*i*-adjective) before it

• *akai hana*
  a red flower

b. Placing an adjectival noun + *na* (*na*-adjective) before it

- *shizuka na heya*
  a quiet room

c. Placing a common (or proper) noun + *no* before it
  - *Eigo no zasshi*
    an English magazine

  Note that when foreign loanwords are used as adjectives in Japanese, *na* is added in most cases.

  - *modan na biru*
    a modern building
  - *romanchikku na sutōrii*
    a romantic story

d. Placing a modifying clause (relative clause) before it

  - *Hon o yonde iru hito wa Tanaka-san desu.*
    The person who is reading a book is Mr. Tanaka.

11. *I*-adjectives function like verbs when used as predicates. They conjugate as follows (plain form):

- *Kēki wa amai.*
  The cake is sweet.
- *Kēki wa amakunai.*
  The cake isn't sweet.
- *Kēki wa amakatta.*
  The cake was sweet.
- *Kēki wa amakunakatta.*
  The cake wasn't sweet.

For a more polite form, add *desu* after the above adjectives.

- *Kēki wa amai desu.*
  The cake is sweet.

12. In subordinate and relative clauses, predicates (verbs and adjectives) are usually in the plain form.

- *Ame ga furu kara, ikimasen.*
  Because it rains, I won't go.
- *Chikai kara, arukimasu.*
  Because it's near, I'll walk.
- *Kinō kita hito wa Yamada-san desu.*
  The person who came yesterday is Miss Yamada.

13. Three important Japanese particles have no equivalents in English.

   Wa follows the topic of a sentence. The topic is what the sentence is about, and *wa* can be thought of as functioning like the English expression "as for."

- *Honda-san wa sensei desu.*
  Mr. Honda is a teacher. (As for Mr. Honda, he is a teacher.)

   Although the subject of a sentence is most frequently topicalized, any part of the sentence can become a topic.

- *Kyō wa Sumisu-san ga kimasu.*
  Mr. Smith comes today. (As for today, Mr. Smith comes.)

   Ga follows the subject of a sentence.

- *Asoko ni hoteru ga arimasu.*
  There is a hotel over there.

O follows the direct object of a verb.

- *Ringo o tabemashita.*
  I ate an apple.

14. Other Japanese particles have functions similar to English prepositions, but they are placed after the words they modify.

- *Ōsaka e kaerimasu.*
  I'll return to Osaka.
- *Kare to hanashimashita.*
  I talked with him.

15. Three sentence-ending particles function as follows:

Ka turns a sentence into a question.

- *Are wa depāto desu ka?*
  Is that a department store?

Ne is used as a request for confirmation, implying "isn't it?" or "aren't you?"

- *Oishii desu ne.*
  It's delicious, isn't it?

Yo is used for emphasis, meaning "I assure you."

- *Kanojo wa kitto kimasu yo.*
  She will surely come.

16. The honorific prefixes *go-* and *o-* are used with nouns, adjectives, and verbs as follows. Generally, *go-* is used with

words of Chinese origin, while *o-* is for those of Japanese origin and some loanwords.

- *go-kekkon* (your marriage)
- *o-shigoto* (your work)
- *o-utsukushii* (beautiful)
- *go-shōtai suru* (to invite)
- *go-chisō* (feast)
- *o-denwa* (telephone)
- *o-biiru* (beer)
- *o-kōto* (your coat)
- *o-somatsu na* (plain)
- *o-hanashi suru* (to talk)

TUTTLE
NEW DICTIONARY OF
LOANWORDS IN JAPANESE

USAGE NOTES

1. Except for words borrowed from English, the origin of each word is indicated as follows:

    abekku アベック [French: *avec*] young unmarried couple

    arubaito アルバイト [German: *Arbeit*] part-time job

    Coined words derived from English are indicated as Japanese Usage.

    mai kā マイ カー [Japanese Usage: my car] one's own car

2. Verbs are listed in their dictionary (infinitive) forms by adding suru (する) to each foreign verb. Verbs that are formed by adding suru to nouns appear after the noun entries as ~**suru**.

    arenji suru アレンジする to arrange

    konbain suru コンバインする to combine

    adobaisu アドバイス advice; ~**suru** する to give advice, to advise

3. All the example sentences are given in a polite style of Japanese spoken widely among adults.

A

ABC *see* **ē-bii-shii**

AI *see* **ē-ai**

A kurasu Aクラス *see* **ē-kurasu**

AV *see* **ōdio bijuaru**

aban-gēru アバンゲール [French: *avant-guerre*] prewar,
prewar generation
  • *Kare-ra wa aban-gēru da kara, kangae ga furui desu.*
    Being from the prewar generation, their ideas are old.

aban-gyarudo アバンギャルド [French: *avant-garde*]
innovative
  • *Aban-gyarudo no bijutsu ni wa tsuite ikemasen.*
    I can't accept avant-garde art.

abekku アベック [French: *avec*] young unmarried couple
  • *Ano kōen wa itsumo abekku de ippai desu.*
    That park is always full of young couples.

aberēji アベレージ average
  • *Bouringu no aberēji wa ikutsu desu ka?*
    What's your bowling average?
  • *Kare no seiseki wa aberēji desu.*
    His grades are average.

abiritii アビリティー ability
  • *Kare wa kono purojekuto o suru abiritii ga arimasu.*
    He has the ability to do this project.

abunōmaru アブノーマル abnormal
  • *abunōmaru na tenkō*
    abnormal weather
  • *Saikin no sōba wa sukoshi abunōmaru desu.*
    Recently the market has been somewhat abnormal.

abusutorakuto アブストラクト abstract
  • *Kono gyararii ni wa abusutorakuto na e ga ōi desu.*

In this gallery there are many abstract paintings.

• *Sono kāten wa abusutorakuto na moyō ga arimasu.*
That curtain has abstract patterns.

• *Kono heya ni wa abusutorakuto na moyō no e ga niaimasu ne.*
A painting with an abstract pattern would go well in this room.

ācherii アーチェリー archery
• *Ācherii wa popyurā na supōtsu desu.*
Archery is a popular sport.

āchi アーチ arch
• *Shōtengai no iriguchi ni āchi ga tatte imasu.*
An arch stands at the entrance of the shopping street.

achiibumento アチーブメント achievement
• *Kagakusha to shite no kare no achiibumento wa mezamashii desu.*
His achievements as a scientist are remarkable.

achiibumento tesuto アチーブメント・テスト achievement test
• *Maitsuki achiibumento tesuto ga okonawaremasu.*
Achievement tests are administered every month.

āchisuto アーチスト artist
• *Koko wa āchisuto no machi to shite shirarete imasu.*
This place is known as an artists' town.

adaputā アダプター adaptor
• *Den'atsu o chōsetsu suru noni, kono adaputā o tsukaimasu.*
This adaptor is used to adjust the voltage.

adaputēshon アダプテーション adaptation
• *Kono eiga wa "Ria Ō" no adaputēshon desu.*
This movie is an adaptation of *King Lear*.

adaruto アダルト adult, grown-up
• *adaruto kankaku no doresu*

tasteful, sophisticated dress
- *Ano mise wa adaruto na mūdo de wakamono o hikitsukete imasu.*

That store's mature atmosphere attracts young people.

adikuto アディクト addict, devout fan
- *Watashi no musuko wa yakyū adikuto desu.*

My son is a baseball addict.

ado アド advertisement
- *Kono zasshi wa ado bakari desu ne.*

This magazine has nothing but advertisements, doesn't it?

adobaisu アドバイス advice; **~suru** する to give advice, advise
- *Shigoto no koto de, tomodachi ni adobaisu o ukemashita.*

I received advice concerning my job from a friend.
- *Kare ni benkyō no shikata o adobaisu shimashita.*

I advised him on how to study.

adobaizā アドバイザー advisor, consultant (in the beauty business)
- *Kanojo wa adobaizā to shite, keshōhin uriba de hataraite imasu.*

She is working at the beauty counter as a consultant.

adobantēji アドバンテージ advantage
- *Kono shōhin no adobantēji wa nan desu ka?*

What are the advantages of this product?

adobarūn アドバルーン [Japanese Usage: ad balloon] advertisement balloon
- *Biru no ue ni adobarūn ga agatte imasu.*

An advertisement balloon is up above the building.

adobenchā アドベンチャー adventure
- *Arashi no naka no funade wa jitsu ni adobenchā deshita.*

Sailing in the storm was truly an adventure.

adoresu アドレス address
- *Tanaka-san no adoresu o shitte imasu ka?*

Do you know Mr. Tanaka's address?

adoribu アドリブ ad lib
- *Kare wa adoribu ga totemo jōzu desu.*
  He is very good at ad-libbing.

Afurika アフリカ Africa
- *Kore wa Afurika no janguru ni sumu yachō desu.*
  This bird lives in the jungles of Africa.

afutā faibu アフター・ファイブ after five (o'clock), after work
- *Kare-ra wa yoku aftā faibu ni bā e ikimasu.*
  They often go to a bar after work.
- *Saikin no wakamono no afutā faibu no sugoshikata o chōsa shite kudasai.*
  Investigate what young people do after work nowadays.

aftā-kea アフター・ケア after-care, after-sales service
- *Ano kutsuya wa shūri nado no aftā-kea mo yatte kuremasu.*
  That shoe store gives you after-sales service such as repairing, etc.
- *Taiingo mo aftā-kea ga hitsuyō desu.*
  You still need after-care even after being released from the hospital.

afutanūn アフタヌーン afternoon
- *Shizuka na afutanūn desu.*
  It's a quiet afternoon.
- *Terebi no afutanūn shō wa imadani nezuyoi ninki ga arimasu.*
  Afternoon television shows still enjoy strong popularity.

afutānūn アフターヌーン *see* **afutanūn**

afutā sābisu アフターサービス [Japanese Usage: after service] after-sales service
- *Hotondo no mise ga o-kyaku ni afutā sābisu o shite imasu.*
  Almost all stores offer after-sales service to their customers.

agensuto アゲンスト against, anti-
- *Amerika de wa bōeki masatsu ga Nihon ni agensuto no kanjō o hikiokoshimashita.*
  In America, trade friction has stirred up anti-Japanese sentiments.
- *Agensuto desu kara 150 yādo wa arimasu ne.*
  Since the wind is blowing against you, it'll be 150 yards (to the green).

aguresshibu アグレッシブ aggressive
- *Kare no aguresshibu na taido wa tanin no kanjō o kizutsukemasu.*
  His aggressive attitude hurts others' feelings.

aguriimento アグリーメント agreement
- *Giron no kekka, aguriimento ni tasshimashita.*
  As a result of discussing the matter, we reached an agreement.

ai banku アイバンク eye bank
- *Kare wa ai banku ni me o kifu suru tsumori desu.*
  He intends to donate his eyes to an eye bank.

aiborii アイボリー ivory
- *Indo kara no o-miyage ni aiborii no saiku o itadakimashita.*
  He brought me an object crafted in ivory when he came back from India.

aidentitii アイデンティティー identity
- *Kare wa jibun no aidentitii o ushinatte imasu.*
  He has lost his identity.

aidea アイデア *see* **aidia**

aidia アイディア idea
- *Ii aidia desu ga, riarisutikku de wa arimasen ne.*
  It's a good idea, but it's not realistic, is it?

aidiaru アイディアル ideal
- *Kanojo wa aidiaru na kankyō ni sodachimashita.*

She was brought up in an ideal environment.

ai-dii kādo アイ・ディー・カード IDカード ID card
- *Soko ni hairu no ni ai-dii kādo ga irimasu ka?*
  Do you need an ID card to get in there?

aidoru アイドル idol
- *Ano kawaii kashu wa Nihon no jūdai no aidoru ni narimashita.*
  That cute singer has become a teen idol in Japan.

ai-kyatchā アイ・キャッチャー eye-catcher
- *Kono hon no hyōshi wa ai-kyatchā desu ne.*
  The cover of this book is an eye-catcher, isn't it?
- *Ai-kyatchā to shite kono irasuto o tsukatte wa dō de shō?*
  How about using this illustration as an attention-getter?

ai-kyū アイ・キュー IQ IQ, intelligence quotient
- *Kono ko no ai-kyū wa amari takaku arimasen.*
  This child's IQ isn't very high.

Ainu アイヌ Ainu
- *Ainu mura o tazuneta koto ga arimasu ka?*
  Have you ever been to an Ainu village?

airon アイロン iron (for pressing clothes)
- *Kono sukāto ni airon o kakete kudasai.*
  Please iron this skirt.

aironii アイロニー irony
- *Kare no sakuhin wa aironii ni michite imasu.*
  His writings are filled with irony.

aironikaru アイロニカル ironical
- *Kare wa sono shōsetsu ni tsuite aironikaru na hihyō o kakimashita.*
  He wrote an ironic review of that novel.

ai shadō アイシャドー eye shadow
- *Ai shadō ga kanojo o betsujin no yō ni misete imasu.*
  The eye shadow makes her look like a different person.

aisu アイス ice

- *Motto aisu o irete kudasai.*
  Please put in some more ice.

aisubān ＡＣＸｏ［ [German: *Eisbahn*] frozen road
- *Aisubān ni natta michi o osoru osoru arukimashita.*
  I walked cautiously on the frozen road.

aisu kōhii アイスコーヒー iced coffee
- *Aisu kōhii wa ii kaori ga shimasen.*
  Iced coffee doesn't have a nice aroma.

aisu kuriimu アイスクリーム ice cream
- *Aisu kuriimu no tsukurikata o oshiete kudasai.*
  Please teach me how to make ice cream.

aisu tii アイスティー iced tea
- *Kōra yori aisu tii no hō ga suki desu.*
  I like iced tea better than cola.

aitemu アイテム item
- *Shōrūmu ni iroiro na aitemu ga narabete arimasu.*
  Various items are on display in the showroom.

ajasuto suru アジャストする to adjust
- *Kono kanjō wa ato de ajasuto shimasu.*
  I'll adjust this bill later.

aji アジ *see* **ajitēshon**

Ajia アジア Asia
- *Ōbeijin no Ajia e no kanshin ga takamarimashita.*
  Westerners' interest in Asia has grown.

ajitēshon アジテーション agitation, provocation
- *Kare no enzetsu wa isshu no ajitēshon desu ne.*
  His speech seems rather provocative, doesn't it?

ajitētā アジテーター agitator
- *Shūkai ni ajitētā ga ōzei kita sō desu.*
  I hear that many agitators came to the meeting.

ajito アジト agitating point, hiding place
- *Koko wa kageki-ha no ajito deshita.*
  This place was a hiding place for extremists.

akademii アカデミー academy
- *Seki-kyōju wa Japan Akademii no menbā desu.*
  Professor Seki is a member of the Japan Academy.

akademikku アカデミック academic
- *Akademikku na hon wa zuibun nedan ga takai desu ne.*
  Academic books are very expensive, aren't they?

ākēdo アーケード arcade
- *Eki mae no ākēdo de kaimono o shimasu.*
  I shop at the arcade in front of the station.

akōdeon アコーデオン accordion
- *Kare wa gakusei no koro akōdeon o hiite imashita.*
  He played the accordion when he was a student.

akōdeon doa アコーデオン・ドア accordion door
- *Akōdeon doa de heya o shikirimasu.*
  The room is partitioned by an accordion door.

akurobachikku アクロバチック acrobatic
- *Kodomo-tachi ga sukēto bōdo de akurobachikku ni subette imasu.*
  Children are skateboarding acrobatically.

akurobatikku アクロバティック *see* **akurobachikku**

akurobatto アクロバット acrobat, acrobatics
- *Kare no akurobatto wa kurōto hadashi desu.*
  His acrobatics could put a professional to shame.
- *kōkūshō de no akurobatto hikō*
  acrobatic flying in an airshow

akusento アクセント accent
- *Kanojo no kuro no doresu wa akai tsubaki ga akusento ni natte imasu.*
  A red camellia adds an accent to her black dress.
- *Kono futatsu no kotoba wa superu wa onaji desu ga akusento ga chigaimasu.*
  These two words have the same spelling but different accented syllables.

akuseru アクセル accelerator
- *Kare wa handoru o nigitta mama inemuri o shite, ashi wa akuseru o funda mama deshita.*
  He fell asleep at the wheel but kept his foot on the accelerator.

akusesarii アクセサリー accessory
- *mingeichō no akusesarii*
  a folkcraft accessory

akusesu アクセス access; **~suru** する to approach
- *Kūkō e no akusesu o kaizen shinakereba narimasen.*
  Access into the airport must be improved.
- *Nihon no keizaikai wa akusesu shigatai desu.*
  The Japanese financial world is difficult to approach.

akushidento アクシデント accident
- *Tetsudō no akushidento de hito ga ōzei shinimashita.*
  Many people died in the railroad accident.
- *Chottoshita akushidento de kare wa shutsujō dekinaku narimashita.*
  He could not participate because of a slight accident.

akushon アクション action
- *akushon no sukunai eiga*
  a movie with little action
- *Kono mondai ni tsuite, keisatsu wa sugu akushon o okosu deshō.*
  The police will take action on this problem immediately.

akutā アクター actor
- *Kare wa chiisai gekidan no akutā deshita.*
  He was an actor in a small troupe.

akutibitii アクティビティー activity
- *Kanojo wa gakkō no akutibitii ni takusan sanka shite imasu.*
  She takes part in many school activities.

akutibu アクティブ active

- *Chichi wa rōjin desu ga mada akutibu desu.*
  My father is an old man but still active.

akutoresu アクトレス actress

- *Musume wa akutoresu ni naritagatte imasu.*
  My daughter wishes to become an actress.

ama アマ *see* **amachua**

amachua アマチュア amateur

- *Kare wa rippa na chōkokuka desu ga shashin wa amachua desu.*
  He is a fine sculptor but an amateur photographer.

amefuto アメフト [Japanese Usage] American football

- *amefuto yōgo no hon*
  a book of American football terminology

amenitii アメニティー amenity (of place, climate)

- *Hikōki no sōon ga shūhen no amenitii o sokonete imasu.*
  The roar of aircraft is disrupting the amenity of the neighborhood.

ameragu アメラグ [Japanese Usage: Ame(rican) Rug(by)] *see* **amefuto**

Amerika アメリカ (the United States of) America, the U.S.A.

- *Ane wa Amerika ni sunde imasu.*
  My older sister lives in U.S.A.

Amerikanaizu suru アメリカナイズする to Americanize

- *Amerikanaizu sareta wakamono ga ōi desu.*
  There are many young people who are Americanized.

Amerikan futtobōru アメリカンフットボール *see* **amefuto**

Amerikan (kōhii) アメリカン(コーヒー) [Japanese Usage: American coffee] weak coffee

- *Amerikan o kudasai.*
  Weak coffee, please.

amyūzumento アミューズメント amusement

- *Shimin no tame ni amyūzumento shisetsu ga hitsuyō desu.*
  Amusement facilities are necessary for city people.

anākizumu アナーキズム anarchism
- *Kare wa ichiji anākizumu ni tsuyoi kanshin o shimeshite imashita.*
  He had a strong interest in anarchism at one time.

anakuronizumu アナクロニズム anachronism
- *Kanryō no anokuronizumu ga sono kuni no hatten o samatageta no desu.*
  The anachronisms of bureaucrats prevented the nation from developing.

anarishisu アナリシス analysis
- *Dēta no anarishisu o shita kekka o happyō shimasu.*
  We'll do an analysis of the data and then announce the results.

anaunsā アナウンサー announcer
- *Kare wa supōtsu tantō no anaunsā desu.*
  He's the head sports announcer.

anaunsu suru アナウンスする to announce
- *Ressha no enchaku ga anaunsu saremashita.*
  The late arrival of the train was announced.

anbaransu アンバランス imbalance
- *Ryōkoku no bōeki no anbaransu ga mondai ni natte imasu.*
  The trade imbalance between the two countries has become a problem.

anbishasu アンビシャス ambitious
- *Kore wa naka naka anbishasu na kikaku desu ne.*
  This is quite an ambitious plan, isn't it?

anchi アンチ anti-
- *anchi-Kyojin*
  hate the Giants

anchiiku アンチーク antique
- *Kare wa anchiiku o atsumete imasu.*

He is collecting antiques.

andārain アンダーライン underline
• *Taisetsu na kotoba ni andārain o hikimashita.*
I underlined the important words.

andāuea アンダーウエア underwear
• *Andāuea wa atsukatte orimasen.*
We don't carry underwear.

anekudōto アネクドート anecdote
• *Sensei ni omoshiroi anekudōto o kikimashita.*
We heard an interesting anecdote from our teacher.

anfea アンフェア unfair
• *Anfea na jōyaku wa haki saremashita.*
The unfair treaty was annulled.

Anguro-sakuson アングロ・サクソン Anglo-Saxon
• *Igirisu-jin wa Anguro-sakuson no chi o hiite imasu.*
English people are related to Anglo-Saxons by blood.

anguru アングル angle
• *Kono anguru kara shashin o totte kudasai.*
Please take a picture from this angle.

anibāsarii アニバーサリー anniversary
• *Kyō wa ryōshin no kekkon nijūgo nen no anibāsarii desu.*
Today is my parents' 25th wedding anniversary.

anime アニメ animation, cartoons
• *Kodomo-tachi wa anime ni muchū ni natte imasu.*
Children are crazy about animation.

animēshon アニメーション *see* **anime**

ankā アンカー anchor (the last runner or swimmer on a team)
• *Kare wa rirē de ankā o tsutomemashita.*
He ran anchor position on the relay.

ankāman アンカーマン anchorman
• *Ankāman wa jiko no genba kara ripōto shimashita.*
The anchorman reported from the scene of the accident.

ankēto アンケート [French: *enquête*] questionnaire
- *shōhizei ni tsuite no ankēto*
  a questionnaire about consumption tax

ankōru アンコール [French] encore
- *Kankyaku wa nando mo ankōru o motomemashita.*
  The audience asked for many encores.

anonimasu アノニマス anonymous
- *Kono shi no sakusha wa anonimasu desu.*
  The author of this poem is anonymous.

anorakku アノラック anorak, parka
- *Anorakku o kite sukii o shimasu.*
  We ski wearing parkas.

anrakkii アンラッキー unlucky
- *Oshii shiai ni makete anrakkii na hi deshita.*
  I just barely lost the game; it was an unlucky day.

ansanburu アンサンブル ensemble, choir, chorus, coordinated clothes
- *Furansu kara shōnen no ansanburu ga kimashita.*
  A boys' ensemble came from France.
- *Supōtii na ansanburu ga hoshii desu.*
  I want a sporty outfit.

antena アンテナ antenna
- *Ie no yane ni terebi no antena ga miemasu.*
  You can see the television antenna on the roof of the house.

antiiku アンティーク *see* **anchiiku**

apāto アパート apartment house
- *Kare wa kōgai no apāto ni sunde imasu.*
  He lives in an apartment house in the suburbs.

apetaizā アペタイザー appetizer
- *Apetaizā ni nani o dashimashō ka?*
  What shall we serve for an appetizer?

apiaransu アピアランス appearance, looks
- *Kare wa apiaransu wa ii desu ga naiyō ga arimasen.*

He looks good but he lacks substance.

apiiru suru アピールする to appeal
  • *Kono dezain wa wakai josei ni apiiru suru to omoimasu.*
  I think that this design will appeal to young women.

apo アポ *see* **apointomento**

apointo アポイント *see* **apointomento**

apointomento アポイントメント appointment
  • *Gogo Tanaka-san to no apointomento ga arimasu.*
  I have an appointment with Mr. Tanaka in the afternoon.

appiiru suru アッピールする *see* **apiiru suru**

appurike アップリケ appliqué
  • *Epuron ni ahiru no appurike ga shite arimasu.*
  The apron has a duck appliqué on it.

appuru アップル apple
  • *Washinton-shū wa appuru no sanchi desu.*
  Washington is an apple-growing state.

appuru pai アップルパイ apple pie
  • *Uchi no niwa no ringo de appuru pai o tsukurimashita.*
  I made an apple pie with the apples from our garden.

appu suru アップする to go up
  • *Shinbun no kōdokuryō wa mainen appu shite imasu.*
  The newspaper subscription rate goes up every year.

appu-tsū-dēto アップ・ツー・デート up-to-date
  • *Kaisha ni totte wa, appu-tsū-dēto na jōhō ga totemo taisetsu desu.*
  As far as the company is concerned, up-to-date information is most crucial.

appu-tū-dēto アップ・トゥー・デート *see* **appu-tsū-dēto**

apure-gēru アプレゲール [French: *après-guerre*] postwar, postwar generation
  • *Apure-gēru wa kachikan ga chigaimasu.*
  The postwar generation has a different sense of values.

apurikēshon アプリケーション application

- *Sono hatsumei wa apurikēshon no han'i ga hiroi desu.*
  That invention has a wide range of applications.

apurōchi アプローチ approach; **~suru** する to approach
- *Kenkyū ni taisuru kare no apurōchi wa yuniiku desu.*
  His approach to doing research is unique.
- *Mazu daikigyō ni apurōchi suru tsumori desu.*
  We intend to approach large corporations first.

Arabia アラビア Arabia
- *Arabia no sabaku o kyaraban ga tōrimasu.*
  Caravans pass through the Arabian desert.

Arabu アラブ Arab
- *Arabu no sekai*
  the Arab world

a-ra-karuto アラカルト à la carte
- *Resutoran de itsumo a-ra-karuto o chūmon shimasu.*
  I always order à la carte in restaurants.

arāmu アラーム alarm
- *Doa ni chikazuku to, arāmu ga narimasu.*
  When you approach the door, the alarm goes off.

aregorii アレゴリー allegory
- *Kono shōsetsu wa furui aregorii ni motozuite kakarete imasu.*
  This novel is based on an old allegory.

arenji suru アレンジする to arrange
- *Enkai wa watashi ga arenji shimashō.*
  I'll arrange the banquet.

arerugii アレルギー allergy
- *Watashi wa mainen haru ni naru to kafun no arerugii desu.*
  Every year when spring arrives I'm allergic to pollen.

aria アリア aria
- *Kanojo wa "Chōchō Fujin" kara utsukushii aria o utaimashita.*

She sang beautiful arias from *Madame Butterfly*.

aribai アリバイ alibi
- *Kare wa aribai ga nai node, utagawarete imasu.*
He is a suspect, because he has no alibi.

ariina アリーナ arena
- *Sono geki wa ariina de kōen saremasu.*
The play will be presented at the arena.

aroha shatsu アロハシャツ [Japanese Usage: aloha shirt]
Hawaiian shirt
- *aroha shatsu no tsūrisuto no ikkō*
a party of tourists wearing Hawaiian shirts

arubaito アルバイト [German: *Arbeit*] part-time job
- *Kanojo wa kamera-shoppu de arubaito o shite imasu.*
She is working part-time at a camera shop.

arubamu アルバム album
- *Kono arubamu o mite mo ii desu ka?*
May I look at this album?

arufabetto アルファベット alphabet
- *Kono kotoba o arufabetto-jun ni narabete kudasai.*
Please put these words in alphabetical order.

arukari アルカリ alkali
- *Arukari wa san o chūwa shimasu.*
Alkali will neutralize an acid.

arukōru アルコール alcohol
- *Arukōru ni izon suru wakamono ga fuete kimashita.*
The number of young people who depend on alcohol has
increased.

arumaito アルマイト [Japanese Usage: alumite] aluminum
oxide
- *arumaito no nabe*
a pan made of aluminum oxide

arumi アルミ *see* **aruminiumu**

arumihoiru アルミホイル aluminum foil

- *Nokori wa arumihoiru de tsutsunde oite kudasai.*
  Please wrap up the leftovers in aluminum foil.

aruminiumu アルミニウム　aluminum

- *aruminiumu no katei yōhin*
  aluminum household goods

aruminyūmu アルミニューム　*see* **aruminiumu**

Arupusu アルプス　Alps

- *Kono natsu ni Nihon-Arupusu ni noboru yotei desu.*
  We plan to climb the Japan Alps this summer.

asainmento アサインメント　assignment

- *Kare wa tokubetsu no asainmento de Sauji-arabia e haken saremashita.*
  He was sent to Saudi Arabia on a special assignment.

asetēto アセテート　acetate

- *Asetēto no burausu wa shiwa ni narimasen.*
  An acetate blouse will not crease.

ashisutanto アシスタント　assistant

- *Isogashii node, ashisutanto o yatoitai desu.*
  I'm so busy, I want to hire an assistant.

ashisutanto direkutā アシスタント・ディレクター
assistant director

- *Kanojo wa yūnō na ashisutanto direkutā desu.*
  She is a capable assistant director.

asoshiēshon アソシエーション　association

- *Mōjin o enjo shite iru asoshiēshon ni hairimashita.*
  I joined an association that helps blind people.

asoshiēto purodyūsā アソシエート・プロデューサー
associate producer

- *Kannu eigasai ni wa asoshiēto purodyūsā ga shusseki shimasu.*
  The associate producer will attend the Cannes Film Festival.

asufaruto アスファルト　asphalt

- *asufaruto no michi*
  an asphalt road

asupirin アスピリン aspirin
- *Asupirin o nijō nomimashita.*
  I took two aspirins.

atakku suru アタックする to attack, take on (something difficult)
- *Tozan tai wa Himaraya o atakku shimashita.*
  The mountaineering expedition took on the Himalayas.

atasshe アタッシェ [French] attaché
- *Buraun-san wa atasshe to shite Amerika taishikan ni tsutomete imasu.*
  Mr. Brown works for the American embassy as an attaché.

atasshe kēsu アタッシェケース [French: *attaché*] briefcase, attaché case
- *Kūkō de otoko ga watashi no atasshe kēsu o tsukande nigemashita.*
  In the ariport a man grabbed my attaché case and ran.

atatchimento アタッチメント attachment
- *Kono kikai no atatchimento wa betsuuri desu.*
  The attachments to this machine are sold separately.

ātifisharu furawā アーティフィシャル・フラワー artificial flower
- *Kore wa ātifisharu furawā ni miemasen.*
  This doesn't look like an artificial flower.

ātisutikku アーティスティック artistic
- *Kono e wa ātisutikku na kachi ga arimasu.*
  This painting shows artistic merit.

ātisuto アーティスト *see* **āchisuto**

āto アート art
- *Āto wa jinsei o yutaka ni shimasu.*
  Art enriches our lives.

āto dezainā アートデザイナー art designer

- *Kanojo wa āto dezainā ni naru tame ni benkyō shite imasu.*
  She is studying to become an art designer.

atomikku ēji アトミック・エージ atomic age
- *Watashi-tachi wa atomikku ēji ni ikite imasu.*
  We live in the atomic age.

atomu アトム atom
- *Arayuru buttai wa atomu kara natte imasu.*
  All physical objects consist of atoms.

atopii アトピー atopy, atopic
- *Musuko wa atopii-sei taishitsu desu.*
  My son has an atopic constitution.

atorakushon アトラクション attraction, something that draws a crowd
- *Bōnenkai de iroiro na atorakushon ga arimashita.*
  There were many different attractions at the year-end party.

atorakutibu アトラクティブ attractive, handsome
- *atorakutibu na sūtsu*
  a handsome suit

ato-hōmu アト・ホーム *see* **atto-hōmu**

ato-randamu アト・ランダム at random
- *Kore was ato-randamu ni seron chōsa shita kekka desu.*
  These are the results from a public poll conducted at random.

atorie アトリエ [French: *atelier*] studio
- *Pari de yūmei na gaka no atorie o hōmon shimashita.*
  I visited a famous painter's studio in Paris.

atoriumu アトリウム atrium
- *Atoriumu ga kono manshon no kyojū-sha no ikoi no ba ni natte imasu.*
  The atrium serves as a place of relaxation for those living in this condominium.

āto shiatā アートシアター art theater

• *Watashi no ie no chikaku ni aru āto shiatā ni wa kireina ārudeko-chō no robii ga arimasu.*
The art theater near my house has a beautiful art deco lobby.

atto-hōmu アット・ホーム at home, relaxed
• *Kaigi wa atto-hōmu na fun'iki de okonawaremashita.*
The conference was held in a relaxed atmosphere.

atto-randamu アット・ランダム *see* **ato-randamu**

auto アウト out
• *Ano bōru wa sen o koemashita. Auto desu.*
That ball crossed the line. It's out.

autobakku アウトバック outback
• *Ōsutoraria no autobakku o miru tabi ni sanka shimashita.*
I joined the trip to see the Australian outback.

autodoa raifu アウトドア・ライフ [Japanese Usage: outdoor life] the outdoors
• *Kyanpu ni itte autodoa raifu o tanoshimimashita.*
We went camping and enjoyed the great outdoors.

autoputto アウトプット output; **~suru** する to output
• *Kono kōjō no ichinichi no autoputto wa sanzen-dai desu.*
This plant's daily output is 3,000 units.
• *Konpyūtā kara jōhō o autoputto shimasu.*
I output information from the computer.

autorain アウトライン outline
• *Shinseihin no autorain ga dekimashita.*
The outlines of the new products have been completed.

autorō アウトロー outlaw
• *Kare wa shakai kara tsuihō sareta autorō desu.*
He is an outlaw who was expelled from society.

autorukku アウトルック outlook
• *Rainen no keizai no autorukku wa yosasō desu.*
The outlook for next year's economy seems to be good.

autosaidā アウトサイダー outsider
• *Autosaidā wa iinkai ni shusseki dekimasen.*

Outsiders can't attend the committee meeting.

autosaido アウトサイド outside

- *Kono jōhō wa autosaido ni morasanaide kudasai.*
  Please don't disclose this information to the outside.
- *Watashi wa autosaido no ningen dakara nantomo iemasen.*
  I'm an outsider here so I can't say anything.

B

BGM *see* **bii-jii-emu**

bā バー bar

- *Yūbe Ginza no bā de nomimashita.*
  We drank in a bar in the Ginza last night.

bābekyū バーベキュー barbecue

- *Pikunikku de bābekyū o shimashita.*
  We had a barbecue picnic.

baburu バブル bubble

- *Keizai no baburu genshō de kabuka ga rankōge shimashita.*
  The bubble phenomenon in the economy caused violent ups and downs in stock prices.

bacherā バチェラー bachelor

- *Tanshin funin de kare wa bacherā seikatsu o tanoshinde iru yō desu.*
  He seems to be enjoying a bachelor's lifestyle since being transferred without his family.
- *Oji wa mada bacherā desu.*
  My uncle is still a bachelor.

bādo-uotchingu バードウオッチング bird-watching

- *Asa hayaku mori de bādo-uotchingu o shimasu.*
  I go bird-watching in the woods early in the morning.

bādo-wotchingu バードウォッチング *see* **bādo-uotchingu**

bagēji kurēmu バゲージクレーム baggage claim
* *Kaban wa bagēji kurēmu de uketotte kudasai.*
  Please collect your suitcases at the baggage claim.

bāgen バーゲン bargain, sale
* *Kono sētā wa bāgen de kaimashita.*
  I bought this sweater at a sale.
* *Depāto de mikkakan bāgen ga arimasu.*
  There will be a three-day sale at the department store.

bāgen-sēru バーゲンセール *see* **bāgen**

baggu バッグ bag
* *Kono baggu wa kaimono ni benri desu.*
  This bag is convenient for shopping.

baiburēshon バイブレーション vibration
* *Denki massāji no baiburēshon ga kimochi ii desu yo.*
  Electromassage vibrations make you feel good.

baiburu バイブル Bible, a book regarded as authoritative
* *Kono zasshi wa bijinesuman no baiburu desu.*
  This magazine is the businessman's bible.

baiingu pawā バイイングパワー buying power
* *Ōte kourigyō no baiingu pawā ga fukōhei na torihiki o hikiokosu kamo shiremasen.*
  The buying power of large retailers may bring about unfair transactions.

baikaruchuraru バイカルチュラル bicultural
* *Nihon de wa gaikoku kara modotta baikaruchuraru na kodomo ga fuete imasu.*
  The number of bicultural Japanese children who have returned to Japan from abroad is increasing.

baikingu バイキング [Japanese Usage: viking] smorgasbord
* *Baikingu ni itte, takusan tabemashita.*
  We went to a smorgasbord buffet and ate a lot.

baiku バイク motorbike, bike, motorcycle, bicycle

- *Baiku de shigoto ni ikimasu.*
  I go to work by motorcycle.

baiogurafii バイオグラフィー biography
- *Ima Mōtsaruto no baiogurafii o yonde imasu.*
  I am reading a biography of Mozart now.

baiorensu バイオレンス violence
- *Kono eiga wa hikakuteki baiorensu ga sukunai desu.*
  This movie has relatively little violence.

baioretto バイオレット violet (color)
- *Baioretto no doresu ga kanojo o issō utsukushiku misete
  imasu.*
  The violet dress makes her look all the more beautiful.

baiorin バイオリン violin
- *Baiorin no ressun wa isshūkan ni ichido desu.*
  I have violin lessons once a week.

baio-tekunorojii バイオテクノロジー biotechnology
- *Baio-tekunorojii no hattatsu de, seibutsugaku no kenkyū
  ga jitsuyōka sarete imasu.*
  Due to the development of biotechnology, some biological
  research is being put to practical use.

baipasu バイパス bypass (highway, surgery)
- *Baipasu no okage de, kōtsū jūtai ga kanwa saremashita.*
  Thanks to the bypass, traffic jams have been alleviated.

baipurēyā バイプレーヤー [Japanese Usage: byplayer]
supporting actor
- *Kare wa baipurēyā to shite wa ichiryū no haiyū desu.*
  He is a top-class supporting actor.

bairingaru バイリンガル bilingual
- *Kōkūgaisha wa bairingaru no jūgyōin o motomete imasu.*
  The airline wants bilingual employees.

baitaritii バイタリティー vitality
- *Kare no piano ensō wa baitaritii ni kakete imasu.*
  His piano performance lacks vitality.

baito バイト *see* **arubaito**

baiyā バイヤー buyer
- *Kokusai mihon'ichi ni baiyā ga zensekai kara atsumarimashita.*
Buyers from all over the world flocked to the international trade fair.

bajji バッジ badge
- *Kare wa sūtsu no eri ni kin'iro no bajji o tsukete imasu.*
He wears a gold badge on the lapel of his suit.

bājon バージョン version
- *Genkō no atarashii bājon o misete kudasai.*
Please show me the new version of the manuscript.
- *Dosu no bājon ga chigau tame, kono puroguramu wa kono kikai de wa ugokimasen.*
This program won't run in this machine because the version of DOS is different.

bakansu バカンス [French: *vacances*] vacation
- *Suisu de bakansu o tanoshimimashita.*
We enjoyed our vacation in Switzerland.

bakēshon バケーション vacation *see* **bakansu**
- *Kūkō wa bakēshon kara kaetta hitobito de konzatsu shite imasu.*
The airport is congested with people returning from their vacations.

baketsu バケツ bucket
- *Mizuumi kara baketsu de mizu o hakobimashita.*
We carried water by bucket from the lake.

bakku バック back, background, backer; **~suru** する to go backwards
- *Kare wa yūryoku na jitsugyōka o bakku ni motte imasu.*
He has an influential businessman as a backer.
- *Garēji kara kuruma o bakku shite dashimashita.*
I backed the car out of the garage.

bakku バック　*see* **baggu**

bakkuappu バックアップ　backup, support
- *Yūjin no bakkuappu ga nakereba, kare wa seikō shinakatta deshō.*
  Without his friends' support, he wouldn't have succeeded.

bakkubōn バックボーン　backbone
- *Kaisha no bakkubōn to naru no wa kinben na shain desu.*
  The backbone of a company is its hard-working employees.

bakkuguraundo バックグラウンド　background
- *Jiken no bakkuguraundo o shirabete mitai desu.*
  I want to look into the events leading up to the incident.

bakkugura(u)ndo myūjikku バックグラ(ウ)ンド・ミュージック　background music　*see* **bii-jii-emu**
- *Bakkuguraundo myūjikku ni utsukushii Shopan ga nagarete imasu.*
  Some beautiful Chopin is being played as background music.

bakku mirā バックミラー　[Japanese Usage: back mirror] rearview mirror
- *Bakku mirā ni pato-kā ga utsutte imasu.*
  A patrol car is reflected in the rearview mirror.

bakku netto バックネット　[Japanese Usage: back net] backstop
- *Fauru bōru ga bakku netto ni atatte ochimashita.*
  A foul ball hit the backstop and fell.

bakku nanbā バックナンバー　back number, back issue
- *Kono zasshi no bakku nanbā wa arimasu ka?*
  Do you have any back issues of this magazine?

bakkuru バックル　buckle
- *Kono bakkuru wa beruto no iro to umaku aimasen.*
  This buckle doesn't go well with the color of the belt.

bakuteria バクテリア　bacteria
- *Natsu wa bakuteria no hanshoku ga hayai desu.*

In summer, bacteria propagate quickly.

bakuteriya バクテリヤ *see* **bakuteria**

banana バナナ banana
- *Banana wa nettai chihō de saibai saremasu.*
  Bananas are grown in the tropics.

bando バンド band (music)
- *Kare wa kodomo-tachi no tame ni bando o tsukurimashita.*
  He formed a band for children.

bandomasutā バンドマスター band leader
- *Watashi-tachi no bandomasutā wa daigakusei desu.*
  Our band leader is a college student.

bangarō バンガロー bungalow
- *Hayashi no naka ni bangarō ga miemasu.*
  You can see bungalows in the grove.

banira バニラ vanilla
- *Aisu kuriimu no furēbā no naka de, banira ga ichiban ii desu.*
  Vanilla is the best of the ice cream flavors.

bankā バンカー banker
- *Kare wa hoshuteki na bankā da to iwarete imasu.*
  He is said to be a conservative banker.

banketto バンケット banquet
- *Banketto wa Purinsu Hoteru de hirakaremasu.*
  The banquet will be held at the Prince Hotel.

banku rōn バンクローン bank loan
- *Banku rōn de manshon o kaimashita.*
  I bought a condominium with a bank loan.

banpā バンパー bumper
- *Kuruma ga denchū ni butsukatte banpā ga magarimashita.*
  A car hit the utility pole and got its bumper twisted.

baraetii バラエティー variety
- *Ano mise wa shinamono no baraetii ga hōfu desu.*
  That store has many varieties of goods.

barakku バラック [Japanese Usage: barracks] decrepit
  buildings
  • *Somatsu na barakku ga naku natte rippa na ie ga
    tachimashita.*
    The shabby buildings were torn down and fine houses were
    built.
baransu バランス balance
  • *Kenkō ni wa baransu no toreta daietto ga hitsuyō desu.*
    A well-balanced diet is necessary for good health.
baransu shiito バランス・シート balance sheet
  • *Kabunushi sōkai ni baransu shiito o teishutsu shinakereba
    narimasen.*
    We must submit a balance sheet at the shareholders' meet-
    ing.
barādo バラード ballad
  • *Jojōteki na barādo wa kokoro ni nagusame o ataete
    kuremasu.*
    A lyrical ballad gives solace to the soul.
barē バレー *see* **barēbōru, baree**
barēbōru バレーボール volleyball
  • *Kaisha ni barēbōru no chiimu ga arimasu.*
    We have a volleyball team in our company.
baree バレエ ballet
  • *Kodomo ni baree o narawasetai desu.*
    I want to have my child learn ballet.
Barentain dē バレンタイン・デー Valentine's Day
  • *Barentain dē ni hātogata no chokorēto o moraimashita.*
    On Valentine's Day I received some heart-shaped choco-
    lates.
bareriina バレリーナ ballerina
  • *Bareriina wa utsukushii taikei o shite imasu.*
    The ballerina has a beautiful figure.
bareru バレル barrel

- *Kinō no Nyū-yōku shijō de sekiyu wa ichi bareru jūhachi doru o warimashita.*
  On the New York market yesterday, oil went below $18 per barrel.

bariēshon バリエーション variation
- *Engan no keshiki wa bariēshon ni tonde imasu.*
  The scenery along the coast is richly varied.

barikan バリカン [Japanese Usage: Barriquand] clippers (for hair)
- *Atarashii barikan de kami o mijikaku kariagete moraimashita.*
  I had my hair cut short with the new scissors.

barikēdo バリケード barricade
- *Machi no achikochi ni barikēdo ga kizukarete imasu.*
  Barricades have been set up all over the city.

bariton バリトン baritone
- *Kanojo wa kare no bariton no koe ni miryoku o kanjimashita.*
  She was charmed by his baritone voice.

bariumu バリウム barium
- *Bariumu o nonde i no kensa o ukemashita.*
  I drank barium and had my stomach examined.

barokku バロック baroque (music, architecture)
- *Kare wa barokku kenchiku o benkyō suru tame ni Yōroppa e ikimasu.*
  He will go to Europe to study baroque architecture.

baromētā バロメーター barometer
- *Kabuka wa keizai no baromētā to iwarete imasu.*
  Stock prices are said to be the barometer of an economy.

barukonii バルコニー balcony
- *Hoteru no barukonii kara gorufujō ga miemasu.*
  You can see a golf course from the hotel balcony.

basshingu バッシング bashing

- *Japan basshingu wa mezurashii koto de wa arimasen.*
  Japan bashing is not uncommon.

basu バス bass

- *Kare wa basu no opera kashu to shite yoku shirarete imasu.*
  He is well-known as a bass in opera.

basu バス bus

- *Basu ni noriokuremashita.*
  I missed the bus.

basu バス bath

- *basu tsuki no heya*
  a room with a bath

bāsudē バースデー birthday

- *Watashi no bāsudē wa Kurisumasu to kasanarimasu.*
  My birthday falls on Christmas.
- *Kare ni bāsudē purezento o moraimashita.*
  I got a birthday present from him.

basuketto バスケット basket *see* **basukettobōru**

- *Basuketto ni orenji ga takusan irete arimasu.*
  Many oranges are put in a basket.

basukettobōru バスケットボール basketball

- *Basukettobōru no senshu wa minna se ga takai desu.*
  All the basketball players are tall.

bāsu kontorōru バースコントロール birth control

- *Bāsu kontorōru wa seiji mondai ni narimashita.*
  Birth control has become a political issue.

basu tāminaru バス・ターミナル bus terminal

- *Basu tāminaru de hito ga ōzei matte imasu.*
  Many people are waiting at the bus terminal.

batā バター butter

- *Batā no kawari ni māgarin o tsukaimasu.*
  I use margarine in place of butter.

batafurai バタフライ butterfly, butterfly stroke

- *Batafurai de wa kanojo no migi ni deru suiei senshu wa imasen.*

  No swimmer surpasses her in the butterfly stroke.

baton バトン baton (for sports, music)

- *Kare wa nagai aida machi no burasu bando de baton o furutte imashita.*

  He wielded the baton for the town's brass band for a long time.

batontatchi suru バトンタッチする [Japanese Usage: to do a baton touch] to pass the torch

- *Kare wa kōnin ni baton tatchi o shite, intai shimashita.*

  He passed the torch to his successor and retired.

battā バッター batter

- *Ichiban battā wa Yamashita desu.*

  The first batter is Yamashita.

battā bokkusu バッターボックス batter's box

- *Kare ga battā bokkusu ni hairu to, daikansei ga agarimashita.*

  When he entered the batter's box, a great cry arose.

batterii バッテリー battery

- *Batterii ga agatta rashikute enjin ga kakarimasen.*

  I cannot start the engine. The battery seems to be dead.

- *Tokei no batterii ga kiremashita.*

  The battery for the watch is dead.

batto バット bat

- *Kare wa batto o kataku nigirimashita.*

  He held his bat firmly.

bea ベア *see* **bēsu appu**

bea shorudā ベアショルダー bare shoulder

- *Kanojo wa bea shorudā no doresu o kite imasu.*

  She is wearing an off-the-shoulder dress.

bebii ベビー baby

- *Nikagetsu mae ni otoko no bebii ga umaremashita.*

A baby boy was born two months ago.
* *bebii yōhin uriba*
a shop for baby supplies

beddo ベッド bed
* *Beddo no naka de hon o yomimasu.*
I read a book in bed.

beddo mēkingu suru ベッドメーキングする [Japanese
Usage: bed making] to make a bed
* *Asa okiru to sugu, beddo mēkingu o shimasu.*
As soon as I get up in the morning, I make my bed.

beddorūmu ベッドルーム bedroom
* *Beddorūmu wa minami ni menshite imasu.*
The bedroom faces south.

beddo taun ベッドタウン [Japanese Usage: bed town]
suburbs
* *Dai-toshi no shūhen ni beddo taun ga takusan dekite
imasu.*
Many suburbs are built on the outskirts of big cities.
* *Kono machi wa Tōkyō no beddo taun to shite sakaete
kimashita.*
This town has begun to thrive as a Tokyo bedroom community.

bei eria ベイ・エリア bay area
* *Shi wa bei eria no kaihatsu o keikaku shite imasu.*
The city is planning to develop the area around the bay.

bejitarian ベジタリアン vegetarian
* *Kare wa bejitarian da kara, metta ni soto de wa
tabemasen.*
Because he is a vegetarian, he seldom dines out.

bēju ベージュ beige
* *Yuka ni wa bēju no kāpetto ga shiite arimasu.*
There is a beige carpet on the floor.

bēkarii ベーカリー bakery

- *Bēkarii de yakitate no pan o kaimasu.*
  I buy freshly-baked bread at the bakery.

bēkon ベーコン bacon

- *Daidokoro kara bēkon no oishisō na nioi ga shite kimashita.*
  An appetizing smell of bacon came from the kitchen.

Bēkuraito ベークライト Bakelite

- *Kono utsuwa wa Bēkuraito de dekite imasu.*
  This container is made of Bakelite.

benchā bijinesu ベンチャー・ビジネス venture business

- *Kare wa kaisha o tochū taishoku shite benchā bijinesu o hajimemashita.*
  He retired from the company midway in his career and set up a venture business.

benchi ベンチ bench

- *Rōfūfu ga kōen no benchi ni koshikakete imasu.*
  An old couple is sitting on a bench in the park.

beranda ベランダ veranda

- *Hiatari no yoi beranda ni hachiue ga narabete arimasu.*
  Potted plants are placed in a row on the sunny veranda.

berē ベレー beret

- *Berē bō o kaburuto Suzuki-san wa Furansu-jin no yō ni miemasu.*
  Mr. Suzuki looks French when he wears a beret.

beru ベル bell

- *Kono beru o oshite kudasai.*
  Please ring this bell.

bēru ベール veil

- *Shinsō wa bēru ni tsutsumarete imasu.*
  The truth is shrouded in a veil.
- *shiroi bēru*
  a white veil

beruto ベルト belt

• *Chichi no hi no purezento ni beruto o kaimashita.*
  I bought a belt for a Father's Day present.

beruto konbeyā ベルト・コンベヤー conveyor belt

• *Seihin o hakobu no ni beruto konbeyā o tsukatte imasu.*
  Conveyor belts are used for carrying products.

bēshikku ベーシック basic

• *bēshikku na chishiki*
  basic knowledge

• *Kanojo wa bēshikku na doresu o kikonasu no ga jōzu
  desu.*
  She is good at making an ordinary dress look attractive.

bēsu ベース base, baseball base, military base

• *chingin no bēsu*
  the wage base

• *sanrui bēsu*
  third base

• *Kare wa Nihon ni aru Beigun no bēsu de hatarakimashita.*
  He worked at the U.S. military base in Japan.

bēsu appu ベースアップ [Japanese Usage: base up] pay
raise

• *Shain wa ōhaba na bēsu appu o kitai shite imasu.*
  The employees expect a big pay raise.

bēsubōru ベースボール baseball

• *Ima bēsubōru shiizun desu.*
  This is the baseball season.

besuto ベスト best

• *Besuto o tsukushimasu.*
  I'll do my best.

besuto serā ベストセラー best seller

• *Kono supōtsu kā wa kotoshi no besuto serā desu.*
  This sports car is this year's best seller.

besuto ten ベストテン [Japanese Usage: best ten] top ten

• *Kare no hon wa uresuji no besuto ten ni haitte imasu.*

His book made the best-selling top ten list.

betā ベター better
- *Motto betā na hōhō wa arimasen ka?*
  Isn't there a better way?

beteran ベテラン veteran
- *Kare wa nijūnen no keiken o motsu beteran kameraman desu.*
  He is an established cameraman with twenty years of experience.

betto ベット *see* **beddo**

bia hōru ビアホール *see* **biya hōru**

bibiddo ビビット vivid
- *Sono shōsetsu no bibiddo na seikaku byōsha ni kanshin shimashita.*
  I was impressed by the vivid character description in the novel.
- *Bibiddo na aka wa nekutai ni wa dame desu ne.*
  Vivid red is no good for a necktie, is it?

bideo ビデオ video
- *Shūmatsu ni tomodachi kara bideo o karimashita.*
  I borrowed a video from my friend for the weekend.

bideo raiburarii ビデオ・ライブラリー video library
- *Bideo raiburarii o katsuyō shite imasu.*
  I use the video library.

biggu ビッグ big
- *Kanojo wa biggu na yume o motte imasu.*
  She has big dreams.

biggu nyūsu ビッグニュース big news
- *Konshū wa biggu nyūsu ga jitsu ni ōkatta desu.*
  There really was a lot of big news this week.

biginā ビギナー beginner
- *Kore wa biginā muke no tekisuto desu.*
  This text is for beginners.

biichi ビーチ beach
- *Biichi made aruite gofun desu.*
  It takes five minutes to walk to the beach.

biifu ビーフ beef
- *Biifu no juyō ga herimashita.*
  The demand for beef has decreased.

bii-jii-emu ビージーエム BGM BGM, background
  music *see* **bakkuguraundo myūjikku**
- *Ano eiga no bii-jii-emu wa totemo kōkateki deshita.*
  The background music in the movie was very effective.

biiru ビール beer
- *Asoko ni biiru no kōjō ga arimasu.*
  There is a beer factory over there.

bijinesu ビジネス business
- *Daigaku de bijinesu o benkyō shimashita.*
  I studied business at college.
- *Bijinesu no hō wa dō desu ka?*
  How's business?

bijinesuman ビジネスマン businessman
- *Tōkyō ni wa gaikoku no bijinesuman ga ōzei imasu.*
  There are many foreign businessmen in Tokyo.

bijinesuraiku ビジネスライク businesslike
- *bijinesuraiku na taido*
  a businesslike attitude
- *Kanojo wa bijinesuraiku ni hanashimashita.*
  She spoke in a businesslike manner.

bijon ビジョン vision, imagination
- *Kare wa hai-teku sangyō no bijon ga arimasen.*
  He has no vision for high-technology industries.
- *Kono kaisha ni wa nijūisseiki e mukete no bijon ga arimasen.*
  This company lacks a vision for the 21st century.

biniiru ビニール vinyl, plastic

- *biniiru no kasa*
  a plastic umbrella

bippu ビップ [Japanese Usage] VIP, very important person

- *Samitto no tame ni kakkoku no bippu ga Tōkyō ni atsumatte imasu.*
  Each country's VIPs gather in Tokyo for the summit.

biriyādo ビリヤード billiards

- *Biriyādo de mata makemashita.*
  I lost at billiards again.

birōdo ビロード [Portuguese: *veludo*] velvet

- *Kore wa birōdo no yō ni kanshoku ga yawarakai desu ne.*
  This feels as soft as velvet, doesn't it?

biru ビル building

- *Ano biru wa sannen mae ni dekimashita.*
  That building was completed three years ago.

birudingu ビルディング *see* **biru**

bitā choko ビターチョコ bitter chocolate

- *Bitā choko ga suki desu.*
  I like bitter chocolate.

bitamin ビタミン vitamin

- *Orenji wa bitamin shii ni tonde imasu.*
  Oranges are rich in vitamin C.

biya hōru ビヤホール beer hall

- *Tokidoki natsu no yūgata o biya hōru de sugoshimasu.*
  Sometimes we spend summer evenings at a beer hall.

biza ビザ visa

- *Yūbin de biza o shinsei shimashita.*
  I applied for a visa by mail.
- *Amerika ni iku ni wa biza ga hitsuyō desu ka?*
  Do you need a visa to go to the U.S.?

bōdā ボーダー border, boundary

- *Ongaku ni bōdā wa arimasen.*
  Music has no boundaries.

bōdārain ボーダーライン borderline
* *Kare no seiseki wa bōdārain jō desu.*
  His grades are borderline.
bodē *see* **bodii**
bodēgādo ボデーガード *see* **bodiigādo**
bodii ボディー body
* *Kono kuruma wa bodii ga shikkari shite imasu.*
  The body of this car is built to last.
bodiibiru ボディービル bodybuilding
* *Kare wa bodiibiru ni isshōkenmei desu.*
  He is working really hard at bodybuilding.
bodiigādo ボディーガード bodyguard
* *Bodiigādo wa minna ansatsusha ni korosaremashita.*
  All the bodyguards were murdered by assassins.
bodii konshasu ボディーコンシャス *see* **bodikon**
bodikon ボディコン [Japanese Usage: body conscious] a
  fashion style emphasizing tight-fitting clothing
* *Bodikon wa karada ni pittari shita shiruetto o kyōchō suru
  fasshon desu.*
  'Body conscious' is a fashion style that emphasizes a slim
  figure.
bōdingu kādo ボーディングカード boarding card, boarding
  pass
* *Kūkō no chekku in kauntā de bōdingu kādo o moraimasu.*
  You will receive a boarding pass at the check-in counter at
  the airport.
bohemian ボヘミアン bohemian
* *Kare wa bohemian no yō ni kiraku ni kurashite imasu.*
  He lives like a bohemian, free from cares.
bōi ボーイ boy, porter
* *Hoteru de bōi ni nimotsu o hakonde moraimashita.*
  A porter carried my baggage for me at the hotel.
bōifurendo ボーイフレンド male friend, boyfriend

- *Kanojo ni wa bōifurendo ga ōzei imasu.*
  She has many male friends.
- *Kanojo wa bōifurendo to tabi ni demashita.*
  She went on a trip with her boyfriend.

boikotto ボイコット boycott
- *Kono seihin wa shōhisha ni boikotto sarete imasu.*
  This product is being boycotted by consumers.

boirā ボイラー boiler
- *Boirā ga koshō de o-yu ga arimasen.*
  The boiler is out of order and we have no hot water.

boiru suru ボイルする to boil
- *Tamago o gofun boiru shite kudasai.*
  Please boil the eggs for five minutes.

bōisshu ボーイッシュ boyish
- *Bōisshu na heasutairu de, kanojo wa wakaku miemasu.*
  With her boyish hairstyle, she looks younger than she is.

Bōi-sukauto ボーイスカウト Boy Scouts
- *Bōi-sukauto no taichō wa dare desu ka?*
  Who is the leader of the Boy Scouts?

bōkaru ボーカル vocal
- *Kanojo wa bōkaru o tantō shite imasu.*
  She handles the vocals.
- *Bōkaru wa piano hodo suki ja arimasen.*
  I don't care for vocals as much as piano.

bokkusu ボックス box
- *Kono bokkusu ni wa nani ga haitte imasu ka?*
  What is in this box?

bokusā ボクサー boxer
- *Kare wa gaikoku umare no bokusā desu.*
  He is a foreign-born boxer.

bokushingu ボクシング boxing
- *Josei no naka ni bokushingu no fan ga kanari iru sō desu.*
  I hear that there are quite a few female boxing fans.

bokyaburarii ボキャブラリー vocabulary
- *Buraun-san wa Nihongo no bokyaburarii ga hōfu desu.*
  Ms. Brown has a large Japanese vocabulary.

bōnasu ボーナス bonus
- *Gekkyū nikagetsu-bun no bōnasu o moraimashita.*
  We received a bonus equivalent to two months' pay.

borantia ボランティア volunteer
- *Borantia katsudō ga hiroku okonawarete imasu.*
  There is a wide range of volunteer activities being carried
  out.

bōringu ボーリング boring
- *Chishitsu chōsa no tame bōringu o shite imasu.*
  They are boring for a geological survey.

bōringu ボーリング *see* **bouringu**

bōru ボール ball
- *Bōru ga atama ni atarimashita.*
  A ball hit me on the head.

bōru-pen ボールペン ball-point pen
- *Kono bōru-pen wa yoku kakemasu.*
  This ball-point pen writes well.

borutēji ボルテージ voltage
- *Kare no taibei hihan wa borutēji ga agatte kimashita.*
  He turned up the voltage on his criticism against the U.S.
- *Borutēji wa kuni ni yotte chigaimasu.*
  Voltage differs depending on the country.

boryūmu ボリューム volume, big
- *Kono mise no tonkatsu wa oishikute boryūmu ga arimasu.*
  The pork cutlets at this restaurant are delicious and the
  servings are big.

bosu ボス boss
- *Bosu ga inai node, minna hayaku kaerimashita.*
  As the boss wasn't around, everybody went home early.

Bosuton baggu ボストンバッグ Boston bag, overnight bag

- *Bosuton baggu o sageta kankōkyaku no ichidan ga densha o orimashita.*

  A group of tourists carrying Boston bags got off the train.

botan ボタン button

- *Shatsu no botan ga toremashita.*

  One of my shirt buttons came off.

bōto ボート boat

- *Bōto de umizuri ni ikō to omotte imasu.*

  We are thinking of going ocean fishing in a boat.

botomu ボトム bottom, the lower half of one's body

- *Kotoshi no josei no ryūkō wa yōfuku no botomu ni pointo o oite imasu.*

  This year women's fashion emphasizes the lower half of a dress.

botomu appu ボトムアップ bottom-up management

- *Sono kaisha wa shita kara no iken o kyūshū suru botomu appu no yarikata o saiyō shite imasu.*

  That company has adopted a bottom-up management style, in which opinions of the lower-level employees are taken into account.

bōto piipuru ボートピープル boat people

- *Betonamu no bōto piipuru no kiji o yomimashita.*

  I read an article about the boat people from Vietnam.

bōto rēsu ボートレース boat race

- *Bōto rēsu wa akutenkō no tame chūshi ni narimashita.*

  The boat race was called off because of the bad weather.

botoru ボトル bottle

- *Tana ni yōshu no botoru ga narande imasu.*

  Bottles of foreign liquor are lined up on the shelf.

botoru kiipu ボトルキープ [Japanese Usage: bottle keep] a system in which one buys a bottle of liquor to be kept at a bar

- *Kare wa ikitsuke no bā ni uisukii no botoru kiipu o shite*

imasu.
He keeps his own bottle of whisky at his favorite bar.

botorunekku ボトルネック bottleneck *see* **nekku**
* *Shokkō wa asenburii-rain no botorunekku o kaiketsu shinai kagiri kōjōchō ni wa naremasen.*
  The foreman will never be plant manager if he can't handle those assembly line bottlenecks better.

botorunekku infure ボトルネック・インフレ bottleneck inflation
* *Rōdōryoku no fusoku ni yoru seisan to juyō no anbaransu ga botorunekku infure o manekimashita.*
  The unbalance of production and demand due to a shortage of manpower brought about bottleneck inflation.

botoru shippu ボトルシップ ship in a bottle
* *Kore wa wain no bin o tsukatte tsukutta botoru shippu desu.*
  This is a miniature ship in a bottle that I made using a wine bottle.

bouringu ボウリング bowling
* *Kinō minna de bouringu o shi ni ikimashita.*
  Yesterday we all went bowling together.

bui ブイ buoy
* *Suimen ni bui ga uite imasu.*
  A buoy is floating on the surface of the water.

bukkuendo ブックエンド bookends
* *Kono bukkuendo wa o-tesei desu ka?*
  Did you make these bookends yourself?

bukku kabā ブックカバー book cover, dust jacket
* *Hyōshi ga yogorenai yō ni bukku kabā o kakemasu.*
  A dust jacket is put on so that the cover won't get soiled.

bukkuretto ブックレット booklet
* *Kono bukkuretto wa benri na mājan no tebiki desu.*
  This booklet is a handy guide to mahjong.

bukkusutoa ブックストア bookstore
- *Bukkusutoa no kōhii shoppu de matte imasu.*
  I'll be waiting for you at the coffee shop in the bookstore.

būmu ブーム boom
- *Kaigai ryokō būmu wa shibaraku tsuzuku deshō.*
  The boom in foreign travel will likely last a little longer.

burabō ブラボー bravo
- *Nekkyō shita kankyaku wa "Burabō!" o renpatsu shimashita.*
  The enthusiastic audience shouted "Bravo!" over and over again.

buraindo ブラインド blind
- *Hi ga hairu kara, buraindo o oroshite kudasai.*
  Because the sun is shining in, please pull the blind down.

burakku ブラック black
- *Burakku wa kanojo no suki na iro desu.*
  Black is a color she likes.
- *Watashi wa kōhii wa burakku wa mattaku dame desu.*
  I absolutely cannot take my coffee black.

burakku bokkusu ブラックボックス black box
- *Burakku bokkusu ni pairotto no saigo no kōshin kiroku ga nokosarete imashita.*
  The pilot's final radio communication was recorded in the black box.

burakku risuto ブラックリスト blacklist
- *Kare no namae wa burakku risuto ni notte imasu.*
  His name is on the blacklist.

burando ブランド brand
- *Kanojo wa burando mono bakari kaimasu.*
  She buys nothing but brand-name articles.

buranketto ブランケット blanket
- *Samui kara, buranketto o motte kite kudasai.*
  As it's cold, could you bring me a blanket, please?

buranku ブランク blank, absence
 • *Sono shingā wa nagai buranku no ato de kamubakku shimashita.*
 The singer made a comeback after a long hiatus.
burashi ブラシ brush
 • *Kōto ni burashi o kakenakereba narimasen.*
 I must brush my coat.
burasshingu ブラッシング brushing
 • *Kanojo wa asaban nagai kami o burasshingu shimasu.*
 She brushes her long hair morning and evening.
burasshu appu suru ブラッシュアップする to brush up
 • *Kare wa Wai-em-shii-ē de Eigo o burasshu appu shite imasu.*
 He is brushing up on his English at the YMCA.
buraun ブラウン brown
 • *buraun no kutsu*
 brown shoes
burausu ブラウス blouse
 • *Kono burausu wa Honkon sei desu.*
 This blouse was made in Hong Kong.
burēki ブレーキ brakes (car), stop
 • *Shōtotsu o sakeru tame gutto burēki o fumimashita.*
 I slammed on the brakes to avoid a collision.
 • *Genshiryoku hatsudensho no kensetsu ni wa burēki ga kakatte imasu.*
 The construction of nuclear power plants has been stopped.
burendo suru ブレンドする to blend
 • *Iroiro na yasai o burendo shite, jūsu o tsukurimasu.*
 I make juice by blending various vegetables.
burēnwosshingu ブレーンウォッシング brainwashing
 • *Kokumin wa seifu no puropaganda de burēnwosshingu sarete imasu.*
 The people are being brainwashed by the government's

propaganda.

buriifingu ブリーフィング briefing
- *Senkyō ni tsuite buriifingu ga okonawaremasu.*
  A briefing will be held about the war situation.

buriifukēsu ブリーフケース briefcase
- *Kono buriifukēsu wa totemo benri ni dekite imasu.*
  This briefcase is very convenient.

burijji ブリッジ bridge
- *Kare wa ryōkoku kan no burijji yaku o tsutomete imasu.*
  He acts as a bridge between the two countries.
- *Tonari no heya de burijji o yatte imasu.*
  They are playing bridge in the next room.

burōchi ブローチ brooch, broach
- *Sono shinju no burōchi wa kirei desu ne.*
  That pearl brooch is pretty, isn't it?

burōkā ブローカー broker
- *Burōkā o tōshite, kabu o kaimashita.*
  I bought stocks through a broker.

burōkun ブロークン broken, imperfectly spoken
- *Kare no Eigo wa burōkun de wakarinikui desu.*
  His English is broken and hard to understand.

burōkun hāto ブロークンハート broken heart
- *Kono tokoro kanojo wa burōkun hāto de fusaide imasu.*
  Recently she's had her heart broken and is depressed.

burondo ブロンド blonde
- *Kanojo wa kami o burondo ni somete imasu.*
  She dyes her hair blonde.

buronzu ブロンズ bronze
- *buronzu no zō*
  a bronze statue

burū ブルー blue
- *Burū no rēnkōto o kita hito ga aruite imasu.*
  A person wearing a blue raincoat is walking along.

- *Ame no hi wa itsumo kibun ga burū desu.*
  On rainy days I always feel blue.

burudōzā ブルドーザー bulldozer
- *Burudōzā de jinarashi o shimashita.*
  They bulldozed the ground.

burujoa ブルジョア bourgeois
- *Kanojo wa burujoa no katei ni sodatta wagamama musume desu.*
  She is a spoilt child from a rich family.

burujowa ブルジョワ *see* **burujoa**

burū-karā ブルーカラー blue-collar worker
- *Koko wa burū-karā no chingin ga hikakuteki takai chiiki desu.*
  In this region the wages of blue-collar workers are relatively high.

būsu ブース booth
- *Denwa no būsu wa minna fusagatte imasu.*
  All the telephone booths are occupied.

butikku ブティック boutique
- *Kono tōri ni wa shōsha na butikku ga narande imasu.*
  This street is lined with fashionable boutiques.

būtsu ブーツ boots
- *Yuki no hi wa būtsu o haite tsūgaku shimashita.*
  On snowy days I went to school wearing boots.

buzā ブザー buzzer
- *Buzā o oshimashita ga, dare mo dete kimasen deshita.*
  I pushed the buzzer, but no one came out.

byuffe ビュッフェ buffet (in a train, station)
- *Shinkansen no byuffe de tabemashō.*
  Let's eat in the bullet train dining car.

byūrokurashii ビューロクラシー bureaucracy
- *Kore wa byūrokurashii no heigai no ichirei desu.*
  This is one example of the ill effects of bureaucracy.

byūtii kontesuto ビューティーコンテスト beauty contest
* *Kanojo wa byūtii kontesuto ni detagatte imasu.*
  She is anxious to enter the beauty contest.

C

CD *see* **shii-dii** (*certificate of deposit*)
CD *see* **shii-dii** (*compact disk*)
CD purēyā CD プレーヤー *see* **shii-dii purēyā**
CEO *see* **shii-ii-ō**
CM *see* **shii-emu**
chaimu チャイム chime
* *Genkan no chaimu ga nido narimashita.*
  The entrance chime rang twice.

Chaina doresu チャイナドレス Chinese dress
* *Chaina doresu o kita bijin*
  a beautiful girl wearing a Chinese dress

Chainataun チャイナタウン Chinatown
* *San-furanshisuko no Chainataun de hisui no yubiwa o kaimashita.*
  I bought a jade ring in San Francisco's Chinatown.

Chainiizu resutoran チャイニーズレストラン Chinese restaurant
* *Chainiizu resutoran de bōnenkai o yarimashita.*
  We had a year-end dinner party at a Chinese restaurant.

chakku チャック fastener, zipper, chuck
* *Zubon no chakku ga kowaremashita.*
  My trousers' zipper is broken.

chakōru gurē チャコールグレー charcoal gray
* *Kono sētā wa chakōru gurē no sukāto to yoku aimasu.*
  This sweater goes well with the charcoal gray skirt.

chāmingu チャーミング charming
- *Kare no fianse wa totemo chāmingu na josei desu.*
  His fiancée is a very charming woman.

chāmu pointo チャームポイント [Japanese Usage: charm point] attractive quality
- *Kanojo no chāmu pointo wa sawayaka na egao deshō.*
  What is most attractive about her is her delightful smile.

chaneru チャネル channel, route
- *Himitsu no chaneru o tsūjite, iroiro na mono ga hanbai sarete imasu.*
  Various items are being sold through clandestine routes.

channeru チャンネル channel, route, channel (for radio or TV)
- *hanbai no channeru*
  a distribution channel
- *Terebi no kyōyō bangumi wa nan channeru desu ka?*
  Which channel has the educational programs?
- *Omoshiroku nai nara hoka no channeru ni shitara dō desu ka?*
  If it's not interesting, why don't you try some other channel?

chanpion チャンピオン champion
- *bokushingu no chanpion*
  a boxing champion

chansu チャンス chance
- *Ima ga fudōsan tōshi ni zekkō no chansu desu.*
  Now is the best chance for investing in real estate.

chaperu チャペル chapel
- *Oka no ue ni shiroi chaperu ga tatte imasu.*
  A white chapel stands on the hill.

chapuren チャプレン chaplain
- *Kono byōin no chapuren wa wakakute hansamu desu.*
  The chaplain in this hospital is young and handsome.

charenjā チャレンジャー challenger, people who try
  • *Charenjā wa chanpion ni makemashita.*
  The challenger was defeated by the champion.
  • *Monogoto o seikō saseru tame ni wa charenjā seishin de iku hoka wa arimasen.*
  To make things successful the only thing you can do is meet them with a spirit of challenge.

charenji suru チャレンジする to challenge, undertake something difficult
  • *Muzukashii shigoto desu ga, charenji shite mimasu.*
  It's a difficult task but I'll try and do it.

charitii konsāto チャリティーコンサート charity concert
  • *Charitii konsāto no kippu o utte imasu.*
  They are selling tickets for a charity concert.

charumera チャルメラ [Portuguese: *charamela*] a street noodle-vendor's flute
  • *Charumera wa rappa no yō na oto ga shimasu.*
  A charamela sounds like a trumpet.

chātā チャーター charter; **~suru** する to charter
  • *Chātā ki de Ōsutoraria e ikimashita.*
  We went to Australia on a charter plane
  • *Dantai ryokō no tame ni basu o chātā shimashita.*
  We chartered a bus for the group tour.

chāto チャート chart
  • *Kono chāto wa kaku toshi no jinkō no tōkei o shimeshite imasu.*
  This chart shows the population statistics for each city.

chekku チェック check, checkered pattern; **~suru** する to check
  • *aka no chekku no burausu*
  a red-checkered blouse
  • *Mō ichido nakami o chekku shite mite kudasai.*
  Please check the contents once more.

chekkuauto チェックアウト check-out; **~suru** する to
   check out
   • *chekkuauto no jikan*
      check-out time
   • *Chekkuauto wa nanji desu ka?*
      What time is check-out?
   • *Kuji goro ni wa hoteru o chekkuauto suru tsumori desu.*
      I intend to check out of the hotel around nine o'clock.

chekkuin チェックイン check-in; **~suru** する to check in
   • *Chekkuin wa go-shuppatsu no ichijikan mae kara
      hajimarimasu.*
      Check-in starts one hour before departure.
   • *Kare wa mō hoteru ni chekkuin shimashita ka?*
      Has he already checked in at the hotel?

chekkupointo チェックポイント checkpoint, main points
   • *Koko ni mensetsu shiken no chekkupointo ga kaite
      arimasu.*
      The main points for the interview are written here.

chēn チェーン chain
   • *Kuruma ga surippu shinai yō ni, taiya ni chēn o
      makimasu.*
      I put chains on the tires so that the car won't skid.

chenji チェンジ change; **~suru** する to change
   • *Shachō no sukejūru ni chenji wa arimasen.*
      There is no change in the company president's schedule.
   • *Giya o rō kara sekando ni chenji shimashita.*
      I changed from first to second gear.

chēn sumōkā チェーンスモーカー chain smoker
   • *Kare wa wakai toki kara chēn sumōkā deshita.*
      He has been a chain smoker since he was young.

chēn sutoa チェーンストア chain store
   • *Kono inaka machi ni mo sūpā no chēn sutoa ga ōpun
      shimashita.*

Even in this country town a chain supermarket has opened.

cherii チェリー cherry
- *Amerikan cherii wa ōkikute amai desu.*
  American cherries are big and sweet.

chero チェロ cello
- *Shizuka na chero no ne ga kikoemasu.*
  The sound of a quiet cello can be heard.

chesu チェス chess
- *Oba wa chesu ni kotte imasu.*
  My aunt is crazy about chess.

chia gāru チアガール [Japanese Usage: cheer girl] cheer-leader (female)
- *Hōmu ran ni chia gāru wa kansei o agemashita.*
  When he hit the home run, the cheerleaders shouted for joy.

chifusu チフス typhus
- *Chifusu wa osoroshii densenbyō desu.*
  Typhus is an extremely contagious disease.

chiifu チーフ chief, head, leader
- *Kare wa sōsakutai no chiifu desu.*
  He is the head of the search party.

chiifu editā チーフエディター chief editor
- *Kare wa kikanshi no chiifu editā desu.*
  He is the chief editor for a quarterly.

chiiku チーク teak
- *chiiku-zai no kagu*
  teakwood furniture

chiiku dansu チークダンス [Japanese Usage: cheek dance] dancing cheek-to-cheek
- *Disuko de kare to chiiku dansu o shimashita.*
  I danced cheek-to-cheek with him at the disco.

chiimu チーム team
- *Kare wa chiimu purē ga dekinai ningen desu.*
  He's not a team player.

- *Puro yakyū ni wa chiimu wa ikutsu arimasu ka?*
  How many professional baseball teams are there?

chiimuwāku チームワーク teamwork
- *Shigoto no seikō wa chiimuwāku ni kakatte imasu.*
  Success at work depends on teamwork.

chiipu shikku チープシック cheap chic
- *Kanojo wa chiipu shikku na oshare ga jōzu desu.*
  She has a way of looking good in inexpensive clothes.

chiizu チーズ cheese
- *Chiizu wa nigate desu.*
  Cheese is not my favorite food.

chiketto チケット ticket
- *Kongetsu no kabuki no chiketto wa mō urikire desu.*
  The tickets for the Kabuki performance this month are already sold out.

chiketto byūrō チケットビューロー [Japanese Usage: ticket bureau] ticket agency
- *Chiketto byūrō de basu no kaisū-ken o kaimasu.*
  I will buy a book of bus tickets at the ticket counter.

chikin チキン chicken
- *Biifu yori chikin no hō ga suki desu.*
  I like chicken better than beef.

chinpanjii チンパンジー chimpanzee
- *Chinpanjii wa dōbutsuen de no ninki mono desu.*
  Chimpanzees are popular animals in the zoo.

chippu チップ tip
- *Nihon ni wa chippu no shūkan wa arimasen.*
  In Japan there is no custom of giving tips.

choisu チョイス choice; **~suru** する to choose
- *Sore ga ichiban yoi choisu da to omoimasu.*
  I think that is the best choice.
- *Hoteru wa jibun de choisu shitai desu.*
  I want to choose the hotel myself.

- *Kore wa kare no choisu desu.*
  This is his choice.

chokki チョッキ [Portuguese: *jaque*] vest
- *Samui hi ni wa sūtsu no shita ni chokki o kimasu.*
  On cold days I wear a vest under my suit.

chokorēto チョコレート chocolate
- *O-miyage ni chokorēto o hitohako motte ikimasu.*
  I'll take a box of chocolates as a gift.

chōku チョーク chalk
- *Kochira no hako ni chōku de shirushi o tsukete kudasai.*
  Please mark these boxes with chalk.

chūba チューバ *see* **tyūba**

chūbu チューブ tube
- *chūbu iri no nerihamigaki*
  a tube of toothpaste

chūin gamu チューインガム chewing gum
- *Kare wa tabako no kawari ni chūin gamu o kande imasu.*
  He is chewing gum instead of smoking cigarettes.

chūn-appu チューンアップ tune-up
- *Kuruma o chūn-appu ni motte ikanakereba narimasen.*
  I must take my car for a tune-up.

chūn-nappu チューンナップ *see* **chūn-appu**

chūtā チューター tutor
- *Nihongo no chūtā o sagashite imasu.*
  I am looking for a Japanese tutor.

D

DM *see* **dairekuto mēru**

Dābii ダービー Derby
- *Dābii ni wa ōzei no yūmeijin ga sugata o misemashita.*
  A large number of celebrities were seen at the Derby.

dabingu ダビング dubbing; **~suru** する to make a copy
* *Tēpu ni ongaku o dabingu shimasu.*
  We dub music on the tape.
* *Sono ongaku o dabingu shite moraemasu ka?*
  Will you dub that music for me?

daburu ダブル double
* *daburu no uwagi*
  a double-breasted coat
* *Daburu no heya o yoyaku shimashita.*
  I made a reservation for a double room.

daburu inkamu ダブルインカム double income
* *Kono hen wa hotondo no katei ga daburu inkamu, tsumari tomobataraki desu.*
  In this area almost all families have two working adults and thus double incomes.

daburu kyasuto ダブルキャスト [Japanese Usage: double cast] casting two actors to play the same role
* *Kono geki no shuyaku wa daburu kyasuto desu.*
  The leading role in this play has been assigned to two actors.

daburu bukkingu ダブルブッキング [Japanese Usage: double booking] overbooking
* *Daburu bukkingu no tame, hikōki no shuppatsu ga okuremashita.*
  Because of overbooking, the plane's departure was delayed.

daburu purē ダブルプレー double play
* *Waga chiimu wa daburu purē de chansu o tsubushimashita.*
  Our team lost an opportunity because of a double play.

daburusu ダブルス doubles
* *Daburusu no gēmu o yarimashō ka?*
  Shall we play doubles?

dagguauto ダッグアウト dugout, bench

- *Senshu wa minna dagguauto ni haitte kōchi to sōdan shimasu.*

  All the players are going into the dugout to have a talk with their coach.

daiaguramu ダイアグラム *see* **daiya**

daiamondo ダイアモンド *see* **daiyamondo**

daiarii ダイアリー diary

- *Kanojo wa mainichi daiarii o tsukete imasu.*

  She writes in her diary every day.

daiaru suru ダイアルする *see* **daiyaru suru**

daibingu ダイビング diving

- *Kanojo no daibingu wa fōmu ga batsugun deshita.*

  Her diving form was preeminent.

- *Daibingu wa taishitsu teki ni watashi ni wa muite inai yō desu.*

  It seems I'm not the right physical type for diving.

daibu ダイブ dive; **~daibu suru** to dive

- *Suichū ni daibu shite, kaitei no shashin o torimashita.*

  They dove into the water and took photos of the seabed.

- *Nigeba o ushinatta sono yūkan na senshi wa gake kara shi no daibu o kankō shimashita.*

  With his escape route cut off, the brave warrior dared to dive from the cliff to his death.

daietto ダイエット diet

- *Yaseru tame ni daietto o shite imasu.*

  I am dieting in order to lose weight.

daijesuto ダイジェスト digest; **~suru** する to digest, summarize

- *supōtsu nyūsu no daijesuto*

  a digest of sports news

- *Kono hon wa gensaku o daijesuto-ban ni shita mono desu.*

  This edition is summarized from the original.

dainamaito ダイナマイト dynamite

- *Dainamaito de biru o bakuha shimashita.*
  They blasted the building with dynamite.
- *Dainamaito o hatsumei shita no wa Arufureddo Nōberu desu.*
  Alfred Nobel was the person who invented dynamite.

dainamikku ダイナミック dynamic
- *Kare wa dainamikku na seijika desu.*
  He is a dynamic politician.
- *Kyodai na sakana ga suisō no naka o dainamikku ni oyoide imasu.*
  A huge fish is swimming vigorously in the water tank.

dainingu kitchin ダイニングキッチン [Japanese Usage: dining kitchen] combined dining room and kitchen
- *Dainingu kitchin no kabe o shiroku nurimashita.*
  I painted the dining-kitchen wall white.

dainingu rūmu ダイニングルーム dining room
- *Hoteru no dainingu rūmu wa kaisōchū desu.*
  The dining room in the hotel is being renovated.

dairekuto ダイレクト direct
- *dairekuto na kōshō*
  a direct negotiation
- *Kono furaito wa dairekuto ni Shikago e ikimasu.*
  This is a direct flight to Chicago.

dairekuto mēru ダイレクトメール direct mail
- *Dairekuto mēru ni yoru kōkoku wa kyōsō ga hageshii desu.*
  There is stiff competition in direct mail advertising.
- *Watashi wa dairekuto mēru wa minaide suteru koto ni shite imasu.*
  I throw out junk mail without looking at it.

daiya ダイヤ diagram *see* **daiyamondo**
- *Ressha no daiya ni tashō henkō ga aru kamo shiremasen.*
  There may be a slight change in the train schedule.

- *Ōyuki no tame ressha daiya wa ōhaba ni okurete imasu.*
  Due to heavy snow, the trains are quite late.

daiyaguramu ダイヤグラム *see* **daiya**

daiyamondo ダイヤモンド diamond
- *Kono daiyamondo wa mozō desu.*
  This diamond is an imitation.

daiyaru suru ダイヤルする to dial
- *Hijō no baai wa hyakutōban o daiyaru shite kudasai.*
  In case of emergency, please dial 110.

dāku hōsu ダークホース dark horse
- *Kare wa kondo no Tochijisen no dāku hōsu desu.*
  He is a dark horse in the next Metropolitan gubernatorial
  election.

dāku saido ダークサイド dark side
- *Kono hon wa shakai no dāku saido o kyōchō shite imasu.*
  This book emphasizes the dark side of society.

dāku sūtsu ダークスーツ dark suit
- *Nihon no bijinesuman wa dāku sūtsu o kite imasu.*
  Japanese businessmen wear dark suits.

damēji ダメージ damage
- *Jishin no damēji wa ōkikunakatta desu.*
  The damage from the earthquake was not great.
- *Sono jiken wa seitō ni chimeiteki na damēji o ataemashita.*
  That incident fatally damaged the political party.

damu ダム dam
- *Damu no kensetsu ga kettei shimashita.*
  They decided to build a dam.

dandii ダンディー dandy
- *Kare no dandii na fukusō ga hitome o hikimasu.*
  His foppish outfits catch peoples' eyes.

danpingu ダンピング dumping
- *Aru kaisha wa kaigai shijō de shinamono o danpingu shite
  imasu.*

Certain companies are dumping goods in overseas markets.

* *Nihon no kigyō no kaigai shijō deno danpingu ga mondai ni natte imasu.*

Japanese companies' dumping in foreign markets has become a problem.

danpu kā ダンプカー [Japanese Usage: dump car] dump truck

* *Danpu kā ga sōko no mae ni tsumini o oroshite imasu.*

A dump truck is unloading its cargo in front of the warehouse.

dansā ダンサー dancer

* *Kanojo no yume wa dansā ni naru koto desu.*

Her dream is to become a dancer.

* *Kanojo wa kurabu de dansā o shite imasu.*

She's a dancer in a club.

dansu ダンス dance; **~suru** する to dance

* *shakō dansu*

social dancing

* *Kare to dansu shita koto wa ichido mo arimasen.*

I have never danced with him.

dasshu ダッシュ dash; **~suru** する to dash

* *Kono kotoba no ato ni dasshu o tsukemasu.*

I'll put a dash after this word.

* *Ōtobai ga kono michi o dasshu shite ikimashita.*

A motorcycle dashed up this road.

* *Kare no sutāto dasshu wa subarashii desu.*

He's a quick starter in running races.

dāsu ダース dozen

* *Biiru wa nandāsu irimasu ka?*

How many dozen bottles of beer do you need?

dasuto shūto ダスト・シュート dust chute

* *Gomi o suteru toki wa dasuto shūto o go-riyō kudasai.*

When you dispose of garbage, use the dust chute.

- *Aru gomi wa dasuto shūto ni nageirete wa ikemasen.*
Certain trash may not be thrown into a dust chute.

daun ダウン down
- *daun o tsumeta makura*
a pillow stuffed with down

daun suru ダウンする to go down, break down
- *Sono bangumi no shichō-ritsu wa go-pāsento ni daun shimashita.*
That program's ratings went down to five percent.
- *Ginkō no konpyūtā ga daun shite gyōmu ga mahi shimashita.*
The bank's computer was down and all operations were paralyzed.

dauntaun ダウンタウン downtown
- *Kūkō kara dauntaun made wa kanari tōi desu.*
It's quite far from the airport to downtown.

deberoppā デベロッパー developer
- *Deberoppā ga hiroi tochi o katte, ie o tatete imasu.*
A developer bought a large amount of land and is building houses on it.

debyū デビュー debut
- *Shinjin sakka ga tsugitsugi ni debyū shite imasu.*
New writers come out one after another.
- *Kare wa kyonen Kānegii-hōru de debyū shimashita.*
He made his debut at Carnegie Hall last year.

deddo bōru デッドボール [Japanese Usage: dead ball] hit by a pitched baseball
- *Deddo bōru o ukete kega o shimashita.*
I was hit by a pitch and got hurt.

deddo hiito デッドヒート dead heat, close game
- *Rēsu wa deddo hiito ni narimashita.*
The race turned into a dead heat.

deddorain デッドライン deadline

- *Gansho uketsuke no deddorain wa itsu desu ka?*
  When is the deadline for the acceptance of applications?
- *Deddorain ga sematte iru noni mada shiryō ga soroimasen.*
  Even though the deadline is drawing near, my materials still aren't complete.

deddorokku デッドロック deadlock
- *Yosan'an no shingi wa deddorokku ni noriagemashita.*
  The budget bill became deadlocked.

deddo sutokku デッドストック dead stock
- *Kaisha no sōko wa deddo sutokku de ippai deshita.*
  The company's warehouse was filled with dead stock.

deforume suru デフォルメする [French: *déformer*] to deform, distort
- *Kono dokyumentarii wa sakusha no shukan ni yotte deforume sarete imasu.*
  This documentary was distorted by the author's subjectivity.

defure デフレ deflation
- *Sono kin'yū seisaku wa defure o maneku osore ga arimasu.*
  It is feared that the financial policy may bring about deflation.

defurēshon デフレーション *see* **defure**

dē gēmu デーゲーム day game
- *Yakyū no dē gēmu wa nanji ni hajimarimasu ka?*
  What time does the baseball day game start?

deirii デイリー daily
- *Mazu deirii ni hitsuyō na mono o kaimasu.*
  First I buy daily necessities.

dejitaru デジタル digital
- *Dejitaru no ketsuatsukei wa tsukai yasui desu.*
  The digital tonometer is easy to use.

dekki デッキ deck
- *Futari de fune no dekki kara yūyake o mimashita.*
  We watched the sunset from the ship's deck.

dekki chea デッキチェア deck chair
- *Dekki chea o mittsu niwa ni hakonde kudasai.*
  Please take three deck chairs to the garden.

dekorēshon デコレーション decoration
- *Kurisumasu no dekorēshon de tōri wa karafuru desu.*
  The streets are colorful with Christmas decorations.

dema デマ [German: *Demagogie*] false rumor
- *Kare no jinin ni tsuite dema ga tobikatte imasu.*
  A rumor about his resignation is circulating.
- *Kare ga jinin suru to iu no wa dema no yō desu.*
  The rumor that he's going to resign seems false.

demeritto デメリット demerit, drawback
- *Kono shin'yaku no demeritto wa fukusayō o okosu koto desu.*
  This new medicine's drawback is its side effects.

demo デモ demonstration *see* **demonsutorēshon**
- *Sensō hantai no demo ga itaru tokoro de arimashita.*
  Demonstrations against the war took place everywhere.

demokurashii デモクラシー democracy
- *Sono kuni no kokumin wa demokurashii o motomete tatakatte imasu.*
  The people of that country are demanding democracy.

demonsutorēshon デモンストレーション
demonstration *see* **demo**
- *Jūdō no demonsutorēshon ni gaijin ga ōzei kimashita.*
  Many foreigners came for the judo demonstration.

denimu デニム denim
- *denimu no sagyōfuku*
  denim working clothes

denomi デノミ *see* **denominēshon**

denominēshon デノミネーション renaming monetary units, redenomination
- *Denominēshon ga jitsugen sareru kamo shiremasen.*
  Currency redenomination might be carried out.

depāto デパート department store
- *Konogoro no depāto wa shichiji made aite imasu.*
  The department store is open until seven o'clock these days.

derakkusu デラックス deluxe
- *Hoteru de derakkusu na suiito ni tomarimashita.*
  We stayed in a deluxe suite at the hotel.

deribarii デリバリー delivery
- *Ano mise wa piza no deribarii o hajimemashita.*
  That store started delivering pizza.

dērii デーリー *see* **deirii**

derikashii デリカシー delicacy, tact
- *Derikashii no nai hito wa gaikō kōshō ni wa mukimasen.*
  A person without tact is not suitable for diplomatic negotiations.

derikēto デリケート delicate
- *Derikēto na mondai desu kara shinchō ni atsukau beki desu.*
  It's a delicate matter so it should be dealt with cautiously.
- *Kono takezaiku wa derikēto ni dekite imasu.*
  This bamboo ware is delicately made.

Derishasu デリシャス Delicious (a kind of apple)
- *Kudamonoya ni rippa na Derishasu ga takusan narande imasu.*
  There are many fine Delicious apples at the fruit store.

dessan デッサン [French: *dessin*] rough sketch
- *Kono e wa dessan ga yoku dekite imasu.*
  The preliminary sketch for this picture is done well.

desuku デスク desk
- *Sono shorui wa desuku no ue ni arimasu.*

The documents are on the desk.

- *Kono repōto o henshūbu no desuku e motte itte kudasai.*

Please take this report to the editorial desk.

desu masuku デスマスク death mask

- *Desu masuku ga jiken kaiketsu no tegakari ni narimashita.*

The death mask was a clue that helped solve the case.

dēta データ data

- *Kono dēta wa sukoshi aimai desu ne.*

This data is a little ambiguous, isn't it?

dētabēsu データベース database

- *Shuju no dēta o fairu shita dētabēsu o riyō shite repōto o kakimasu.*

I write reports using a database that files various kinds of data.

detēru デテール *see* **ditēru**

dēto suru デートする to date

- *Kanojo wa onaji shokuba no dansei to yoku dēto shite imasu.*

She often dates men from her workplace.

dezain デザイン design

- *Kono doresu wa Mori Hanae no dezain desu.*

This dress was designed by Hanae Mori.

dezainā デザイナー designer

- *Kare wa shitsunai sōshoku no shinshin dezainā desu.*

He is a rising star in interior design.

dezāto デザート dessert

- *Dezāto ni aisu kuriimu o tabemashita.*

I ate ice cream for dessert.

dibeito ディベイト *see* **dibēto**

diberoppā ディベロッパー *see* **deberoppā**

dibēto ディベート debate

- *Sono koto ni kanshite hageshii dibēto ga arimashita.*

There was a heated debate over that matter.

digitaru ディジタル *see* **dejitaru**

dii-emu ディーエム DM [Japanese Usage: d(irect) m(ail)] *see* **dairekuto mēru**

diirā ディーラー dealer
- *Otōto wa chūkosha no diirā o shite imasu.*
  My younger brother is a used car salesman.

diiringu ディーリング dealing
- *Gaikoku kawase no diiringu wa gozen hachiji-han kara hajimarimasu.*
  The foreign exchange dealing starts at 8:30 A.M.

diizeru enjin ディーゼルエンジン diesel engine
- *diizeru enjin o tōsai shita kuruma*
  a car with a diesel engine

dikutēshon ディクテーション dictation
- *Tokidoki Nihongo no dikutēshon no tesuto ga arimasu.*
  Sometimes we have dictation tests in Japanese.

dinā ディナー dinner
- *Hoteru de Furansu-ryōri no dinā o tabemashita.*
  We had French cuisine for dinner at the hotel.

dinā pātii ディナーパーティー dinner party
- *Dinā pātii de kare ni shōkai saremashita.*
  I was introduced to him at a dinner party.

dinā shō ディナーショー dinner show
- *Yūbe no dinā shō no uta wa subarashikatta desu ne.*
  The singing at the dinner show last night was terrific, wasn't it?

direkutā ディレクター director
- *Kare wa terebi no ninki bangumi no direkutā desu.*
  He is the director of a hit TV program.

direnma ディレンマ *see* **jirenma**

disukasshon ディスカッション discussion
- *Kaihi no neage ni tsuite disukasshon o shimasu.*
  We'll have a discussion about the increase in membership

fees.

disukaunto ディスカウント discount
 • *Nijuppāsento no disukaunto de kōkūken o kaimashita.*
 I bought an air ticket at a 20% discount.

disuko ディスコ disco, discotheque
 • *Disuko de yoru osoku made odorimashita.*
 We danced at a disco until late at night.

disuku ディスク disk
 • *San-ten-go inchi no disuku o tsukatte kudasai.*
 Please use a 3.5-inch disk.

disuku jokkii ディスクジョッキー disc jockey, deejay
 • *Rajio de disuku jokkii o kikinagara, asagohan o tabemashita.*
 I ate breakfast while listening to the deejay on the radio.

disukurōjā ディスクロージャー disclosure
 • *Insaidā torihiki bōshi no tame disukurōjā wa hitsuyō desu.*
 Disclosure is necessary in order to prevent insider trading.

disupōzā ディスポーザー disposer
 • *Disupōzā de nama gomi o kudaite nagashimasu.*
 Garbage is ground by a disposer and flushed away.

disupurē ディスプレー display; **~suru** する to display
 • *Imariyaki no disupurē wa ninki o yobimashita.*
 The Imari ware display was popular.
 • *Robii ni shōhin ga disupurē shite arimasu.*
 The merchandise is displayed in the lobby.

disutoribyūtā ディストリビューター distributor
 • *Kono chiiki no disutoribyūtā ni natte itadakitai no desu.*
 We would like you to be our distributor in this area.

ditēru ディテール detail
 • *Keikaku no ditēru wa nochihodo o-shirase shimasu.*
 We will tell you the details of the plan later.

doa ドア door
 • *Doa wa jidōteki ni hirakimasu.*

The doors open automatically.

doa ai ドアアイ [Japanese Usage: door eye] peep hole
- *Doa o akeru mae ni doa ai o nozoite mimasu.*
  Before opening the door I try to look out the peep hole.

doa bōi ドアボーイ [Japanese Usage: door boy] doorman
- *Resutoran no toguchi ni doa bōi ga tatte imasu.*
  A doorman is standing in the doorway of the restaurant.

Doitsu ドイツ [German: *Deutsch*] Germany
- *Doitsu tōitsu wa kakkiteki na dekigoto deshita.*
  The reunification of Germany was an epoch-making event.

dokutā ドクター doctor
- *Dokutā no adobaisu de tabako o yamemashita.*
  I gave up smoking at my doctor's advice.

dokyumentarii ドキュメンタリー documentary
- *Sono dokyumentarii wa shō o moraimashita.*
  That documentary received a prize.
- *Kono eiga wa yasei dōbutsu no dokyumentarii desu.*
  This movie is a documentary about wild animals.

domesuchikku ドメスチック domestic
- *Soko de domesuchikku ni norikaete kudasai.*
  Please board your domestic flight there.

domesutikku ドメスティック *see* **domesuchikku**

dōmu ドーム dome
- *Kyōkai no dōmu no ue o tori ga tonde imasu.*
  Birds are flying over the church dome.

dōnatsu ドーナツ doughnut
- *Ano bēkarii no dōnatsu wa saikō desu.*
  The doughnuts at that bakery are the best.

dōnattsu ドーナッツ *see* **dōnatsu**

dorafuto ドラフト draft
- *Yatto shōsetsu no dorafuto ga dekiagarimashita.*
  Finally a draft of the novel was completed.
- *puro yakyū no dorafuto kaigi*

a draft conference for professional baseball players

dorai ドライ dry, businesslike, hard-boiled
- *Kare wa dorai na manējimento de shirarete imasu.*
  He is known for his hard-boiled management style.
- *dorai biiru*
  dry beer
- *Kanojo wa dorai ni mondai o shori shimashita.*
  She dealt with the matter in a businesslike manner.

doraibā ドライバー driver
- *Sono jiko de doraibā dake tasukarimashita.*
  In that accident, only the driver was saved.

doraibu ドライブ drive; ~suru する to drive
- *yoru no doraibu*
  a night drive, night driving
- *Supōtsu kā de Biwa-ko made doraibu shimashita.*
  I drove to Lake Biwa in a sports car.

doraibu-in ドライブイン drive-in
- *Doraibu-in de hanbāgā o kaimashita.*
  We bought some hamburgers at a drive-in.

dorai kuriiningu ドライクリーニング dry cleaning
- *Kono sētā o dorai kuriiningu shite kudasai.*
  Please have this sweater dry-cleaned.

doraiyā ドライヤー dryer
- *Doraiyā de kami o kawakashimashita.*
  I dried my hair with a hair dryer.

dorama ドラマ drama
- *Konban Shēkusupia no dorama ga hōei saremasu.*
  A Shakespearean drama will be televised tonight.

doramachikku ドラマチック dramatic
- *Jiken no doramachikku na tenkai ni odorokimashita.*
  I was surprised at the incident's dramatic developments.
- *Kare no enzetsu wa nakanaka doramachikku deshita.*
  His speech was quite dramatic.

doramatikku ドラマティック *see* **doramachikku**

doramu ドラム drum
- *Sono gakudan de dare ga doramu o tantō shite imasu ka?*
  Who plays drums in that band?

dorasuchikku ドラスチック drastic
- *Dorasuchikku na shudan ga toraremashita.*
  Drastic measures have been adopted.
- *Kaisha no manējimento ga dorasuchikku ni kaikaku saremashita.*
  The company management was drastically reorganized.

dorasutikku ドラスティック *see* **dorasuchikku**

doresshii ドレッシー dressy
- *Doresshii na burausu wa kirai desu.*
  I dislike dressy blouses.
- *Konnani doresshii ni yosootta kanojo wa mita koto ga arimasen.*
  I have never seen her in such dressy clothes.

doresshingu ドレッシング dressing
- *Sarada ni wa oiru no haitte inai doresshingu o tsukaimasu.*
  I use oil-free dressing for salads.

doresu ドレス dress
- *Doresu wa wan-piisu mo tsū-piisu mo gozaimasu.*
  We carry both one-piece and two-piece dresses.
- *Ano burū no doresu wa kanojo ni pittari desu.*
  That blue dress is perfect for her.

doresu appu suru ドレスアップする to dress up
- *Kanojo wa itsumo doresu appu shite dekakemasu.*
  She always dresses up to go out.

dorippu ドリップ [Japanese Usage: drip] dripping; **~suru** する to drip
- *Kōhii mame o hiite dorippu shimasu.*
  I grind coffee beans and drip them.

doriru ドリル drill
* *Gaikokugo no shūtoku ni, doriru wa kaku koto ga dekimasen.*
Drills are indispensable for mastering a foreign language.

dorinku ドリンク drink
* *Dorinku wa jūsu ka aisu tii ni shimasu.*
I'll have juice or iced tea to drink.

doron gēmu ドロンゲーム drawn game
* *Enchōsen no kekka, doron gēmu ni narimashita.*
After an extra inning, the game ended in a draw.

doroppuauto ドロップアウト dropout; ~**suru** する to drop out
* *Kare wa Nihon no shakai no doroppuauto desu.*
He is a dropout from Japanese society.
* *Kōkōsei no go-nin ni hitori wa doroppuauto suru to iwarete imasu.*
It's said that one in five high school students drop out.

doru ドル dollar
* *Kyō no doru sōba wa dō natte imasu ka?*
What is today's quotation on the dollar?

E

ea baggu エアバッグ air bag
* *Ea baggu no tsuita kuruma wa anzen desu.*
A car with an air bag is safe.
* *Ea baggu no sōbi ga gimuzukerareru to iu no wa hontō desu ka?*
Is it true that air bag equipment is going to be compulsory?

eabasu エアバス Airbus
* *Eabasu de yoku Tōkyō–Ōsaka kan o ōfuku shimasu.*
I often make the round trip between Tokyo and Osaka by

Airbus.

ē-ai エーアイ AI AI, artificial intelligence
- *Ē-ai to wa keisan dake de naku gakushū mo suiron mo dekiru konpyūtā no koto desu.*
  Artificial intelligence means computers which not only can calculate but also can learn and reason.

eakon エアコン air conditioner (both cooling and heating)
- *Natsu ni wa zettai ni eakon ga irimasu yo.*
  You definitely need an air conditioner in summer.

ea kondishonā エアコンディショナー *see* **eakon**

eamēru エアメール airmail
- *Kozutsumi o eamēru de okurimasu.*
  I will send the packages by airmail.

ea poketto エアポケット air pocket, blind spot
- *Hikōki ga ea poketto ni haitte, jōkyaku ga sūnin kega o shimashita.*
  The airplane hit an air pocket and several passengers got hurt.
- *Nanmin no mondai wa shakai fukushi no ea poketto ni natte imasu.*
  The refugee problem is a blind spot in the social welfare system.

eapōto rimujin エアポートリムジン airport limousine
- *Eapōto rimujin de kūkō made ikimashō.*
  Let's take an airport limousine to the airport.

earain エアライン airline
- *Kanojo wa gaikoku no earain no suchuwādesu desu.*
  She is a flight attendant on a foreign airline.

ea tāminaru エアターミナル [Japanese Usage: air terminal] airport terminal
- *Ea tāminaru de bagēji o chekku-in dekimasu.*
  You can check in your baggage at the airport terminal.

ē-bii-shii エービーシー ABC ABCs, fundamentals

- *Kare wa hoteru keiei no ē-bii-shii mo shirimasen.*
  He doesn't even know the fundamentals of hotel management.

echiketto エチケット etiquette
- *Sonna kōi wa echiketto ni han-shimasu.*
  That kind of behavior is not good etiquette.

edishon エディション edition
- *Kono edishon wa ima deta bakari desu.*
  This edition just came out now.

Efubiiai エフ・ビー・アイ FBI FBI, Federal Bureau of Investigation
- *Neruson-san wa Efubiiai ni ita toki Nihongo o naratta no desu.*
  Mr. Nelson learned Japanese when he was with the FBI.

efuē エフエー FA FA, factory automation
- *Sono kaisha wa efuē de Amerika no kaisha to teikei shita kekka, ima ya sōgyō no rokujūppāsento o mujinka shite imasu.*
  The company has cooperated with an American firm in FA, and now their operations are 60% unmanned.

efuemu エフエム FM FM (frequency modulation)
- *Efuemu hōsō de kurashikku o kikimasu.*
  I listen to classical music on FM radio.

eggu エッグ egg
- *Sukuranburu eggu ni shimasu ka pōchido eggu ni shimasu ka?*
  Would you prefer scrambled or poached eggs?

ego エゴ ego, self
- *Kare wa iji o tōshite jibun no ego o manzoku sasemasu.*
  He gratifies his ego by getting his own way.

egoisutikku エゴイスティック egoistic
- *Kare no egoisutikku na teian wa kyohi saremashita.*
  His egoistic proposal was rejected.

egoisuto エゴイスト egoist
- *Kanojo wa egoisuto da kara, tomodachi ga arimasen.*
  Because she is an egoist, she has no friends.

egoizumu エゴイズム egoism
- *Egoizumu ga kare o hametsu sasemashita.*
  His egoism ruined him.

eguzekutibu エグゼクティブ company executive
- *Kono bā no jōren wa kaisha no eguzekutibu ga hotondo desu.*
  This bar's regular customers are mostly company executives.

eijingu エイジング aging
- *Maroyaka na koku o dasu tame ni wain o eijingu shite imasu.*
  They are aging wine to give it fine body.

eipuriru fūru エイプリルフール *see* **ēpuriru fūru**

eizu エイズ [acquired immune deficiency syndrome] AIDS
- *Eizu wa ōkina shakai mondai no hitotsu desu.*
  AIDS is one of the big social problems.

ējenshii エージェンシー agency
- *Biru no ikkai ni ryokō ya kōkoku no ējenshii ga arimasu.*
  There are travel and advertising agencies on the first floor of the building.

ējento エージェント agent
- *Kono mise wa Nihon no denki kiki no kaisha no hanbai ējento desu.*
  This store is a sales agent for a Japanese electronics company.
- *Kare wa gaikoku seifu kara haken sareta ēgento kamo shiremasen.*
  He might be an agent sent from a foreign government.

ējingu エージング *see* **eijingu**

Ejiputo エジプト Egypt

- *Ejiputo de piramiddo o mimashita.*
  We saw the pyramids in Egypt.

ejji エッジ edge
- *sukēto no ejji*
  the edge of a skate

ēkā エーカー acre
- *Oji wa Amerika ni sen-ēkā no nōjō o motte imasu.*
  My uncle owns a one-thousand-acre farm in America.

ekijibishon エキジビション *see* **ekishibishon**

ekisaitingu エキサイティング exciting
- *Sore wa mottomo ekisaitingu na shō de wasureraremasen.*
  It was such an exciting show—I'll never forget it.

ekisaito suru エキサイトする to excite
- *Kankyaku wa shiai ni totemo ekisaito shite imasu.*
  The audience is very excited watching the game.

ekisasaizu エキササイズ exercise
- *Mainichi karui ekisasaizu o shita hō ga ii desu.*
  You should do some light exercise every day.

ekisentorikku エキセントリック eccentric
- *Abe-kyōju wa ekisentorikku na gakusha desu.*
  Professor Abe is an eccentric scholar.
- *Kare wa chotto ekisentorikku na tokoro ga arimasu.*
  He has some eccentric qualities.

ekishibishon エキシビション exhibition
- *Bijutsukan de modan āto no ekishibishon ga
  hirakaremashita.*
  An exhibition of modern art was held at the art gallery.

ekisu エキス extract, essence
- *Gyūniku kara ekisu o torimasu.*
  They extract essence from beef.
- *Puramu no ekisu wa kenkō ni ii to iwarete imasu.*
  Plum extract is said to be good for your health.

ekisupāto エキスパート expert

- *Kare wa māketingu no ekisupāto desu.*
  He is a marketing expert.

ekisutora エキストラ extra
- *Eiga de ekisutora o yatta koto ga arimasu.*
  I have played an extra in a movie.

ekizochikku エキゾチック exotic
- *Kohan ni ekizochikku na resutoran ga arimasu.*
  There is an exotic restaurant on the lakefront.

ekizochishizumu エキゾチシズム exoticism
- *Saikin bungaku ni okeru ekizochishizumu ga mote-hayasarete imasu.*
  Recently exoticism in literature is being valued.

ekkisu エッキス *see* **ekisu**

ekkusu エックス X X
- *ekkusu gata no burōchi*
  an X-shaped brooch
- *Kūkō de tenimotsu wa ekkusu sen kensa saremasu.*
  Baggage will be X-rayed at the airport.

ekō エコー echo
- *Sakebigoe ga sankan de ekō o kaeshimasu.*
  A shout echoes between the mountains.
- *Ekō o kakeru to uta ga jōzu ni kikoemasu.*
  Singing sounds better when there's an echo.

ekonomikku animaru エコノミック・アニマル economic animal
- *Ekonomikku animaru wa rieki o motomeru tame ni shudan o erabimasen.*
  An economic animal will stop at nothing to make profits.
- *Nihon wa ekonomikku animaru no omei o henjō suru tame ni nani o subeki deshō ka?*
  What must Japan do to lose its stigma of being an economic animal?

ekonomii kurasu エコノミークラス economy class

- *Hikōki no ekonomii kurasu wa dantai kyaku de konde imashita.*
  The economy class section of the plane was crowded with group travelers.

ekonomisuto エコノミスト economist
- *Kabushiki shijō no mitōshi wa ekonomisuto ni yotte chigaimasu.*
  Prospects for the stock market differ depending upon the economist.

ekorojii エコロジー ecology
- *Kore wa ekorojii no ken'i ni yotte kakareta hon desu.*
  This is a book written by an authority on ecology.

ekorojisuto エコロジスト ecologist
- *Shizen hogo o tonaeru ekorojisuto ga kōjō no kensetsu ni hantai shite imasu.*
  Ecologists who advocate the protection of the environment oppose the building of the factory.

ekujibishon エクジビション *see* **ekishibishon**

ē-kurasu エークラス or Aクラス top-class, first-rate
- *ē kurasu no ryokan*
  a top-class Japanese inn

ekusasaizu エクササイズ *see* **ekisasaizu**

ekusentorikku エクセントリック *see* **ekisentorikku**

ekuserento kanpanii エクセレント・カンパニー excellent company
- *Kono zasshi ni ekuserento kanpanii hyaku no risuto ga notte imasu.*
  This magazine has a list of one hundred excellent companies.

ekusuchenji rēto エクスチェンジ・レート exchange rate
- *Kyō no ekusuchenji rēto wa ichi doru hyakuhachi-en desu.*
  Today's exchange rate is 108 yen to the dollar.

ekusupāto エクスパート *see* **ekisupāto**

ekusutashii エクスタシー ecstasy
- *Sono amaku merankorikku na senritsu wa watashi o ekusutashii ni izanaimashita.*
The sweet, melancholy melodies lured me into ecstasy.

ekusuteria エクステリア exterior
- *Sono ie no ekusuteria wa mada kansei shite imasen.*
The exterior of the house has not been completed yet.

ekuzotikku エクゾティック *see* **ekizochikku**

ekuzotishizumu エクゾティシズム *see* **ekizochishizumu**

emājenshii エマージェンシー emergency
- *Emājenshii no baai wa itsu de mo denwa shite kudasai.*
Please call me if there is an emergency, no matter what time it is.

emerarudo エメラルド emerald
- *Emerarudo wa go-gatsu no tanjōseki desu.*
Emerald is the birthstone for May.

emōshonaru エモーショナル emotional
- *Kono machi de emōshonaru na hogei hantai undō ga hajimarimashita.*
A passionate anti-whaling movement started in this city.

emu エム M M (medium)
- *Watashi no saizu wa emu desu.*
My size is medium.

emu-ando-ē エム・アンド・エー M&A M & A, merger and acquisition
- *Kinnen kigyō no emu-ando-ē ga sekkyokuteki ni okonawarete imasu.*
In recent years mergers and acquisitions have been carried out agressively.

emuemushii エム・エム・シー MMC MMC, money market certificate
- *Emuemushii wa kinri ga mankibi made kotei sarete imasu.*
The MMC has a fixed interest rate until the date of maturity.

enameru エナメル enamel
* *enameru no kutsu*
patent leather shoes

endingu エンディング ending
* *Ano eiga no endingu wa akkenakatta desu ne.*
The ending of that movie wasn't satisfying, was it?

endōsumento エンドースメント endorsement
* *Endōsumento ga areba, kōkūken wa hoka no kaisha ni tsūyō shimasu.*
With an endorsement, an air ticket can be used on another airline.

endo yūzā エンドユーザー end user
* *Kore wa konpyūtā no endo yūzā no tame no manyuaru desu.*
This is a manual for end users of computers.

enerugii エネルギー energy
* *enerugii no hozon*
the conservation of energy
* *Kare-ra wa atarashii shigoto ni enerugii o sosoide imasu.*
They are pouring their energies into a new task.

enerugisshu エネルギッシュ [German: *energisch*] energetic
* *Kare wa sōnen no enerugisshu na kigyōka desu.*
He is an energetic entrepreneur in the prime of his life.

engēji ringu エンゲージリング engagement ring
* *Kanojo wa ōkina daiya no engēji ringu o moratte, totemo shiawasesō desu.*
She received a big diamond engagement ring and looks very happy.

enjeru エンジェル angel
* *Sono ko wa enjeru no yō desu.*
That young girl looks like an angel.

enjin エンジン engine

- *Yamamichi de kuruma no enjin ga tomarimashita.*
  On a mountain path, the car's engine stopped.

enjinia エンジニア engineer
- *Gaikoku no enjinia ga Nihon e kenshū ni kimasu.*
  Foreign engineers come to Japan to study and do research.

enjiniaringu エンジニアリング engineering
- *Sugureta enjiniaringu o minarai ni kōjō e itte kimasu.*
  I'm going to the factory to receive training in fine engineering.
- *Waga sha demo enjiniaringu bumon o kyōka suru hitsuyō ga arimasu.*
  Even our company has a need to build up its engineering department.

enjoi suru エンジョイする to enjoy
- *Kurūzu de gōka na tabi o enjoi shimashita.*
  We enjoyed a luxurious trip on a cruise ship.

ensuto エンスト [Japanese Usage: engine stop] engine stall
- *Fubuki no naka de ensuto shimashita.*
  The engine stalled in a snowstorm.

entāteimento エンターテイメント entertainment
- *Suiri shōsetsu wa ii entāteimento ni narimasu.*
  Detective stories are entertaining.

entāteinā エンターテイナー entertainer
- *Enkai de amachua no entāteinā ga katsuyaku shite imasu.*
  Amateur entertainers play active parts at banquet parties.

entāteinmento エンターテインメント *see* **entāteimento**

entoransu エントランス entrance
- *Entoransu o hairu to, migite ni uketsuke ga arimasu.*
  When you go through the entrance, you will find the reception desk on the right.

enzeru エンゼル *see* **enjeru**

enzerufisshu エンゼルフィッシュ angelfish
- *Enzerufisshu ga tamago o umimashita.*

The angelfish spawned.

epirōgu エピローグ epilogue
- *Sono geki no epirōgu wa dasoku desu.*

The epilogue of the play is superfluous.

episōdo エピソード episode
- *Kore-ra no episōdo wa sakusha no mezurashii keiken ni motozuite imasu.*

These episodes are based on the author's unusual experiences.

epokku エポック epoch
- *Reisen no shūketsu ga sekai heiwa ni totte hitotsu no epokku ni narimashita.*

The end of the cold war heralded an epoch of world peace.

epokku-mēkingu エポックメーキング epoch-making
- *Konpyūtā no hatsumei wa epokku-mēkingu na dekigoto to ieru deshō.*

You can say that the invention of computers was an epoch-making event.

ēpuriru fūru エープリルフール April Fools' Day
- *Ēpuriru fūru ni mata damasaremashita.*

I was tricked again on April Fools' Day.

epuron エプロン apron
- *Suchuwādesu ga epuron o kakete shokuji o dashite imasu.*

Stewardesses wearing aprons are serving food.

erā エラー error
- *Kono repōto ni wa taihen na erā ga arimasu.*

There is a serious error in this report.

erebētā エレベーター elevator
- *Kono erebētā wa kaku-kai ni tomarimasu.*

This elevator stops at each floor.

eregansu エレガンス elegance
- *Kono chōkoku ga shitsunai ni eregansu o soete imasu.*

This sculpture adds elegance to the room.

ereganto エレガント　elegant
- *Sakuhin no ereganto na buntai ni kanshin shimashita.*
  I was impressed by the work's elegant style.
- *Kanojo wa gesuto to shite ereganto ni furumaimashita.*
  She conducted herself elegantly as the guest of honor.

erejii エレジー　elegy, old ballad
- *Mukashi hitto shita erejii ga fukkatsu shimashita.*
  A ballad that was a hit a long time ago has been revived.

erekutoronikusu エレクトロニクス　electronics
- *Nihon wa erekutoronikusu de sekai no sentan o itte imasu.*
  Japan leads the world in electronics.

eremento エレメント　element
- *Chiimuwāku wa kōritsuteki na seisan ni hitsuyō na eremento desu.*
  Teamwork is a critical element for efficient production.

eria エリア　area
- *Kono eria wa kaimono ni fuben desu.*
  This area is inconvenient for shopping.

eriito エリート　elite
- *Kare wa shōrai o yakusoku sareta eriito desu.*
  He's cream of the crop with a promising future.

erochikku エロチック　erotic
- *Sono erochikku na shashinshū wa hidoku hinan saremashita.*
  The erotic photograph collection was severely criticized.

erochishizumu エロチシズム　eroticism
- *Sono buyōgeki wa erochishizumu ni okeru bi o tsuikyū shite imasu.*
  The dance drama searches for the beauty in eroticism.

erotishizumu エロティシズム　see **erochishizumu**

erotikku エロティック　see **erochikku**

eru エル L　L (large)
- *Kono sētā no eru o misete kudasai.*

Please show me this sweater in a large size.

erueru エルエル LL LL (extra large)

* *erueru no doresu*
an extra large-sized dress

erueru エルエル LL LL (language laboratory)

* *Isshūkan ni nido erueru ni iku koto ni natte imasu.*
We are to go to the language laboratory twice a week.

esē エセー *see* **essē**

essē エッセー essay

* *Kono essē wa ninjō no kibi o atsukatta mono desu.*
This essay deals with the secrets of human nature.

esseisuto エッセイスト essayist

* *Kanojo wa surudoi dōsatsu-ryoku de shirareta esseisuto desu.*
She is an essayist known for her keen insight.

essensu エッセンス essence

* *banira essensu*
vanilla essence

esu エス S S (small)

* *Esu wa chotto kyūkutsu desu.*
The small is a little too tight for me.

ēsu エース ace

* *Sono tōshu wa chiimu no ēsu desu.*
That pitcher is the ace of the team.

esuefu エスエフ SF SF, science fiction

* *Hon'ya de zasshi no kaigai esuefu tokushū ga me ni tsukimashita.*
The magazine's special issue on foreign science fiction caught my eye in the bookstore.

esukarētā エスカレーター escalator

* *Esukarētā de ikkai kara hachikai made agarimashita.*
I went up from the first to the eighth floor by escalator.

esukarēto suru エスカレートする to escalate

- *Kōron ga esukarēto shite ōgenka ni narimashita.*
A quarrel escalated into a big fight.

esukarugo エスカルゴ escargot
- *Esukarugo no oishii Furansu ryōri no mise o go-shōkai shimashō.*
Let me recommend a French restaurant that serves delicious escargot.

esukēpu suru エスケープする to escape
- *Tōkyō no atsusa o esukēpu shite, Shiga-kōgen de natsu o sugoshimashita.*
I spent the summer in the Shiga highlands, escaping the Tokyo heat.

Esukimō エスキモー Eskimo
- *Esukimō wa samui chihō de genshiteki na seikatsu o okutte imasu.*
Eskimos lead pristine lives in cold regions.

esukōto suru エスコートする to escort
- *Kare wa gārufurendo o esukōto shite konsāto ni ikimashita.*
He escorted his girlfriend to the concert.

esunikku エスニック ethnic
- *Doko e itte mo esunikku ryōri ga būmu desu.*
Ethnic food is booming everywhere.

esu-ō-esu エス・オー・エス SOS SOS
- *Sono fune wa esu-ō-esu o hasshimashita.*
The ship sent out an SOS.

Esuperanto エスペラント Esperanto
- *Esuperanto wa sekai kyōtsū no kotoba to shite tsukuraremashita.*
Esperanto was created to be the world's common language.

esupuri エスプリ esprit
- *Kare no sakuhin wa esupuri no kiita kaiwa de ninki ga arimasu.*

His works are popular because the conversations are so dynamic.

esutetikku エステティック [French: *esthétique*] esthetics, improving one's own beauty
- *Kanojo wa esutetikku ni kotte imasu ga kōka wa nasasō desu.*
  She is obsessed with beauty aids but she doesn't seem to be getting any more beautiful.

etoranze エトランゼ [French: *étranger*] stranger, alien
- *Kotoba ga wakaranakute Pari de wa mattaku no etoranze deshita.*
  Without knowing the language, we were total aliens in Paris.
- *Puraha deno etoranze toshite no keiken wa kare no sakuhin ni ōkina eikyō o ataemashita.*
  His experience as a stranger in Prague had a big influence on his work.

F

FA *see* **efuē**
FBI *see* **Efubiiai**
FM *see* **efuemu**
fā ファー fur
- *Kankoku wa fā seihin no mekka desu.*
  Korea is a mecca for fur products.

faiaman ファイアマン fireman, relief pitcher
- *Faiaman ga kodomo o nikai kara sukuidashimashita.*
  A fireman rescued a child from the second floor.
- *Saikin sono tōshu wa faiaman to shite katsuyaku shite imasu.*

He has been active as a relief pitcher recently.

faibā ファイバー fiber
- *Faibā no ōi yasai wa karada ni ii desu.*
Vegetables with lots of fiber are good for the health.

fainansu ファイナンス finance; **~suru** する to finance
- *Sono mēkā wa Amerika ni fainansu gaisha o tsukurimashita.*
The manufacturer established a finance company in America.
- *Aru ginkō ga sono kaisha no shinki jigyō o fainansu shite imasu.*
A certain bank finances the new ventures of that company.

fainarisuto ファイナリスト finalist
- *Kanojo wa piano no konkūru de fainarisuto no hitori deshita.*
She was one of the finalists in the piano contest.

fainaru ファイナル final
- *Gorufu no konpe wa ashita ga fainaru desu.*
Tomorrow will be the golf tournament final.

faindā ファインダー finder, view finder
- *Faindā de mita kanojo no egao wa totemo utsukushikatta desu.*
Her smiling face in the view finder was very beautiful.

fain purē ファインプレー fine play
- *Pitchā wa hisashiburi ni fain purē o misete kuremashita.*
It has been a long time since the pitcher played so well.
- *Aite chiimu no sādo no fain purē de gyakuten no chansu o nogashimashita.*
The other team's third baseman made a great play and we lost our chance to come from behind.

fairu ファイル file; **~suru** する to file
- *Fairu o shirabemashita ga mitsukarimasen deshita.*
I went through the file but couldn't find it.

* *Jinmeibo wa koko ni fairu shite arimasu.*
  The lists of names are filed here.

faitā ファイター fighter

* *Kare wa faitā da kara, ichido no shippai de wa kujikemasen.*
  Because he is a fighter, he won't be daunted by a single failure.

faitingu supiritto ファイティングスピリット fighting spirit

* *Kare wa faitingu supiritto o motte nagai tōbyō seikatsu o taemashita.*
  He endured his long illness with fighting spirit.

faito ファイト fight

* *Kesshōsen ni katō to chiimu wa faito ni moete imasu.*
  The team is full of fight because they want to win the finals.

fajii konpyūtā ファジーコンピューター [Japanese Usage: fuzzy computer] a computer that has fuzzy logic

* *Ningen no yō ni jōhō shori no dekiru fajii konpyūtā ga kaihatsu sareru deshō.*
  A fuzzy logic computer that can handle information almost like humans will probably be developed.

fakkusu ファックス *see* **fakusu**

fakushimiri ファクシミリ *see* **fakusu**

fakusu ファクス fax

* *Kono jimusho ni wa fakusu ga nidai arimasu.*
  There are two fax machines in this office.

fakutā ファクター factor

* *Doryoku to kōun ga kare no seikō no fakutā desu.*
  Effort and good luck are factors in his success.

fakutorii ōtomēshon ファクトリー・オートメーション factory automation

* *Robotto o katsuyō shita fakutorii ōtomēshon ga susunde imasu.*

Factory automation utilizing robots is making progress.

famikon ファミコン [Japanese Usage: fami(ly) com(puter)]
home entertainment system
- *Tokidoki kodomo to famikon de gēmu o shimasu.*
Sometimes I play computer games at home with my child.

famirii ファミリー family
- *Nihon no kaisha wa famirii ishiki ga tsuyoi desu.*
Japanese companies have a strong sense of family.
- *Kondo no Nichiyō wa famirii sābisu o suru yotei desu.*
I'm planning to spend this Sunday with my family.

famirii kā ファミリーカー family car
- *Famirii kā yori supōtsu kā o kaitai desu.*
I want to buy a sports car rather than a family car.

famirii konpyūtā ファミリー・コンピューター *see*
famikon

famirii resutoran ファミリー・レストラン family restau-
rant
- *Tsuki ni ichido kazokuzure de famirii resutoran e ikimasu.*
We go to a family restaurant once a month with our family.

fan ファン fan
- *Rokku shingā ni wa wakai fan ga ōi desu.*
Rock singers have a large number of young fans.

fanachikku ファナチック fanatic
- *Sono shūkyō no fanachikku na shinja ga shūdan jisatsu o shimashita.*
The fanatic followers of that religion committed mass
suicide.

fandamentaruzu ファンダメンタルズ fundamentals
- *Keizai no fandamentaruzu ga kawase sōba o kimeru no desu.*
Fundamental elements in the economy determine the ex-
change rate.

fanatikku ファナティック *see* **fanachikku**

fandēshon ファンデーション foundation (cosmetic)
- *Fandēshon wa natsu no hizashi kara hada o mamorimasu.*
  Foundation protects your skin from the summer sunlight.

fando manējā ファンドマネージャー fund manager
- *Kare wa yarite no fando manējā desu.*
  He is a capable fund manager.

fanii fēsu ファニーフェース funny face
- *Kanojo wa fanii fēsu de uridashimashita.*
  Her funny face won her popularity.

fankushon ファンクション function, output
- *Kikai no fankushon ga teika shimashita.*
  The machine's output has dropped.

fanshii ファンシー fancy
- *Kanojo no wādorōbu ni wa fanshii na yōfuku ga takusan kakatte imasu.*
  There are many fancy clothes hanging in her wardrobe closet.

fanshii shopppu ファンシーショップ [Japanese Usage: fancy shop] shop for fancy goods
- *Fanshii shopppu de kono keshōbako o mitsukemashita.*
  I found this cosmetic case in a fancy gift shop.

fantajii ファンタジー fantasy
- *Sono monogatari wa kodomo-tachi o fantajii no sekai e michibikimasu.*
  The story leads children into a world of fantasy.

fantasuchikku ファンタスチック fantastic, great
- *fantasuchikku na aidia*
  a fantastic idea
- *Mori no naka no shiro wa fantasuchikku ni miemashita.*
  The castle in the woods looked fantastic.

fantasutikku ファンタスティック *see* **fantasuchikku**
fāru ファール *see* **fauru**
fasādo ファサード facade

• *Sono biru no fasādo wa fantasuchikku na dezain ga
  hodokosarete imasu.*
  The building's facade is decorated with a fantastic design.

fashizumu ファシズム fascism
• *Senzen sekai kakuchi de fashizumu undō ga taitō
  shimashita.*
  Before the war, fascist movements arose in various parts of
  the world.

fassho ファッショ [Italian: *Fascio*] *see* **fashizumu**

fasshon ファッション fashion
• *Dono mise mo haru no fasshon de akaruku miemasu.*
  Spring fashions brighten all the stores.

fasshonaburu ファッショナブル fashionable
• *Kanojo wa fasshonaburu na hea sutairu o shite imasu.*
  Her hair style is very fashionable.
• *Machiaishitsu wa hoteru no raunji no yō ni fasshonaburu
  ni narimashita.*
  The waiting room became as fashionable as a hotel lounge.

fasshon moderu ファッションモデル fashion model
• *Ano joyū wa moto fasshon moderu deshita.*
  That actress used to be a fashion model.

fasshon shō ファッションショー fashion show
• *Kyō no fasshon shō de aki no shinsaku ga happyō
  saremasu.*
  New designs for the fall will be presented at today's fashion
  show.

fasunā ファスナー fastener, zipper, zip
• *Senaka no fasunā o shimete kudasai.*
  Please do up the fastener on my back.

fāsuto ファースト first, first base
• *Fāsuto (no senshu) wa dare desu ka?*
  Who is the first baseman?

fāsuto fūdo ファーストフード fast food

- *Isogashii toki wa, fāsuto fūdo de sumasete shimaimasu.*
  When I'm busy, I get by on fast food.

fāsuto kurasu ファーストクラス first class

- *Narita kara San-furanshisuko made fāsuto kurasu de tobimashita.*
  I flew first class from Narita to San Francisco.

Fāsuto redii ファーストレディー First Lady

- *Fāsuto redii ni yotte fasshon ga tsukurareru koto ga arimasu.*
  There are times when the First Lady sets the fashion.

faundēshon ファウンデーション *see* **fandēshon**

fauru ファウル foul

- *Kare no utta bōru wa fauru ni narimashita.*
  The ball he hit was a foul.
- *Hōmuran ka to omowareta ōkina furai wa fauru deshita.*
  I thought it was a home run but it was a long fly that went foul.

Fāzā ファーザー Father (Christian priest)

- *Shingakkō o detate no wakai Fāzā ga kyōkai ni kimashita.*
  A young priest fresh from the seminary came to our Church.

fea フェア fair

- *Kare ni wa fea na seishin ga arimasen.*
  He is not a fair-minded person.
- *Kanojo wa hito o fea ni atsukaimasu.*
  She treats people fairly.

fea フェア fair *see* **fea purē**

- *Nihon de wa, teikiteki ni iroiro na fea ga hirakaremasu.*
  In Japan, various kinds of fairs are routinely held.
- *Sō iu koto o suru no wa fea de wa arimasen.*
  It's not fair to do that kind of thing.

fea purē フェアプレー fair play

- *Kare-ra wa fea purē o kokoro ni chikatte, shutsujō shimashita.*

Pledging to play fair, they took the field.

- *Wareware wa fea purē ni tesshite seisei dōdō to tatakau koto o chikaimasu.*

We swear we will fight fair and square.

fēdo auto フェードアウト fadeout; **~suru** する to fade out

- *Sono shūkan wa izure fēdo auto suru deshō.*

That custom will fade out eventually.

feiku fā フェイクファー fake fur

- *Feiku fā ga shin fasshon to shite chūmoku sarete imasu.*

Fake fur is getting attention as a new fashion.

feinto フェイント feint

- *Teki ni feinto o kakete itten iremashita.*

I made a feint against the opponent and gained one point.

feminisuto フェミニスト gallant

- *Kare wa shanai kitte no feminisuto desu.*

He is the most gallant man in the whole company.

fēmu フェーム fame

- *Fēmu o motometa amari, kanojo wa shikujirimashita.*

Because she was too eager in her search for fame, she failed.

fēn フェーン [German: *Föhn*] hot, dry wind blown down from a mountain

- *Nihon-kai gawa no kakuchi de fēn genshō ga oki, kion ga jōshō shimashita.*

Because of the hot, dry wind blowing from the Japan Sea coast, the temperature has risen.

fendā フェンダー fender

- *Kuruma no fendā ga magatte imasu.*

The car's fender is bent.

fenshingu フェンシング fencing

- *Issho ni fenshingu no shiai o mi ni ikimashō.*

Let's go to see the fencing match together.

fensu フェンス fence

- *Sono shikichi wa takai fensu de kakomarete imasu.*

The site is surrounded by a high fence.

ferii フェリー ferry
- *Ferii de kaikyō o watarimashita.*
  I crossed the channel by ferry.

ferōshippu フェローシップ fellowship
- *Kare wa Nihon de bungaku kenkyū o suru tame ni ferōshippu o ukemashita.*
  He received a fellowship to do literary research in Japan.

feruto フェルト felt
- *Feruto no surippa wa karukute hakigokochi ga ii desu.*
  Felt slippers are light and comfortable to wear.

fesutibaru フェスティバル festival
- *Nihon de wa ichinenjū arayuru shurui no fesutibaru ga okonawaremasu.*
  In Japan all kinds of festivals take place throughout the year.

fezākatto フェザーカット feathercut
- *Chūnen no josei no fezākatto ga hayatte imasu.*
  The feathercut is in fashion among middle-aged women.

fēzu フェーズ phase
- *Kono kōsu no kaku fēzu no owari ni shiken ga arimasu.*
  An examination is given at the end of each phase of this course.
- *Kankeisha no aida de fēzu awase o shite oku hitsuyō ga arimasu.*
  It is necessary to check each phase with the persons concerned.

fianse フィアンセ fiancé, fiancée
- *Kanojo no fianse wa Shidonii no shiten ni tenkin shimasu.*
  Her fiancé will be transferred to a branch office in Sydney.

figyua フィギュア *see* **figyua sukēto**

figyua sukēto フィギュアスケート figure skating
- *Amerika wa figyua sukēto de kin-medaru o torimashita.*

America won a gold medal in figure skating.

fiibā フィーバー fever, enthusiasm; **~suru** する to be enthusiastic
- *Tōshika wa sekiyu kabu ni tai shite fiibā o misete imasu.*
  The investors are exhibiting oil stock fever.

fiidobakku フィードバック feedback; **~suru** する to give/receive feedback
- *Shiken no ato de itsumo fiidobakku ga arimasu.*
  Feedback is always given after an examination.
- *Shinseihin ni taisuru kouriten no koe o mēkā ni fiidobakku shimasu.*
  Retailers' opinions of the new products will be fed back to the manufacturer.

fiiringu フィーリング feeling
- *Sore wa rikutsu de wa naku, fiiringu no mondai desu.*
  That's not a matter of logic, but of emotion.

fiirudo フィールド field
- *Kanojo wa otoko no fiirudo de katsuyaku shite imasu.*
  She is active in a male field.

fiirudo wāku フィールドワーク field work
- *Chishitsugaku ya kōkogaku de fiirudo wāku ga jūshi sarete imasu.*
  Much importance is attached to field work in geology and archaeology.

fiito フィート feet (foot)
- *Ichi fiito wa yaku sanjussenchi desu.*
  One foot is about 30 centimeters.

fijikaru フィジカル physical
- *Nanigoto ni yorazu, mazu fijikaru na tairyoku ga hitsuyō desu.*
  First and foremost you need physical strength.

fikkusu suru フィックスする to fix
- *Kaigi no nittei o narubeku hayaku fikkusu shite kudasai.*

Please fix the date for the conference as soon as possible.

fikushon フィクション fiction

- *Sono hanashi wa hontō dokoro ka mattaku no fikushon desu.*

Far from the truth, what you hear is pure fiction.

fināre フィナーレ finale

- *Fināre de shutsuensha ga minna sutēji ni soroimashita.*

All the performers gathered on the stage for the finale.

finisshu フィニッシュ finish; **~suru** する to finish

- *Sono itten de shiai no finisshu ga kimarimashita.*

That one point determined the finish of the game.

- *Kore wa raishū no Suiyōbi made ni finisshu shite kudasai.*

Please finish this by next Wednesday.

firansoropii フィランソロピー philanthropy

- *Firansoropii-katsudo ni sanka shite, kigyō ga shakai no tame ni kifu o shite imasu.*

Joining the philanthropy movement, industries are making donations to society.

fire フィレ *see* **hire**

firosofii フィロソフィー philosophy

- *Gakusei no koro watashi-tachi wa yoku firosofii o ronjimashita.*

When we were students, we often talked about philosophy.

firuhāmonikku フィルハーモニック philharmonic

- *Shikago Firuhāmonikku Ōkesutora ga Tōkyō de ensō shimashita.*

The Chicago Philharmonic Orchestra played in Tokyo.

firumu フィルム film

- *Kono firumu o nihon kudasai.*

Please give me two rolls of this film.

firutā フィルター filter

- *Kare wa firutā tsuki no tabako shika suimasen.*

He smokes only filter-tip cigarettes.

fisshingu フィッシング fishing
- *Konshūmatsu wa fisshingu ni ikimasu.*
  I'm going fishing this weekend.

fisshu フィッシュ fish
- *Fisshu ni wa kono wain ga yoku aimasu.*
  This wine goes very well with fish.

fittingu rūmu フィッティング・ルーム fitting room
- *Fittingu rūmu de doresu o kite mimashita.*
  I tried on dresses in the fitting room.

fitto suru フィットする to fit
- *Kono saizu wa ōkisugite fitto shimasen.*
  This size is too big and doesn't fit me.

fittonesu フィットネス fitness
- *Fittonesu ni maiasa uōkingu o shimasu.*
  I walk to improve my physical fitness every morning.
- *Fittonesu kurabu ni maishū kayotte imasu.*
  I go to a fitness club every week.

foa bōru フォアボール [Japanese Usage: four balls] base on balls
- *Foa bōru de rannā ga ichirui ni demashita.*
  Base on balls, and the runner went to first base.
- *Oshidashi no foa bōru de kesshōten ga hairimashita.*
  A base on balls forced the winning run home.

fōkasu フォーカス focus; **~suru** する to focus
- *Kono shashin wa fōkasu ga amai desu ne.*
  This photo is out of focus, isn't it?
- *Kare no shiseikatsu ga shūkanshi ni fōkasu saremashita.*
  A weekly magazine focused on his private life.

fōku フォーク fork
- *Yōshoku wa fōku to naifu de tabemasu.*
  We eat Western food with a knife and fork.

fōku songu フォークソング folk song
- *Gitā o hikinagara fōku songu o utaimasu.*

I sing folk songs while playing the guitar.

fōmaru フォーマル formal

- *Fōmaru na bansankai ni manekaremashita.*
  I was invited to a formal dinner party.
- *Kono koto wa mada fōmaru ni happyō sarete imasen.*
  This matter has not been announced formally yet.

fōmatto フォーマット format; **~suru** する to format

- *Kongetsu kara kono zasshi no fōmatto ga kawarimashita.*
  Starting this month, the format of this magazine has been changed.
- *Pasokon de tsukau mae ni furoppii o fōmatto shinakereba narimasen.*
  You have to format the floppy before using it in a P.C.

fōmēshon フォーメーション formation

- *Hikōki ga fōmēshon o kunde tonde imasu.*
  The airplanes are flying in formation.

fōmu フォーム form

- *Kare no suiei no fōmu wa subarashii desu.*
  His swimming form is excellent.

fōmu フォーム *see* **hōmu** (*platform*)

fon フォン *see* **hon**

fōramu フォーラム forum

- *Tsugi no fōramu no tēma wa "hataraku josei" desu.*
  The next forum will focus on working women.

forō suru フォローする to follow, help out

- *Kare ga umaku forō shite kureta no de, purezentēshon wa seikō shimashita.*
  Because he tactfully helped me out, my presentation was successful.

forō uindo フォローウインド [Japanese Usage: follow wind] favorable wind

- *Kōkeiki no forō uindo o ukete, kaisha no seiseki ga agarimashita.*

With the wind of good fortune, the company's business earnings have gone up.

forudā フォルダー folder
• *Gansho wa minna forudā ni irete oite kudasai.*
Please keep all the applications in a folder.

forumu フォルム *see* **fōmu** (*form*)

foto フォト *see* **fotogurafi**

fotogurafā フォトグラファー photographer
• *Kanojo wa fotogurafā to shite mi o tatete imasu.*
She has established herself as a photographer.

fotogurafi フォトグラフィ photography
• *Kare no fotogurafi wa inshōha no eikyō ga tsuyoi desu.*
His photography shows strong impressionistic influences.

fotojenikku フォトジェニック photogenic
• *Shuyaku ni erabareta nyū fēsu wa fotojenikku na kao o shite imasu.*
The new unknown selected for the leading part has a photogenic face.

fuan フアン *see* **fan**

fūdo フード hood
• *fūdo tsuki no kōto*
a coat with a hood

fueruto フエルト *see* **feruto**

fuirumu フイルム *see* **firumu**

furai フライ deep-fry, fry
• *ebi furai*
fried prawns
• *Sakana wa furai ni shimashō.*
Let's fry the fish.

furai フライ fly ball
• *Niruishu ga hashitte furai o torimashita.*
The second baseman ran to catch the fly ball.

furaiingu フライイング *see* **furaingu**

furaingu フライング [Japanese Usage: flying] false start
- *Kyōei de kare wa gōhō ga naru mae ni furaingu o shimashita.*
  In the swimming race he made a false start just before the gun was fired.

furai pan フライパン frying pan
- *Furai pan de sakana o sotē ni shimasu.*
  I fry fish in a frying pan.

furaito フライト flight
- *Furaito jikan wa san-jikan tarazu desu.*
  The flight's duration is less than three hours.

furanchaizu フランチャイズ franchise (store), home ground
- *Watashi-tachi wa Makudonarudo no furanchaizu ten desu.*
  We are a McDonald's franchise.
- *Sono chiimu no furanchaizu wa yoso ni utsusareru kamo shiremasen.*
  That team's franchise may be moved to somewhere else.

furanku フランク frank
- *Kare no furanku na taido wa hito ni kōkan o ataemasu.*
  His frank attitude makes a favorable impression on people.
- *Shūkai de furanku ni hanashiaimashita.*
  We talked frankly at the meeting.

furanneru フランネル flannel
- *furanneru no pajama*
  flannel pajamas

Furansu フランス France
- *Imōto wa Furansu e itta mama ichido mo kaettekimasen.*
  My younger sister went to France and has never come back.

furasshu フラッシュ flash; **~suru** する to flash
- *Rokku shingā wa hōdōjin no furasshu o abimashita.*
  The rock singer was flooded in the press corps' camera flashes.
- *Kono kamera wa serufu taimā o tsukau toki akai ranpu ga*

furasshu shimasu.
When you use the self-timer on this camera, the red light
flashes.

furasshubakku フラッシュバック flashback; ~**suru** する
to flash back

* *Furasshubakku de kako no dekigoto o katarimasu.*
Flashbacks are used to portray past events.
* *Kono eiga wa furasshubakku o takumi ni tsukatte
kinchōkan o moriagete imasu.*
This movie skillfully uses flashbacks to build up tension.
* *Totsuzen kare no omokage ga nōri ni furasshubakku
shimashita.*
Suddenly his image flashed across my mind.

furasshu-kādo フラッシュカード flashcard

* *Furasshu-kādo o tsukatte, tango o oboemasu.*
Using flashcards, I memorize vocabulary words.

furasuko フラスコ [Portuguese: *flasco*] flask

* *Kagaku no jikken ni furasuko o tsukaimasu.*
Flasks are used for chemical experiments.

furasutorēshon フラストレーション frustration

* *Keikaku ga umaku ikazu, nando mo furasutorēshon o
ajiwaimashita.*
The plan did not go smoothly and it caused me a lot of
frustration.

furawā arenjimento フラワーアレンジメント flower
arrangement

* *Dorai furawā wa yōfū no furawā arenjimento desu.*
Dried flowers are European-style ikebana, or flower arrangement.

furē フレー hurray

* *"Furē! Furē!" to sakende, chiimu no ōen o shimashita.*
We cheered on the team, shouting "Hurray! Hurray!"

furekishibiritii フレキシビリティー flexibility

- *Kare wa furekishibiritii ga nai no de, buka ni uke ga warui desu.*

  Because he lacks flexibility, he is unpopular among those who work under him.

furekishiburu フレキシブル flexible

- *furekishiburu na rōdō jikan*
  flexible working hours
- *Sukejūru wa furekishiburu ni kunde arimasu.*
  The schedule is made flexibly.

furekkusutaimu フレックスタイム flextime

- *Furekkusutaimu no dōnyū ga kaisha gawa ni yotte kentō sarete imasu.*

  The management is considering the introduction of flexible work time.
- *Jūgyōin no hotondo wa furekkusutaimu desu.*
  Most workers are on flextime.

furekushibiritii フレクシビリティー *see* **furekishibiritii**
furekushiburu フレクシブル *see* **furekishiburu**
furēmu フレーム frame

- *Kanojo wa pinku no furēmu no sangurasu o kakete imasu.*
  She is wearing pink-framed sunglasses.

furēmuwāku フレームワーク framework

- *Yosan no furēmuwāku o kimemashita.*
  We set up the framework for the budget.

Furenchi furai フレンチフライ French fries

- *Hanbāgā to Furenchi furai o teikuauto shimashita.*
  I ordered a hamburger and French fries takeout.

Furenchi suriibu フレンチスリーブ French sleeve

- *Furenchi suriibu no burausu*
  a French-sleeved blouse

Furenchi tōsuto フレンチトースト French toast

- *Furenchi tōsuto wa watashi no kōbutsu desu.*
  French toast is my favorite food.

furendorii フレンドリー friendly
- *Shokuba wa furendorii na fun'iki de tanoshii desu.*
  My workplace has a friendly atmosphere and I enjoy it.

furesshu フレッシュ fresh
- *furesshu na kudamono*
  fresh fruit
- *Asa no kūki wa kibun o furesshu ni shimasu.*
  The morning air makes me feel fresh.

furesshuman フレッシュマン freshman, new employee
- *Kare wa kotoshi nyūsha shita bakari no furesshuman desu.*
  He is a new employee who joined the firm just this year.

furēzu フレーズ phrase
- *Senden posutā ni sendōteki na furēzu ga kaite arimasu.*
  There are provocative phrases written on that propaganda poster.
- *Eigo no furēzu ni wa mattaku imi ga sōzō dekinai yōna mono ga arimasu.*
  In English there are phrases for which I can't even imagine the meanings.

furii フリー free *see* **furiiransu**
- *Furii na tachiba de shigoto o shitai desu.*
  I want to work in a freer position.
- *Shinbunsha o yamete furii ni narimashita.*
  I quit my job at the newspaper company and became a freelancer.

furii daiaru フリーダイアル [Japanese Usage: free dial] toll-free number
- *Go-chūmon wa furii daiaru o go-riyō kudasai.*
  Please use the toll-free number for your orders.

furii daiyaru フリーダイヤル *see* **furii daiaru**

furii pasu フリーパス free pass
- *Watashi wa suizokukan no furii pasu o motte imasu.*

I have a free pass to the aquarium.

furiiransā フリーランサー *see* **furiiransu**

furiiransu フリーランス freelancer, freelance
- *Kanojo wa furiiransu de iroiro na zasshi ni kaite imasu.*
  She writes freelance for various magazines.

furiisutairu フリースタイル freestyle
- *Kare wa suiei no furiisutairu de ichiban ni narimashita.*
  He won first place in the freestyle swimming race.

furii taimu フリータイム free time
- *Furii taimu ga jūbun ni aru dantai ryokō ni sanka shitai to omoimasu.*
  I would like to join a group tour that has plenty of free time.

furii tōkingu フリートーキング [Japanese Usage: free talking] free discussion
- *Iroiro na koto o furii tōkingu de hanashiaimashita.*
  We had a free discussion about various matters.

furiiuē フリーウエー freeway
- *Akai supōtsu kā ga furiiwē o tobashite imasu.*
  A red sports car is speeding down the freeway.

furiiwē フリーウェー *see* **furiiuē**

furiiwei フリーウェイ *see* **furiiuē**

furiizā フリーザー freezer
- *Niku o furizā ni irete okimasu.*
  I keep meat in the freezer.

furoa フロア floor
- *Henshūbu wa kono furoa desu ka?*
  Is the editorial office on this floor?

furoa shō フロアショー floor show
- *Ima furoa shō ga hajimaru tokoro desu.*
  The floor show is just starting now.

furokku フロック fluke
- *Kare-ra no shōri wa furokku to minasarete imasu.*
  Their victory is regarded as a fluke.

furokku kōto フロックコート frock coat
- *Furokku kōto o kita shinshi ga kuruma o orimashita.*
  A gentleman wearing a frock coat got out of the car.

furontia フロンティア frontier, untapped territory
- *Kagakusha wa kagaku no furontia ni chōsen shite imasu.*
  Scientists are challenging the frontiers of science.

furonto フロント front, front desk
- *Kichōhin wa furonto ni azukete okimasu.*
  I leave my valuables at the front desk.

furoppii フロッピー floppy disk
- *Kono furoppii wa hoka no konpyūtā ni mo tsukaemasu.*
  This floppy disk can be used in other computers.

furoppii disuku フロッピーディスク *see* **furoppii**

furōringu フローリング flooring, boarding the floor
- *chairo no furōringu*
  a brown floor
- *Kitchin no yuka o furōringu ni shitai desu.*
  I want to have flooring put on the kitchen floor.

furōzun fūdo フローズン・フード frozen food
- *Furōzun fūdo wa hataraku josei ni totte mo dokushin dansei ni totte mo totemo benri desu.*
  Frozen food is very convenient for working women, and single men too.

furu フル full
- *Tairyō chūmon o ukete kōjō wa furu kaiten shite imasu.*
  Because of the large order, the factory is running at full speed.
- *Kyanpu seikatsu o furu ni tanoshimimashita.*
  We fully enjoyed camping out.

furu bēsu フルベース [Japanese Usage: full base] load the bases, with the bases loaded
- *Kyūkai no ura de furu bēsu desu.*
  Bases are loaded in the bottom of the ninth inning.

furu kōsu フルコース [Japanese Usage: full course] full-course dinner
- *Furu kōsu no shokuji o go-chisō ni narimashita.*
  I was treated to a full-course dinner.

furu nēmu フルネーム full name
- *Koko ni adoresu to furu nēmu o kaite kudasai.*
  Please write your full name and address here.

furu supiido フルスピード full speed
- *Shōbōsha ga furu supiido de hashitte imasu.*
  A fire engine is running at full speed.

furu taimu フルタイム full time
- *Raigetsu kara furu taimu de hatarakimasu.*
  Starting next month I'll be working full time.

furūto フルート flute
- *Tonari no ie no furūto ga urusakute benkyō dekimasen.*
  I can't study because the annoying sound of a flute is coming from next door.

furūtsu フルーツ fruit
- *Tokidoki asagohan ni furūtsu o tabemasu.*
  Sometimes I eat fruit for breakfast.

furūtsu jūsu フルーツジュース fruit juice
- *Gyūnyū no kawari ni furūtsu jūsu o nomimashita.*
  I had fruit juice instead of milk.

furūtsu pārā フルーツパーラー [Japanese Usage: fruit parlor] coffee shop that also sells fruit
- *Furūtsu pārā wa taitei wakai josei de konde imasu.*
  "Fruit parlors" are usually crowded with young women.

furyūto フリュート *see* **furūto**

futtobōru フットボール football
- *Terebi de futtobōru no gēmu o mimashita.*
  I watched a football game on TV.

futtoraito フットライト the footlights
- *Kare no kyakuhon ga hajimete futtoraito o abimashita.*

His play was put on stage for the first time.

futtouea フットウエア footwear

- *Futtouea no uriba wa gokai desu.*

  Footwear is sold on the fifth floor.

futtowāku フットワーク footwork

- *Kanojo no dansu wa futtowāku ga subarashii desu.*

  Her footwork in dance is excellent.

fyūzu フューズ *see* **hyūzu**

G

GATT *see* **Gatto**

GI *see* **jii-ai**

G-men Gメン *see* **jii-men**

GNP *see* **jii-enu-pii**

G-pan Gパン *see* **jii-pan**

gāden pātii ガーデンパーティー garden party

- *Ame de gāden pātii wa dainashi ni narimashita.*

  The rain ruined the garden party.

gādo ガード girder bridge, railroad overpass

- *Gādo o kugutte senro no mukōgawa ni demashita.*

  Passing under a girder bridge, I came out on the other side of the railroad.

gādoman ガードマン [Japanese Usage: guardman] security guard

- *Mon no mae ni gādoman ga tatte imasu.*

  A security guard is standing in front of the gate.

gādorēru ガードレール guardrail

- *Torakku ga gādorēru o tsukiyabutte gake kara ochimashita.*

  A truck crashed through the guardrail and fell off the cliff.

gaidansu ガイダンス guidance
  • *Gakusei ni zemi ni kan shite gaidansu o shimasu.*
  I am counseling my students about the seminar.
gaido ガイド guide
  • *Bijutsukan de wakai gaido no setsumei o kikimashita.*
  We listened to a young guide's explanation at the art museum.
gaidobukku ガイドブック guidebook
  • *Hon'ya de yoku gaidobukku o tachiyomi shimasu.*
  I often read guidebooks while standing in the bookstore.
gaidorain ガイドライン guideline
  • *Kore wa kaunseringu ni kan suru gaidorain desu.*
  These are the guidelines for counseling.
gamu ガム chewing gum
  • *Michi o arukinagara gamu o kande wa ikemasen yo.*
  You really should not chew gum while walking on the street.
gan ガン gun, pistol, rifle
  • *Kare-ra wa gan o mitsuyu shite iru to iu uwasa desu.*
  Rumor has it that they are smuggling guns.
garasu ガラス [Dutch: *glas*] glass, pane
  • *garasu no kabin*
  a glass flower vase
garēji ガレージ garage
  • *Kono biru no chika wa garēji ni natte imasu.*
  There's a garage in the basement of this building.
garēji sēru ガレージセール garage sale
  • *Kinjo no garēji sēru de honbako o kaimashita.*
  I bought a bookcase at a garage sale in my neighborhood.
gārikku ガーリック garlic
  • *Gārikku o tsukau to, aji ga ichidan to yoku narimasu.*
  Using garlic greatly improves the flavor.
garon ガロン gallon

• *Ima gasorin wa ichi garon ichi doru jussento desu.*
Gasoline costs $1.10 per gallon now.

gārufurendo ガールフレンド girlfriend
• *Kare no atarashii gārufurendo wa Kanada-jin desu.*
His new girlfriend is Canadian.

gāru hanto ガールハント [Japanese Usage: girl hunt]
picking up a girl
• *Kare wa tenisu kōto e gāru hanto ni ikimasu.*
He goes to tennis courts to pick up girls.

Gāru-sukauto ガールスカウト Girl Scouts
• *Shōjo no koro, Gāru-sukauto no unifōmu ni
akogaremashita.*
As a little girl, I was attracted by the Girl Scouts' uniform.

gasorin ガソリン gasoline, gas
• *Gasorin no nedan wa antei shite kimashita.*
The price of gasoline has stabilized.

gasorin sutando ガソリンスタンド [Japanese Usage:
gasoline stand] gas station
• *Ano gasorin sutando wa sābisu ga ii desu.*
That gas station gives good service.

gasu ガス gas
• *Gasu yori denki o yoku tsukaimsu.*
I use more electricity than gas.

gasu masuku ガスマスク gas mask
• *Kūshūkeihō ga naru to, minna gasu masuku o
tsukemashita.*
Everybody put on a gas mask when the air raid alarm went
off.

Gatto ガット GATT GATT, General Agreement on Tariffs
and Trade
• *Danpingu yushutsu wa Gatto de kinjirarete imasu.*
Export dumping is prohibited under GATT.

gaun ガウン dressing gown

- *Kanojo wa gaun o kite ima de kutsuroide imasu.*
  Wearing a robe, she is making herself comfortable in her living room.

gāze ガーゼ [German: *Gaze*] gauze

- *Kizuguchi ni kusuri o nutte gāze o atemashita.*
  I applied medicine to the wound and put some gauze on it.
- *Keshō o otosu no ni gāze o tsukaimasu.*
  I use cotton to remove my make-up.

gei ゲイ gay

- *Kare ga gei da to iu uwasa wa hontō desu ka?*
  Is the rumor true that he's gay?

gei bā ゲイバー gay bar

- *Gei bā de kare rashii hito o mikakemashita.*
  I saw someone like him in a gay bar.

gēmu ゲーム game

- *Konpyūtā de iroiro na gēmu ga tanoshimemasu.*
  You can enjoy a variety of games on a computer.

gēmu ōbā ゲームオーバー [Japanese Usage: game over] the end of play (for video games), the game's over

- *Taimurii-hitto de gēmu ōbā ni narimashita.*
  The timely hit ended the game.

gēmu sentā ゲームセンター [Japanese Usage: game center] video game arcade

- *Gēmu sentā de kodomo ga yoru osoku made asonde imasu.*
  Children play until late at night in video game arcades.

gera ゲラ galley

- *Sono genkō wa gera-zuri de yomimashita.*
  I read that manuscript in the galley proof stage.

gerira ゲリラ guerrilla

- *Gerira ga yōsai o kishū shimashita.*
  A guerrilla made a surprise attack on the fortress.

gesuto ゲスト guest

- *Kanojo wa terebi bangumi ni gesuto to shite shutsuen shimashita.*
  She made a guest appearance on a TV program.

gesuto-hausu ゲストハウス guesthouse
- *Koko wa gaikoku no bijinesuman muke no gesuto-hausu desu.*
  This is a guesthouse for foreign businessmen.

gēto ゲート gate
- *Kōjō no gēto wa yakan wa heisa saremasu.*
  The factory gate is closed at night.

gētoru ゲートル [French: *guêtre*] gaiters
- *Ashi ni gētoru o maite hatake shigoto o shimasu.*
  I work in a field with gaiters on my legs.

gettō ゲットー ghetto
- *Kare wa yōnen jidai o Shikago no gettō de sugoshimashita.*
  He spent his childhood in a ghetto in Chicago.

gia ギア gear
- *Kuruma ga sakamichi ni sashikakatta toki, gia o kaemashita.*
  As my car approached the slope, I changed gears.

gibu-ando-tēku ギブ・アンド・テーク give-and-take
- *Gibu-ando-tēku no jōken de ryōsha wa jōhō o kōkan shite imasu.*
  The two companies exchange information on a give-and-take basis.

gibuappu suru ギブアップする to give up
- *Kare wa shōshin no nozomi o gibuappu shimashita.*
  He gave up his hope for promotion.
- *Marason rēsu no tochū de gibuappu shimashita.*
  He dropped out in the middle of the marathon.

gibusu ギブス *see* **gipusu**

gifuto kādo ギフトカード [Japanese Usage: gift card] gift

certificate
- *Shinamono no kawari ni gifuto kādo o purezento shimashita.*
  I gave a gift certificate as a present.

gifuto shoppu ギフトショップ gift shop
- *Kanojo wa oya no isan de gifuto shoppu o hajimemashita.*
  She started a gift shop using the inheritance she received when her parents died.

gipusu ギプス [German: *Gips*] gyps, plaster cast
- *Hone o otte gipusu o hamete imasu.*
  I broke a bone and am wearing a plaster cast.

gitā ギター guitar
- *Kare wa gitā no meishu desu.*
  He is an accomplished guitarist.

giya ギヤ *see* **gia**

giyā ギヤー *see* **gia**

gō ゴー go *see* **gō sain**

gochikku ゴチック *see* **goshikku**

gō-gō dansu ゴーゴーダンス go-go dance
- *Konban no furoa shō wa gō-gō dansu desu.*
  Tonight's floor show is go-go dancing.

gōjasu ゴージャス gorgeous, luxurious
- *Shinkon ryokō de gōjasu na hoteru ni tomarimashita.*
  We stayed at a gorgeous hotel on our honeymoon.
- *Heya wa gōjasu ni kazatte arimasu.*
  The room is decorated luxuriously.

gomu ゴム [Dutch: *gom*] rubber
- *Haikingu ni wa gomu zoko no kutsu ga ii desu.*
  Rubber-soled shoes are good for hiking.

gondora ゴンドラ gondola
- *Gondora wa Benisu no meibutsu no hitotsu desu.*
  Gondolas are one of the attractions in Venice.

gongu ゴング gong

- *Gongu ga natte bokushingu no shiai ga shūryō shimashita.*
  The boxing match finished at the sound of the gong.

gorira ゴリラ gorilla
- *Gorira ga ori no naka o ittari kitari shite imasu.*
  A gorilla is prowling about in its cage.

gōru ゴール goal, target; **~suru** する to reach a goal
- *Wahei kyōtei ni mukete no hanashiai wa yōyaku gōru ni tasshimashita.*
  The peace accord conference finally achieved its goal.
- *Keiyaku kōshō wa gōru ni tasshimashita.*
  The contract negotiation reached its target.
- *Kare wa rakuraku to ichii de gōru shimashita.*
  He easily came in first place in the marathon.

gōruden awā ゴールデン・アワー [Japanese Usage: golden hour] prime time
- *Gōruden awā ni wakamono muke no terebi bangumi ga fuemashita.*
  Prime time television shows targeted for young people have increased.

gōruden taimu ゴールデン・タイム *see* **goruden awā**

gōruden uiiku ゴールデン・ウイーク [Japanese Usage: golden week] consecutive holidays from April 29th to May 5th
- *Gōruden uiiku wa doko e itte mo hito de ippai desu.*
  No matter where you go during Golden Week, you find nothing but people.

gōruden wiiku ゴールデン・ウィーク *see* **gōruden uiiku**

gōrudo ゴールド gold
- *Kono sofā ni wa gōrudo no kusshon ga yoku aimasu.*
  Gold-colored cushions go well with this sofa.

gorufā ゴルファー golfer
- *Kanojo wa sekai kusshi no gorufā desu.*
  She is one of the most outstanding golfers in the world.

gorufu ゴルフ golf
- *Chikagoro gorufu o yaru jikan ga arimasen.*
  I have had no time for golf lately.

gorufu uidō ゴルフウイドー golf widow
- *Gorufu uidō ga uwasabanashi ni kyōjite imasu.*
  The golf widows are having fun gossiping.

gōruin suru ゴールインする [Japanese Usage: goal in] to reach the goal, get married (finally)
- *Kare-ra wa itsu kekkon ni gōruin suru no kashira?*
  I wonder when they will finally get married.

gō sain ゴーサイン green light
- *Tsui ni kono purojekuto ni gō sain ga demashita.*
  This project was finally given the green light.

goshikku ゴシック Gothic
- *Yōroppa ni wa goshikku-shiki no kenchiku-butsu ga takusan arimasu.*
  There is much Gothic-style architecture in Europe.

goshippu ゴシップ gossip
- *Mūbi sutā no rikon ga goshippu ran o nigiwashite imasu.*
  A movie star's divorce is good material for the gossip columns.

gō sutoppu ゴーストップ [Japanese Usage: go stop] traffic signal
- *Ano gō sutoppu de migi ni magatte kudasai.*
  Please turn right at that traffic signal.

guddo aidia グッド・アイディア good idea
- *Genchi o shisatsu shite miru to iu no wa guddo aidia desu.*
  It's a good idea to make an on-site inspection.

guddobai グッドバイ goodbye
- *Guddobai to ittara, shōjo wa damatte te o furimashita.*
  When I said goodbye, the girl waved to me silently.

guddo taimingu グッド・タイミング good timing
- *Jinji-idō wa ima ga guddo taimingu da to omoimasu.*

I think that now is a good time for personnel changes.

gurabia グラビア (photo)gravure
- *Kono gurabia no shashin wa sensō no hisan o monogatatte imasu.*

These photos at the front of the magazine show us the ravages of war.

gurabu グラブ *see* **gurōbu**

gurafikku dezain グラフィックデザイン graphic design
- *Gurafikku dezain wa kōkoku ni hitoyaku katte imasu.*

Graphic design plays an important role in advertising.

gurafu グラフ graph
- *Kono sūji o gurafu ni shite kudasai.*

Please make a graph of these figures.

guramā グラマー grammar
- *Nihongo no guramā no hon o suisen shite itadakemasen ka?*

Would you please recommend a Japanese grammar book to me?

guramā グラマー glamour
- *Bikini sugata no guramā na josei ga nikkōyoku o shite imasu.*

Glamour girls wearing bikinis are sunbathing.

guramarasu グラマラス glamorous
- *Geinōkai no pātii de guramarasu na mūdo o ajiwaimashita.*

I felt the glamorous atmosphere at the show-biz party.
- *Kanojo wa guramarasu ni kikazatte imasu.*

She is dressed up glamorously.

guramu グラム gram
- *Gyūniku o nihyaku guramu kudasai.*

Give me 200 grams of beef, please.

gurando グランド *see* **guraundo**

gurando sēru グランドセール [Japanese Usage: grand sale]

big sale

• *Gurando sēru de depāto wa miugoki dekinai hodo konde imasu.*

There's a big sale and the department store is so crowded that I can hardly move.

guranpuri グランプリ [French: *grand prix*] grand prize

• *Kono eiga wa kokusai eigasai de guranpuri o kakutoku shimashita.*

This movie won the grand prize at an international film festival.

gurasu グラス glass

• *Gurasu ni wain o ippai tsugimashita.*

I filled the glass with wine.

guraundo グラウンド playground, stadium

• *Yakyū no senshu ga guraundo de renshū shite imasu.*

Baseball players are practicing on the field.

gurē グレー gray

• *gurē na kibun*

a gray mood, the blues

• *Shatsu ga yogorete sentakuki no naka de gurē ni natte shimaimashita.*

My shirt got dirty and turned gray in the washing machine.

gurēdo グレード grade

• *Kare wa itsumo gurēdo no takai sūtsu o kite imasu.*

He always wears high-quality suits.

gurēdo appu グレードアップ [Japanese Usage: grade up] upgrade

• *Kuruma no gurēdo appu o kangaete imasu.*

I am thinking of upgrading my car.

gurei グレイ *see* **gurē**

gurēpu グレープ grape

• *Gurēpu no shiizun wa mō owarimashita.*

The season for grapes is over.

gurēpufurūtsu グレープフルーツ grapefruit
- *Kono gurēpufurūtsu wa Kariforunia san desu ka?*
  Are these grapefruits from California?

gurii kurabu グリークラブ glee club
- *Kare wa gurii kurabu no shiki-sha desu.*
  He is the conductor for the glee club.

guriin グリーン green
- *guriin no shibafu*
  a green lawn

guriin bijinesu グリーンビジネス [Japanese Usage: green business] gardening business
- *Shitsunai yō no puranto o atsukau guriin bijinesu ga hayatte imasu.*
  Gardening businesses that sell indoor plants are thriving.

guriin fii グリーンフィー green fee
- *Gorufu jō o shiyō suru no ni guriin fii ga irimasu.*
  You must pay a green fee to use a golf course.

guriin-karā グリーンカラー [Japanese Usage: green collar] worker in the computer software industry
- *Konpyūtā no puroguramā ya shisutemu enjinia wa guriin-karā to yobarete imasu.*
  Computer programmers and system engineers are called "green collar workers."

guriin piisu グリーンピース green peas
- *Shinsen na guriin piisu o reitō ni shimasu.*
  I freeze fresh green peas.

guriitingu kādo グリーティングカード greeting card
- *Guriitingu kādo wa doko de utte imasu ka?*
  Where do they sell greeting cards?

gurippu グリップ grip
- *Tozanka wa rōpu no gurippu o ushinatte tani ni tenraku shimashita.*
  A mountain-climber lost his grip on his rope and fell into

the ravine.

- *Ase de raketto no gurippu ga mawatte bōru o umaku utemasendeshita.*

Because of sweat her hand slipped on the racket and she didn't hit the ball well.

guriru グリル grill

- *O-kyaku o tsurete kaisha no chikaku no guriru e chūshoku ni ikimasu.*

I'll take the guest for lunch to a grill near the company.

gurōbarizēshon グローバリゼーション globalization

- *Keizai no gurōbarizēshon ga yoku wadai ni narimasu.*

The globalization of the economy often becomes a topic of conversation.

gurōbaru グローバル global, international

- *Kodomo o gurōbaru na ningen ni sodatetai desu.*

I want to raise my child to be an international person.

- *Māketingu wa gurōbaru ni okonau beki desu.*

Marketing should be conducted on a global scale.

gurōbu グローブ glove, boxing glove

- *Kono gurōbu wa bokushingu ni tsukaimasu.*

These gloves are used for boxing.

gurokkii グロッキー groggy, exhausted

- *Tetsuya de shigoto shite, kesa wa mattaku gurokkii desu.*

I was up all night working and feel totally groggy this morning.

gurotesuku グロテスク grotesque

- *gurotesuku na kaibutsu*

a grotesque monster

- *Kabe ga kebakebashii iro de gurotesuku ni nurarete imasu.*

The wall is painted grotesquely with gaudy colors.

gurume グルメ gourmet

- *Gurume būmu de yunyū shokuhin ga yoku urete imasu.*

Imported food is selling well due to the boom in gourmet cuisine.

gurūpii グルーピー groupie
- *Ryūkō kashu no kare wa tsune ni wakai gurūpii ni tsukimatowarete imasu.*
  Being a popular singer, he is constantly followed around by young groupies.

gurūpu グループ group
- *Gurūpu ni wakarete, disukasshon o shimashita.*
  We were divided into groups and had discussions.

gurūpu dainami(k)kusu グループ・ダイナミ(ッ)クス group dynamics
- *Gurūpu dainamikkusu no jikken wa shokuba no fuwa ya mondai o kaiketsu suru tame ni tsukawaremasu.*
  Exercises in group dynamics are used to remove discord and other problems from the workplace.

gyabajin ギャバジン garbardine
- *gyabajin no rēnkōto*
  a garbardine raincoat

gyanburu ギャンブル gamble
- *Kare wa gyanburu de zen-zaisan o ushinaimashita.*
  He lost his whole fortune gambling.

gyangu ギャング gang, gangster
- *Kare wa sūnin no gyangu ni torikakomaremashita.*
  He was surrounded by several gangsters.

gyappu ギャップ gap
- *Sedai no gyappu wa ōkiku naru ippō desu.*
  The generation gap keeps widening.

gyara ギャラ guarantee, performance fee, appearance fee
- *Kanojo no gyara wa haneagarimashita.*
  Her performance fee jumped.

gyararii ギャラリー gallery, spectators
- *Kare wa Ginza no gyararii de koten o hirakimashita.*

He held a one-man exhibition at a gallery on the Ginza.
* *Ōzei no gyararii ga gorufu no tōnamento ni tsumekakemashita.*
A large number of spectators flocked to the golf tournament.

gyarēji ギャレージ *see* **garēji**

H

hābu ハーブ herb
* *Ano mise de kakushu no hābu ga kaemasu.*
You can buy all kinds of herbs at that store.

hābu tii ハーブティー herb tea
* *Tsukareta toki ni hābu tii wa totemo ii desu yo.*
Herb tea is very good when you are tired.

hādo ハード hard
* *Kono shigoto wa totemo hādo desu.*
This work is very hard.

hādo ハード hardware
* *Sono kaisha wa konpyūta no hādo o seisan shite imasu.*
The company manufactures hardware for computers.

hādo-boirudo ハードボイルド hard-boiled, unfeeling
* *Kare wa hādo-boirudo no suiri shōsetsu o kakimasu.*
He writes hard-boiled mysteries.
* *Kare no shōsetsu no shujinkō wa minna hādo-boirudo desu.*
The protagonists of his novels are all unfeeling.

hādo doraggu ハード・ドラッグ hard drug
* *Heroin ya kokain wa hādo doraggu to iwarete imasu.*
Heroin and cocaine are known as hard drugs.

hādokabā ハードカバー hardcover

- *hādokabā no hon*
  a hardcover book

hādo-koa poruno ハードコア・ポルノ hard-core pornography

- *Hādo-koa poruno no tsuihō undō o keikaku shite imasu.*
  They are planning a campaign aimed at doing away with
  hard-core pornography.

hādoru ハードル hurdle

- *Kare wa karugaru to hādoru o tobikoshimashita.*
  He jumped over the hurdles with ease.

hādo torēningu ハードトレーニング hard training

- *Supōtsu no senshu wa minna hādo torēningu o
  ukenakereba narimasen.*
  All sports players must go through hard training.

hādouea ハードウエア *see* **hādo** (*hardware*)

hādo wāku ハードワーク hard work

- *Ichinichi jūnijikan no hādo wāku desu.*
  It's 12 hours a day of hard work.

hāfu ハーフ [Japanese Usage: half] person of mixed race

- *Ano otoko no ko wa Nihon-jin to Amerika-jin no hāfu
  desu.*
  That boy is half-Japanese and half-American.

hāfu kōto ハーフコート [Japanese Usage: half coat] short
coat

- *Hāfu kōto wa ryokō ni benri desu.*
  A short coat is convenient for traveling.

hai ハイ high

- *Sukoshi wain o nonde hai na kibun ni narimashita.*
  I drank a little wine and got high.

hai-bijon ハイビジョン high-vision, HDTV (high definition
television)

- *Hai-bijon no honkakuteki na shiken hōsō ga
  okonawaremashita.*

A large-scale experimental high-vision broadcast was conducted.

hai-fai ハイファイ hi-fi
- *Kono hai-fai wa onshitsu ga ii desu.*
This stereo has good sound.

haifun ハイフン hyphen
- *Aru Eigo no kotoba wa haifun de tsunagatte imasu.*
Some English words are connected by a hyphen.

hai gurēdo ハイグレード high grade
- *Kanojo wa hai gurēdo na yunyūhin o kaimasu.*
She buys high grade imported goods.

haihiiru ハイヒール high-heeled shoes
- *Moderu ga haihiiru o haite sassō to aruite imasu.*
The models are walking breezily in their high-heeled shoes.

haihon ハイホン *see* **haifun**

haijakku ハイジャック hijack
- *Kyūba yuki no hikōki ga haijakku saremashita.*
An airplane bound for Cuba was hijacked.

haikā ハイカー hiker
- *Haikā ga michibata de yasunde imasu.*
Hikers are resting by the road.

haikara ハイカラ high collar, stylish, foreign-style
- *haikara na dansei*
a stylish man
- *Sobo wa kami o haikara ni yutte imashita.*
My grandmother did her hair up in a foreign style.

hai kuoritii ハイクオリティー high quality
- *Ano kaisha no seihin wa hai kuoritii de shirarete imasu.*
That company's products are known for their high quality.

hai-kurasu ハイクラス high-class
- *Kanojo wa hai-kurasu na bā no hosutesu desu.*
She is a hostess at a high-class bar.

hai-nekku ハイネック high-necked

- *hai-nekku no burausu*
  a high-necked blouse

hai-pitchi ハイピッチ high-pitched, high-speed

- *hai-pitchi no koe*
  a high-pitched voice
- *Shimekiri ni maniau yō ni hai-pitchi de genkō o kaite imasu.*
  I'm quickly writing the manuscript so that I can meet the deadline.

hairaito ハイライト highlight

- *Maiban terebi de kyō no supōtsu no hairaito o mimasu.*
  I watch the day's sports highlights on TV every night.

hai-risuku ハイリスク high-risk

- *Hai-risuku no aru tōshi wa sakeru beki desu.*
  High-risk investments should be avoided.

hai sukūru ハイスクール high school

- *Sono jānarisuto wa hai sukūru no droppuauto desu.*
  That journalist is a high school dropout.

hai supiido ハイスピード high speed

- *Kōji wa hai supiido de susunde imasu.*
  The construction is progressing at a high speed.

hai sensu ハイセンス [Japanese Usage: high sense] good taste, elegant taste

- *Hai sensu no akusesarii ga doresu o hikitatete imasu.*
  Elegant accessories enhance the beauty of the dress.

hai-teku ハイテク high tech, high-tech *see* **hai tekunorojii**

hai tekunorojii ハイテクノロジー high technology, high tech

- *Kon seiki no hai tekunorojii no hatten wa mezamashii mono ga arimasu.*
  The development of high technology this century is remarkable.

hai-tiin ハイティーン [Japanese Usage: high teen] late teens

- *Musume wa hai-tiin de te ni oemasen.*
  My daughter is in her late teens and unmanageable.

haiuē ハイウエー highway
- *Haiuē de pato-kā ni tomeraremashita.*
  I was stopped by a patrol car on the highway.

haiyā ハイヤー limousine
- *Haiyā de kenbutsu ni ikimashita.*
  We went sightseeing in a limousine.

hamingu ハミング humming
- *Rajio no kyoku ni awasete hamingu shimashita.*
  I hummed along with the music on the radio.

Hamondo orugan ハモンド・オルガン Hammond organ
- *Usugurai chaperu de dare ka ga Hamondo orugan o hiite imasu.*
  Someone is playing the Hammond organ in the dimly-lit chapel.

hāmonii ハーモニー harmony
- *Shitsunai sōshoku ni wa shikisai no hāmonii ga taisetsu desu.*
  The harmony of colors is important in interior decoration.

hāmonika ハーモニカ harmonica
- *Nikai no kodomo ga asa kara ban made hāmonika o fuite imasu.*
  A child upstairs plays the harmonica from morning till night.

hamu ハム ham
- *Haha wa yaita hamu wa Kanshasai ni shika tabemasen.*
  My mother eats baked ham only on Thanksgiving.

hamu eggu ハムエッグ ham and eggs
- *Kesa wa hamu eggu ni shimasu.*
  I'll have ham and eggs this morning.

hāmuresu ハームレス harmless
- *Sake wa nomisuginakereba, hāmuresu desu.*

If you don't drink too much, alcohol is harmless.

hanbāgā ハンバーガー hamburger
- *Kōra o nominagara hanbāgā o tabemasu.*
  I eat a hamburger while drinking a cola.

hanbāgu ハンバーグ *see* **hanbāgu sutēki**

hanbāgu sutēki ハンバーグステーキ hamburger (meat)
- *Kono resutoran no hanbāgu sutēki wa aburakkoi desu.*
  The hamburger at this restaurant is greasy.

hanchingu ハンチング hunting cap
- *Hanchingu o kabutta otoko no hito ga mori no naka o aruite imasu.*
  A man wearing a hunting cap is walking in the woods.

hande ハンデ *see* **handikyappu**

handi ハンディ *see* **handii, handikyappu**

handii ハンディー handy
- *chiisakute handii na jisho*
  a small and handy dictionary

handikyappu ハンディキャップ handicap
- *Kōchingin wa Amerika kigyō no handikyappu to ieru deshō.*
  You might say that high wages are a handicap for American corporations.

handobaggu ハンドバッグ handbag
- *Wanigawa no handobaggu ga hoshii desu.*
  I want an alligator handbag.

handobukku ハンドブック handbook
- *Kono Nihongo no bunpō no handobukku wa wakariyasui desu.*
  This handbook of Japanese grammar is easy to understand.

handomēdo ハンドメード handmade
- *Kono mingeihin wa handomēdo desu.*
  This piece of folkcraft is handmade.

handoru ハンドル handle, steering wheel

- *Sono shunkan kuruma no handoru o migi ni kirimashita.*
  At that moment I turned the wheel of my car to the right.

hanemūn ハネムーン honeymoon

- *Kare-ra wa nido me no hanemūn ni dekakemashita.*
  They set out on their second honeymoon.

hangā ハンガー hanger

- *Kono hangā o tsukatte mo ii desu ka?*
  May I use this hanger?

hangā sutoraiki ハンガーストライキ *see* **hansuto**

hangurii ハングリー hungry

- *hangurii seishin o motsu bokusā*
  a boxer with a hungry spirit

hankachi ハンカチ handkerchief

- *Furansu sei no kirei na hankachi o itadakimashita.*
  I received a pretty handkerchief made in France.

hankachiifu ハンカチーフ *see* **hankachi**

hankechi ハンケチ *see* **hankachi**

hanmā ハンマー hammer

- *Hanmā de oyayubi o uchitsukete, mada itai desu.*
  I hit my thumb with a hammer and it still hurts.

hanmokku ハンモック hammock

- *Kare wa hanmokku de nemutte imasu.*
  He is sleeping in a hammock.

hansamu ハンサム handsome

- *Kanojo wa hansamu na wakai dansei to dēto shite imasu.*
  She is dating a handsome young man.

hansuto ハンスト [Japanese Usage] hunger strike

- *Sensō ni hantai suru gakusei ga hansuto o hajimemashita.*
  The students who opposed the war started a hunger strike.

hantā ハンター hunter

- *Hantā ga nagaredama ni atatte kega o shimashita.*
  A hunter was wounded by a stray bullet.

hantingu ハンティング hunting

- *Aki ni nattara hantingu ni dekakemashō.*
  Let's go hunting in the fall.

happii ハッピー happy
- *Kyūyū to nonde itara happii na kibun ni narimashita.*
  I had a drink with my old friend and felt happy.
- *Shinkon no futari wa happii ni kurashite imasu.*
  The newlyweds are living together happily.

happii endo ハッピーエンド happy ending
- *Eiga wa happii endo de owarimashita.*
  The movie had a happy ending.
- *Sono eiga wa happii endo desu ka?*
  Does that movie have a happy ending?

hāpu ハープ harp
- *Hāpu no oto de dainingu rūmu ga ereganto na mūdo de mitasaremashita.*
  The sound of the harp filled the dining room with an elegant atmosphere.

hapuningu ハプニング happening, unexpected event
- *Kare no shi wa yosōgai no hapuningu deshita.*
  His death was an unexpected event.
- *Chottoshita hapuningu ga atte kyō wa ikarenaku narimashita.*
  Due to an unexpected event, I cannot come today.

hareruya ハレルヤ hallelujah
- *Hareruya no gasshō ga kaijō ni hibikiwatarimashita.*
  The hallelujah chorus resounded through the hall.

harō ハロー hello
- *Amerika-jin ga watashi ni "Harō!" to aisatsu shimashita.*
  The American greeted me with "Hello!"

hassuru suru ハッスルする to hustle
- *Kanojo wa repōto o kyōjū ni shiage yō to hassuru shite imasu.*
  She is hustling about to get the report finished by the end of

today.

hasukii ハスキー husky *see* **hasukii boisu**
- *Kanojo wa hasukii na koe o shite imasu.*
  She has a husky voice.

hasukii boisu ハスキーボイス husky voice
- *Sono singā wa hasukii boisu de utaimasu.*
  That singer sings in a husky voice.

hāto ハート heart
- *Kare wa tsui ni kanojo no hāto o itomemashita.*
  He finally won her heart.

hātofuru ハートフル [Japanese Usage: heartful] sweet-hearted, full of tenderness
- *Kanojo no hātofuru na kotoba ni kandō shimashita.*
  I was moved by her tender words.

haujingu ハウジング housing
- *Kotoshi wa tōsha no haujingu-bumon ga jitsu ni kōchō deshita.*
  The housing division of our company made a very good showing this year.

hausubōi ハウスボーイ houseboy
- *Kare wa hausubōi o shinagara Amerika no daigaku ni kayoimashita.*
  He put himself through an American college while working as a houseboy.

hausukiipā ハウスキーパー housekeeper
- *Hausukiipā wa ichinichi oki ni kimasu.*
  The housekeeper comes every other day.

hautsū ハウツー how to, method
- *Kono hon wa tōshi no hautsū o oshiete kuremasu.*
  This book tells you how to invest.

hayashi raisu ハヤシライス [Japanese Usage: Hayashi rice] beef and vegetables seved over rice
- *Kono hayashi raisu wa chotto amasugimasu.*

This "Hayashi rice" is a little too sweet.

hazu ハズ *see* **hazubando**

hazubando ハズバンド husband
- *Kanojo no ima no hazubando wa yoninme desu.*
  Her present husband is her fourth.

heapin ヘアピン hairpin
- *Heapin de kamikazari o tomemasu.*
  I hold up my hair ornament with a hairpin.
- *Nikkō no Iroha-zaka wa heapin kābu de yūmei desu.*
  The Iroha-zaka slopes in Nikko are famous for their hairpin curves.

heasutairu ヘアスタイル hairstyle
- *Kanojo wa maishū heasutairu o kaete terebi ni dete imasu.*
  She appears on TV with a different hairstyle every week.

hea tonikku ヘアトニック hair tonic
- *Shanpū no ato de hea tonikku o tsukaimasu.*
  After shampooing I use hair tonic.

hebii ヘビー heavy
- *hebii na shigoto*
  a heavy task

hebii sumōkā ヘビースモーカー heavy smoker
- *Kare wa ichinichi ni gohako mo suu hebii sumōkā desu.*
  He is a heavy smoker who smokes up to five packs of cigarettes a day.

heddingu ヘッディング *see* **hedingu**

heddo ヘッド head, chief
- *Kono risāchi gurūpu no heddo wa Tanaka-kyōju desu.*
  The head of this research group is Professor Tanaka.

heddofon ヘッドフォン headphone
- *Heddofon de rajio o kikimasu.*
  I listen to the radio with headphones.

heddohantingu ヘッドハンティング headhunting, scouting
- *Kigyō no aida de heddohantingu ga tsune ni okonawarete*

imasu.

Headhunting is common practice among companies.

heddohon ヘッドホン *see* **heddofon**

heddo kōchi ヘッドコーチ head coach

- *Basuketto bōru no heddo kōchi wa senshu ni hijō ni shitawarete imasu.*

The head basketball coach is adored by his players.

heddorain ヘッドライン headline

- *Shinbun wa heddorain shika yomimasen.*

I only read the headlines of newspapers.

heddoraito ヘッドライト headlight

- *Fukai kiri no naka o kuruma ga heddoraito o tsukete jokō shite imasu.*

In the heavy fog, cars are crawling with their headlights on.

hedingu ヘディング heading

- *Hedingu shūto ga migoto ni kimarimashita.*

The ball was headed skillfully into the goal.

hejji ヘッジ hedge; **~suru** する to hedge

- *infure no hejji*

hedge against inflation

- *Bunsan tōshi o shite risuku o hejji shimasu.*

I hedge risk by diversifying investments.

herikoputā ヘリコプター helicopter

- *Herikoputā ga ki no ue o suresure ni tonde ikimashita.*

A helicopter skimmed over the top of a tree.

heripōto ヘリポート heliport

- *Biru no okujō ni heripōto o setchi suru koto ga dekimasu.*

A heliport can be built on the roof of the building.

heroin ヘロイン heroin

- *Heroin no mitsubainin ga keisatsu ni taiho saremashita.*

The heroin smugglers were arrested by the police.

herumetto ヘルメット helmet

- *Ōtobai ni noru toki wa herumetto o kaburanakereba*

narimasen.
You must wear a helmet when you ride a motorcycle.

herupā ヘルパー helper
 • *Byōnin no sewa o shi ni mainichi herupā ga kimasu.*
 A helper comes every day to take care of the sick.

herupu ヘルプ help; **~suru** する to help
 • *Hitori de dekimasu kara, herupu wa irimasen.*
 Since I can do it alone, I don't need any help.
 • *Heya no kazaritsuke o herupu shite kudasai.*
 Please help me decorate the room.

herushii ヘルシー healthy
 • *Herushii shikō de washoku ga minaosarete imasu.*
 With health-consciousness on the rise, Japanese food is gaining popularity again.
 • *Kono daietto wa herushii ja arimasen.*
 This diet isn't healthy.

herusu mētā ヘルスメーター [Japanese Usage: health meter] bathroom scale
 • *Maiban furoba no herusu mētā de taijū o hakarimasu.*
 Every night I weigh myself on the bathroom scale.

hiaringu ヒアリング hearing, aural comprehension
 • *Ashita hiaringu no shiken ga arimasu.*
 We have an aural comprehension exam tomorrow.

hiirō ヒーロー hero
 • *Sūpāman wa kodomo-tachi no hiirō desu.*
 Superman is a children's hero.

hiitā ヒーター heater
 • *Hiitā ga ugokimasen.*
 The heater doesn't work.

hinto ヒント hint
 • *Kare wa suiri shōsetsu kara satsujin no hinto o emashita.*
 He got a hint about the murder from a detective story.

hippii ヒッピー hippie

- *Kare wa hippii no seikatsu o hōki shite shakai ni fukki shimashita.*

He abandoned his hippie lifestyle and returned to society.

hippu ヒップ hip, waist

- *hippu no hosoi josei*

a slim-hipped woman

- *hippu no ōkii onna*

a wide-hipped woman

- *Kono doresu wa hippu ga sukoshi kitsui desu.*

This dress is a little tight in the hips.

hire ヒレ [French: *filet*] fillet, tenderloin

- *Gokujō no hire o chūmon shimashita.*

I ordered fillet of the finest quality.

hiroikku ヒロイック heroic

- *Keisatsukan no hiroikku na kōi wa shōsan saremashita.*

The policeman's heroic deed was praised.

hiroin ヒロイン heroine

- *Hiroin no kanashii unmei ni watashi wa nakimashita.*

I wept at the heroine's sad fate.

hisuterii ヒステリー [German: *Hysterie*] hysterics, hysteria

- *Kare wa hisuterii o okoshite sakebimashita.*

He became hysterical and began shouting.

hisuterikku ヒステリック hysteric

- *Kare-ra wa sono hanketsu ni hisuterikku na hannō o shimeshimashita.*

They had a hysterical reaction to the court's decision.

- *Kanojo wa hisuterikku ni nakidashimashita.*

She started to cry hysterically.

hisutorii ヒストリー history

- *Sono jiken wa mō hisutorii ni natte shimaimashita.*

That incident has already become history.

hitchihaiku suru ヒッチハイクする to hitchhike

- *Hitchihaiku shite mokutekichi made ikimashita.*

I hitchhiked to my destination.

hitto ヒット hit; **~suru** する to hit, be a hit

- *Kono geki wa dai hitto desu.*
  This play is a big hit.
- *Kono shōhin wa yosō dōri ni wa hitto shimasen deshita.*
  This article was not the hit it was expected to be.

hiyaringu ヒヤリング (public) hearing *see* **hiaringu**

- *Genshiryoku hatsudensho no kensetsu ni tsuite kōkai hiyaringu ga okonawaremasu.*
  There will be a public hearing regarding nuclear power plants.

hobii ホビー hobby

- *Ningyōzukuri o hobii ni shite imasu.*
  My hobby is making dolls.

hokku ホック hook, snap hook

- *Doresu o hokku de tomemasu.*
  I hook up my dress.
- *Hokku o tomete kuremasen ka?*
  Can you hook me up?

hōku ホーク *see* **fōku**

hōmā ホーマー *see* **hōmuran**

homo ホモ homosexual, gay

- *Kanojo wa homo no musuko o tōzakete imasu.*
  She keeps away from her homosexual son.

homosekushuaru ホモセクシュアル *see* **homo**

hōmu ホーム platform

- *Ōsaka yuki wa sanban hōmu kara demasu.*
  A train bound for Osaka will depart from platform number three.

hōmu ホーム home

- *Onsenchi ni rōjin hōmu ga tachimashita.*
  An old age home was built in a hot spring resort.

hōmu dorama ホームドラマ [Japanese Usage: home drama]

TV drama based on family affairs

• *Hōmu dorama wa sesō o han'ei shimasu.*

TV dramas based on family affairs reflect social conditions.

hōmu gurando ホームグランド *see* **hōmu guraundo**

hōmu guraundo ホームグラウンド home ground

• *Kono kyūjō wa waga chiimu no hōmu guraundo desu.*

This stadium is our team's home ground.

• *Kare no hōmu guraundo de no senkyo undō wa kappatsu deshita.*

His home turf election campaign was vigorous.

hōmu herupā ホームヘルパー [Japanese Usage: home helper] a person who helps with housework or cares for shut-ins

• *Hōmu herupā ga netakiri rōjin no sewa ni kite kuremasu.*

The home helper comes to take care of a bedridden old person.

hōmumēdo ホームメード homemade

• *hōmumēdo no kukkii*

homemade cookies

hōmuran ホームラン home run

• *Kare wa (dai)sanjūgō hōmuran o uchimashita.*

He hit his 30th home run.

hōmuresu ホームレス homeless

• *Hōmuresu o tasukeru undō ga okotte imasu.*

A movement to help the homeless is being carried out.

hōmurūmu ホームルーム homeroom

• *Anata-gata no homurūmu no sensei wa donata desu ka?*

Who is your homeroom teacher?

• *Kyō no ichijikan me wa hōmurūmu desu.*

The first hour today I'm in homeroom.

hōmushikku ホームシック homesick

• *Gaikoku ni ita toki wa tokidoki hōmushikku ni kakarimashita.*

I was sometimes homesick when I lived abroad.

hōmu sutei ホームステイ home stay; **~suru** する to stay with a host family
- *Hōmu sutei wa bunka kōryū no tame ni ii puroguramu desu.*
  Home stay programs are good for cultural exchange.
- *Amerika no katei ni sanshūkan hōmu sutei shimashita.*
  I stayed with an American host family for three weeks.

hon ホン phon
- *Sono ressha no sōon wa hachijū hon ika deshita.*
  The sound of the train registered less than 80 phons.

hōn ホーン *see* **hon**

hōpu ホープ hope, a person with a promising future
- *Kanojo wa taisōkai no hōpu desu.*
  She is the hope of the gymnastics world.

hōru ホール hall
- *Ashita chikaku no hōru de piano no risaitaru ga arimasu.*
  There will be a piano recital at a nearby hall tomorrow.

hōrudoappu ホールドアップ holdup
- *Ginkō de hōrudoappu ga atta sō desu.*
  I hear there was a holdup at the bank.

horumon ホルモン [German: *Hormon*] hormone
- *Horumon no fukinkō de taichō ga warui no desu.*
  Due to a hormone imbalance, I am in poor physical shape.

hōsu ホース [Dutch: *hoos*] hose
- *Hōsu de niwa ni mizu o makimasu.*
  I water the garden with a hose.

hosupisu ホスピス hospice
- *Kanojo wa isan o hosupisu ni kifu shimashita.*
  She donated her inheritance to the hospice.

hosupitaritii ホスピタリティー hospitality
- *Tabisaki de omowanu hosupitaritii o ukemashita.*
  We received unexpected hospitality while traveling.

hosutesu ホステス hostess, barmaid
- *Kōkyu bā dake atte kirei na hosutesu o soroete imasu.*
  As might be expected from a high class bar, only pretty hostesses work there.

hosuto ホスト host
- *Kare wa bansankai de shachō ni kawatte hosuto-yaku o tsutomemashita.*
  He played host at the banquet instead of the company president.

hosuto famirii ホスト・ファミリー host family
- *Kariforunia no hosuto famirii ni reijō o dashimashita.*
  I mailed a thank-you letter to my host family in California.

hoteru ホテル hotel
- *Kono hoteru wa shiriai ga keiei shite imasu.*
  An acquaintance of mine runs this hotel.

hotto ホット hot
- *Nihon de ichiban hotto na singā*
  the hottest singer in Japan
- *Hotto o kudasai.*
  Hot coffee, please.

hottodoggu ホットドッグ hot dog
- *Ranchi ni hottodoggu to poteto chippu o tabemashita.*
  I ate a hot dog and potato chips for lunch.

hotto nyūsu ホットニュース hot news
- *Kare no jishoku wa seikai no hotto nyūsu desu.*
  His resignation is hot news in the political world.

hotto rain ホットライン hot line
- *Wāpuro ni kansuru go-shitsumon wa hotto rain o o-tsukai kudasai.*
  Please use our hot line for questions concerning word processors.

howaito ホワイト white
- *howaito no shiruku sukāfu*

a white silk scarf

howaito ホワイト correction liquid
- *Machigai wa howaito de keshite kudasai.*
Please white out the mistakes.

Howaito-hausu ホワイトハウス White House
- *Howaito-hausu no shashin o torimashita.*
I took a photo of the White House.

howaito-karā ホワイトカラー white-collar worker
- *Howaito-karā no shitsugyō ritsu ga takaku natte imasu.*
The white-collar unemployment rate is increasing.

hyūman ヒューマン human
- *Kanojo ni wa hyūman na atatakami ga arimashita.*
There was human warmth about her.

hyūmanisuto ヒューマニスト humanist
- *Kare wa hyūmanisuto da kara, sossen shite mazushii hito o tasukemasu.*
Being a humanist, he takes the lead in helping the needy.

hyūmanitii ヒューマニティー humanity, human nature
- *Kare no sakuhin wa hyūmanitii o fukaku horisagete imasu.*
His work probes deeply into human nature.

hyūmanizumu ヒューマニズム humanism
- *Hyūmanizumu ni afureta hon o yonde kandō shimashita.*
I read a book full of humanistic values and I was moved.

hyūzu ヒューズ fuse
- *Hyūzu ga tonda node, tsukekaemashita.*
Because the fuse had blown, I put a new one in.

I

ID kādo ID カード *see* **ai-dii kādo**
IQ *see* **ai-kyū**
iahōn イアホーン *see* **iyahon**

iaringu イアリング *see* **iyaringu**

ibento イベント event

- *Torihikisaki kara iroiro na ibento ni shōtai saremashita.*
  We were invited to various events by our business connections.

ibu イブ eve

- *Kurisumasu ibu ni Shidonii ni iru shujin ni denwa o kakemashita.*
  On Christmas Eve, I telephoned my husband in Sydney.

ibuningu doresu イブニングドレス evening dress

- *Taishi fujin ga gōka na ibuningu doresu de resepushon ni arawaremashita.*
  The ambassador's wife showed up at the reception in a gorgeous evening dress.

ideorogii イデオロギー [German: *Ideologie*] ideology

- *Ryōsha no aida ni ideorogii no tairitsu ga miraremasu.*
  We can see an ideological conflict between the two parties.

idiomu イディオム idiom

- *Nihongo no idiomu o naraitai desu.*
  I want to learn Japanese idioms.

ierō イエロー yellow

- *ierō no sētā*
  a yellow sweater
- *Kono aki no fasshon no kichō wa ierō desu.*
  Yellow is the underlying tone in fashion this fall.

iesu イエス yes

- *Iesu ka nō ka ashita made ni shirasete kudasai.*
  Please let us know yes or no by tomorrow.

iesu man イエスマン yes man, person who agrees with everything

- *Iesu man no kare ga hajimete nō to iimashita.*
  Usually a yes man, he said no for the first time.

Igirisu イギリス [Portuguese: *Inglez*] England

- *Chōjo wa Igirisu de umaremashita.*
  Our oldest daughter was born in England.

iibun イーブン even, tie, draw
- *Ryō chiimu no tokuten wa iibun desu.*
  The two teams are tied.
- *Kore de watashi-tachi wa iibun desu ne.*
  With this we're even, right?

iijii イージー easy, comfortable
- *Kare no iijii na taido de wa ii shigoto wa kitai dekimasen.*
  Because of his easygoing attitude, he can't be expected to
  do a good job.
- *Bunkatsu-barai wa shiharai o iijii ni shimasu.*
  It makes it easier if you pay in installments.

iijiigōingu イージーゴーイング easygoing *see* **iijii**
- *Kare wa iijiigōingu na taipu desu.*
  He is an easygoing type.
- *Toshi o toru ni tsurete, iijiigōingu ni narimashita.*
  As I grew older, I became more easygoing.

iijiiōdā イージーオーダー [Japanese Usage: easy order]
semi-tailored suit
- *Iijiiōdā wa redii-mēdo yori ii desu.*
  A semi-tailored suit is better than a ready-made one.

iijii-ōpun イージーオープン [Japanese Usage: easy open]
easily-opened
- *Iijii-ōpun no kan-jūsu wa pikunikku ni benri desu.*
  Easily-opened cans of juice are convenient for a picnic.

Iisutā イースター Easter
- *Iisutā ni wa kyōkai wa kikazatta hito de ippai deshita.*
  On Easter, the church was full of people dressed in their
  Sunday best.

Iisuto-kōsuto イーストコースト East Coast (of the U.S.A.)
- *Sono kazoku wa Iisuto-kōsuto kara Kariforunia ni
  utsurimashita.*

The family moved to California from the East Coast.

iizeru イーゼル easel
- *Iizeru ni kanbasu ga kakete arimasu.*

A canvas was put on the easel.

ikōru イコール equal
- *Shūshoku ikōru jiritsu de wa arimasen.*

Employment does not necessarily mean self-support.

imajinēshon イマジネーション imagination
- *Kanojo no sakufū wa dokusha no imajinēshon o shigeki shimasu.*

Her literary style stimulates the reader's imagination.

imēji イメージ image
- *Kaku shōhin no ii imēji o tsukuru koto ga kanjin desu.*

It is essential to create a good image for each product.

imēji appu イメージアップ [Japanese Usage: image up] to improve an image
- *Kaisha wa ureyuki no warui shōhin no imēji appu ni tsutomete imasu.*

The company is trying to improve the image of their slower-selling products.

imēji chenji イメージチェンジ [Japanese Usage: image change] to change an image
- *Ninki no nai kōhosha wa imēji chenji kara hajimenakereba narimasen.*

Unpopular candidates must start by changing their images.

imigurēshon イミグレーション immigration
- *Kūkō no imigurēshon de nyūkoku kyoka o moraimashita.*

I received an entry permit at the immigration desk in the airport.

imitēshon イミテーション imitation
- *Kōkyūhin no imitēshon ga demawatte imasu.*

Imitations of high quality goods appear on the market.

inbaransu インバランス imbalance

- *Keizaijō no inbaransu wa zesei sarenakereba narimasen.*
  The economic imbalance must be corrected.

inbesutomento インベストメント investment

- *Kono inbesutomento wa nen ni ichiman doru no rieki o umimasu.*
  This investment yields a profit of $10,000 a year.

inchi インチ inch

- *Kono beruto wa ichi inchi mijikai desu.*
  This belt is one inch short.

indasutoriaru dezain インダストリアル・デザイン industrial design

- *Indasutoriaru dezain wa jūyōshi sarete imasu.*
  Industrial design is regarded as important.

indekkusu インデックス index

- *Kono hon ni wa indekkusu ga arimasen.*
  This book has no index.

Indian インディアン (American) Indian, Native American

- *Kono shū ni wa Indian no shūraku wa hotondo nokotte imasen.*
  There are hardly any Indian villages left in this state.

Indian samā インディアンサマー Indian summer

- *Indian samā ga otozurete kyū ni atsuku narimashita.*
  Indian summer arrived and it suddenly became hot.

indiizu インディーズ indies (independent production)

- *Indiizu no seisaku shita rekōdo ni wa dokusōteki na sakuhin ga ōi desu.*
  There are many creative records among those produced by the indies.

Indo インド India

- *Indo no eiga o mite, ikitaku narimashita.*
  I saw a movie about India and felt like going there.

indoa supōtsu インドアスポーツ indoor sport

- *Indoa supōtsu yori autodoa supōtsu no hō ga suki desu.*

I like outdoor sports better than indoor sports.

Indoneshia インドネシア Indonesia

- *Kare wa Indoneshia kara kita bijinesuman desu.*
  He is a businessman from Indonesia.

inferioritii konpurekkusu インフェリオリティー・コンプ
レックス inferiority complex *see* **konpurekkusu**

- *Kanojo wa bijin no ane ni inferioritii konpurekkusu o
  motte imasu.*
  She has an inferiority complex because of her beautiful
  older sister.

infōmaru インフォーマル informal

- *Sono koto wa infōmaru na miitingu de hanashiaimashita.*
  We discussed the matter in an informal meeting.
- *Infōmaru ni tsūchi ga arimashita.*
  We were notified informally.

infomēshon インフォメーション information

- *Chūgoku no naijō ni kanshite infomēshon o atsumete
  imasu.*
  I am collecting information about conditions inside China.
- *Iriguchi no migi ni infomēshon ga arimasu kara soko de
  kiite kudasai.*
  There's an infomation booth at the right of the entrance, so
  ask there.

infura インフラ infrastructure

- *Infura wa keizai katsudō no kiban o keisei suru kisoteki na
  setsubi desu.*
  Infrastructure means the basic facilities that form the foundation for economic activities.
- *Infura o seibi suru koto ga senketsu desu.*
  Maintenance of the infrastructure is an issue that needs to be
  settled ahead of time.

infurasutorakuchā インフラストラクチャー *see* **infura**
infure インフレ *see* **infurēshon**

infure hejji インフレヘッジ inflationary hedge
- *Infure hejji ni kin o kaimashita.*
  I bought gold as an inflationary hedge.

infurēshon インフレーション inflation
- *Infurēshon wa kontorōru sarete imasu.*
  Inflation is under control.

infuruenza インフルエンザ influenza, flu
- *Ima Tōkyō de wa infuruenza ga hayatte imasu.*
  The flu is raging in Tokyo now.

Ingurando イングランド England
- *Ingurando ni taizaichū, Tōmasu Hādi no shusseichi o otozuremashita.*
  While in England, I visited Thomas Hardy's birthplace.

Ingurisshu-mafin イングリッシュマフィン English muffin
- *Ingurisshu-mafin to kōcha de kantan na chōshoku o torimashita.*
  I had a simple breakfast of English muffins and tea.

inisharu イニシャル *see* **inishiaru**

inishiachibu イニシアチブ initiative
- *Kare wa itsumo hanbai sokushin no inishiachibu o torimasu.*
  He always takes the initiative in sales promotions.

inishiaru イニシアル initial
- *Kare wa itsumo inishiaru no haitta waishatsu o kiteimasu.*
  He always wears dress shirts with his initials on them.
- *Koko ni inishiaru de shomei o shite kudasai.*
  Please initial here.

inishiatibu イニシアティブ *see* **inishiachibu**

inki インキ *see* **inku**

inku インク ink
- *Kono shinbun wa inku no nioi ga shimasu.*
  This newspaper smells of ink.

inku kātorijji インクカートリッジ ink cartridge

- *Mannenhitsu no inku kātorijji wa ippai desu.*
  This fountain pen's ink cartridge is full.

inmoraru インモラル immoral

- *Sono yōna inmoraru na koto wa yaritaku arimasen.*
  I don't wish to do such an immoral thing.
- *Inmoraru na shōsetsu ga yoku urete imasu.*
  Immoral novels are selling well.

inobēshon イノベーション innovation

- *Fakushimiri wa bijinesu ni okeru subarashii inobēshon desu.*
  The facsimile is a wonderful innovation for business.
- *Shinki jigyō mo ii ga hongyō no inobēshon ga jūyō de wa nai desu ka?*
  New ventures are fine, but isn't it important to innovate your main business?

inobētibu イノベーティブ innovative

- *inobētibu na kigyō*
  an innovative enterprise

inpakuto インパクト impact

- *Naikaku no kaizō wa seikai ni ōki na inpakuto o ataeru deshō.*
  The cabinet change will have a great impact on the political world.

inpōto インポート import

- *Kono mise de wa inpōto mono no baggu ga yoku urete imasu.*
  Imported bags are selling well in this store.

inputto suru インプットする to put in, input

- *Bōdai na shiryō ga konpyūtā ni inputto sarete imasu.*
  A vast amount of data has been put into the computer.

insaidā インサイダー insider

- *Kin'yūkai de wa insaidā torihiki wa kibishiku kisei sarete imasu.*

Insider trading is strictly regulated in the financial world.

insaido インサイド inside
- *Kono kiji wa seikai no insaido o abaita mono desu.*

This article discloses the inside of the political world.

insaido ripōto インサイドリポート [Japanese Usage: inside report] exposé
- *Kore wa insaido ripōto bakari nosete iru shinbun desu.*

This newspaper carries nothing but exposés.
- *Konshū wa kin'yū gyōkai no insaido ripōto o o-okuri shimasu.*

This week we bring you an inside report from the financial world.

insupirēshon インスピレーション inspiration
- *Sono gaka wa Mone no sakuhin kara insupirēshon o ukemashita.*

The painter received inspiration from Monet's work.

insutanto インスタント instant
- *Insutanto shokuhin ni wa mō akimashita.*

I got tired of instant foods.

insutanto kamera インスタントカメラ [Japanese Usage: instant camera] Polaroid
- *Insutanto kamera de kazoku no shashin o torimashita.*

I took pictures of my family with a Polaroid.

insutorakushon インストラクション instruction
- *Tsukau mae ni insutorakushon o yoku yonde kudasai.*

Please read the instructions carefully before you use it.

insutorakutā インストラクター instructor
- *Kare wa hiruma wa gakusei de yoru wa jūdō no insutorakutā desu.*

He is a student in the day and a judo instructor at night.

intābaru インターバル interval
- *Ki ga ittei no intābaru o oite uwatte imasu.*

Trees are planted at regular intervals.

intabyū インタビュー interview; **~suru** する to interview
- *Kare wa terebi no intabyū de kotoshi no hōfu o katarimashita.*
  He spoke of his aspirations for this year in the TV interview.
- *Shinbun kisha ga Sōri-daijin ni intabyū shimashita.*
  A newspaper reporter interviewed the Prime Minister.

intāchenji インターチェンジ interchange
- *Kōsoku dōro no intāchenji de taiya ga panku shimashita.*
  A tire blew out on the interchange of the freeway.

intāhon インターホン intercom
- *Intāhon da to oshiuri o kotowaru no wa kantan desu.*
  You can easily turn away door-to-door salesmen using an intercom.

intāhōn インターホーン *see* **intāhon**

intān インターン intern
- *Kanojo wa toshin no byōin de intān o tsutomete imasu.*
  She is serving her internship at a hospital in the heart of the city.

intānashonaru インターナショナル international
- *intānashonaru na kyōgikai*
  an international sports meet
- *Kare no namae wa intānashonaru ni shirarete imasu.*
  His name is known internationally.
- *Motto intānashonaru na shigoto o shitai to omotte imasu.*
  I think I'd like to do work that's more international.

intavyū インタヴュー *see* **intabyū**

interekuchuaru インテレクチュアル intellectual
- *Kare-ra wa interekuchuaru na shigoto ni tazusawatte imasu.*
  They are engaged in intellectual work.

interi インテリ intellectuals, intelligentsia
- *Kare no dokusha wa wakai interi ga hotondo desu.*
  His readers are mostly young intellectuals.

interia インテリア interior
- *Kono heya no interia wa Supein-fū desu.*

  The interior of this room is done in a Spanish style.

interigenchia インテリゲンチア *see* **interi**

interijensu インテリジェンス intelligence
- *Interijensu o kanjisaseru katarikuchi ga kanojo no mochiaji desu.*

  Her distinctive quality is that when she speaks you think she is intelligent.

intonēshon イントネーション intonation
- *Onaji hatsuon no kotoba de mo intonēshon ni yotte imi ga chigaimasu.*

  Even words with the same pronunciation can differ in meaning depending on intonation.

intoro イントロ introduction
- *Kono kyoku wa intoro ga sukoshi nagasugimasu ne.*

  The introduction of this music is a little too long, isn't it?

intorodakushon イントロダクション *see* **intoro**

irasuto イラスト illustration
- *Suteki na irasuto ga hon o hikitatete imasu.*

  The wonderful illustrations enhance the book.

irasuto mappu イラストマップ illustrated map
- *Ryokō-dairiten de kankō yō no irasuto mappu o moraimashita.*

  I got an illustrated sightseeing map at the travel agency.

irasutorēshon イラストレーション *see* **irasuto**

irasutorētā イラストレーター illustrator
- *Kanojo wa irasutorētā shibō desu.*

  She wants to be an illustrator.

iriigaru イリーガル illegal
- *iriigaru na torihiki*

  illegal transactions
- *Kare-ra wa iriigaru ni nyūkoku shimashita.*

They entered the country illegally.

iruminēshon イルミネーション illumination
- *Iruminēshon no okage de yoru no machi wa akarukute utsukushii desu.*

The city at night is bright and beautiful with illumination.

iryūjon イリュージョン illusion
- *Kanojo wa mada Pari ni iru yō na iryūjon ni ochiirimashita.*

She fell into the illusion that she was still in Paris.

iryuminēshon イリュミネーション *see* **iruminēshon**

Itaria イタリア Italy
- *Itaria wa opera no honba desu.*

Italy is the birthplace of opera.

Itarian resutoran イタリアン・レストラン Italian restaurant
- *Kono machi ni Itarian resutoran ga kyū ni fuemashita.*

In this city the number of Italian restaurants has suddenly increased.

itarikku イタリック italic
- *Kasen o hiita kotoba wa itarikku ni shite kudasai.*

Please change the underlined words to italic type.

ivu イヴ *see* **ibu**

ivuningu イヴニング *see* **ibuningu doresu**

iyahon イヤホン earphone
- *Iyahon de rajikase o kikinagara jogingu suru no wa kiken desu.*

It's dangerous to jog while listening to a cassette with earphones.

iyahōn イヤホーン *see* **iyahon**

iyaringu イヤリング earring
- *Kanojo no pāru no iyaringu ga totemo suteki deshita.*

Her pearl earrings were very attractive.

izumu イズム ism, principle

- *izumu no nai hito*
  a person without any isms

J

JAS māku JASマーク *see* **Jasu-māku**
JIS māku JISマーク *see* **Jisu-māku**
JR *see* **Jeiāru**
jā ジャー jar, thermos
- *Tana no ue ni garasu no jā ga narande imasu.*
  Glass jars are placed in a row on the shelf.
- *denki suihan jā*
  an electric rice cooker
- *Jā ni kōhii o irete okimasu.*
  I keep coffee in a thermos.
jāgon ジャーゴン jargon
- *Sono supiichi wa jāgon ga ōkute wakarinikukatta no desu.*
  The speech had a lot of jargon in it and was hard to understand.
jaianto ジャイアント giant
- *Kare wa jazu kai no jaianto desu.*
  He is a giant in the jazz world.
- *Jaianto panda ga dōbutsuen e kimashita.*
  A giant panda came to the zoo.
jāji ジャージ *see* **jājii**
jājii ジャージー jersey
- *jājii no tsū-piisu*
  a two-piece jersey dress
- *jājii o kita ragubii senshu*
  rugby players in their jerseys
jajji ジャッジ judge, decision

- *Kankyaku wa shinpan no jajji ni gimon o idakimashita.*
  The spectators had doubts about the umpire's decision.

jaketto ジャケット jacket
- *Kono jaketto wa Kurisumasu purezento ni moraimashita.*
  I received this jacket as a Christmas present.

jakki ジャッキ jack
- *Taiya o kaeru no ni jakki de kuruma o mochiagemasu.*
  I jack up the car to change a tire.

jakkunaifu ジャックナイフ jackknife
- *Jakkunaifu de odosaremashita.*
  I was threatened with a jackknife.

Jāman bureddo ジャーマン・ブレッド German bread
- *Katai Jāman bureddo ga suki desu.*
  I like hard German bread.

jamu ジャム jam
- *Ichigo ya ringo de jamu o tsukurimasu.*
  We make jam with strawberries and apples.

jānarisuto ジャーナリスト journalist
- *Jānarisuto ga ōzei saibansho no mae ni atsumatte imasu.*
  Many journalists are gathering in front of the courthouse.

jānarizumu ジャーナリズム journalism
- *Kono shinbun no henshūchō wa jānarizumu gakka no shusshin desu.*
  The chief editor of this newspaper was a student of journalism.
- *Jānarizumu wa kenryoku ni geigō subeki de wa arimasen.*
  Journalism shouldn't cater to those in power.

janbo ジャンボ jumbo, jumbo jet
- *janbo na hanbāgā*
  a jumbo hamburger
- *Janbo de Taihei-yō o watarimasu.*
  I cross the Pacific by jumbo jet.

janbō jetto ジャンボージェット *see* **janbo**

janguru ジャングル jungle
- *Hikōki ga janguru ni tsuiraku shimashita.*
  An airplane crashed into the jungle.

janku ジャンク junk
- *Ano mise no mono wa janku bakari desu.*
  That store has only got junk.

janku bondo ジャンクボンド junk bond
- *Janku bondo wa takai rishi ga tsukimasu ga, risuku mo ōkii desu.*
  Junk bonds bear high interest but have high risks as well.

janku fūdo ジャンクフード junk food
- *Janku fūdo wa tabenai yō ni shite imasu.*
  I try not to eat junk food.

janbā ジャンバー *see* **janpā**

janpā ジャンパー jumper, jacket for sports or work
- *Chairo no janpā o kita hito ga fensu o tatete imasu.*
  A man wearing a brown jumper is putting up a fence.

janpu ジャンプ jump; ~**suru** する to jump, skip
- *Kanojo wa sukii no janpu de atarashii kiroku o tsukurimashita.*
  She set a new record in ski-jumping.
- *Igirisu de wa dekiru gakusei wa kōkō o janpu shite daigaku ni hairemasu.*
  In England, capable students can skip high school and enter university.

janru ジャンル [French: *genre*] kind
- *Watashi no ichiban suki na e no janru wa inshōha desu.*
  My favorite kind of painting is impressionist.

Japan manē ジャパンマネー Japanese money
- *Japan manē ga kaigai no tochi o kaishimete imasu.*
  They are buying up real estate in foreign countries with Japanese money.

Japanaizu suru ジャパナイズする to Japanize

- *Japanaizu sareta gairaigo ga takusan arimasu.*
  There are many Japanized loanwords.

Japaniizu-Ingurisshu ジャパニーズ・イングリッシュ
  Japanese-English, Japlish
  - *Kare no Japaniizu-Ingurisshu wa totemo Amerika-jin ni wa tsūjinai deshō.*
    Americans won't understand his Japlish at all.

Jasu-māku ジャスマーク JASマーク JAS mark (Japan Agricultural Standard)
  - *Nippon-nōrin-kikaku ni gōkaku shita shokuhin ni wa Jasu-māku ga tsukeraremasu.*
    A JAS mark is attached to food that is up to the Japan Agricultural Standard.

jasumin ジャスミン jasmine
  - *Jasumin no kaori ga kasuka ni tadayotte imasu.*
    The faint scent of jasmine hangs in the air.

jasumin tii ジャスミンティー jasmine tea
  - *Sobo wa ryokucha yori mo jasumin tii o aiyō shite imasu.*
    My grandmother has jasmine tea more often than green tea.

jasuto ジャスト just, exactly
  - *Ima goji jasuto desu.*
    It's exactly five o'clock.
  - *Kono teiki yokin no risoku wa roku pāsento jasuto desu.*
    The interest rate for this time deposit is exactly six percent.

jazu ジャズ jazz
  - *Kare wa naito kurabu de jazu o ensō shite imasu.*
    He is playing jazz at a nightclub.

Jeiāru ジェイ・アール JR JR (Japan Railways)
  - *Jeiāru de Nihonjū hotondo doko e de mo ryokō dekimasu.*
    You can travel to practically every part of Japan by JR.

jenerēshon ジェネレーション generation
  - *Tsugi no jenerēshon o seou wakamono wa sekinin jūdai desu.*

The young people who will lead the next generation have a
serious responsibility.

jenerēshon gyappu ジェネレーション・ギャップ generation gap
- *Shakai no arayuru men ni jenerēshon gyappu ga miraremasu.*

A generation gap can be seen in all aspects of society.

jentoruman ジェントルマン gentleman
- *Dono men kara mite mo kare wa jentoruman desu.*

He is a gentleman in every respect.

jerii ジェリー *see* **zerii**

jesuchā ジェスチャー gesture
- *Sono gaijin wa jesuchā de imi o tsūjisasemashita.*

The foreigner made himself understood by using gestures.

jetto ジェット jet, jet plane
- *Jetto-ki de iku to, nijikan shika kakarimasen.*

It takes only two hours if you go by jet.

jetto kōsutā ジェットコースター [Japanese Usage: jet coaster] roller coaster
- *Yūenchi de jetto kōsutā ni notte tanoshimimashita.*

We enjoyed riding the roller coaster at the amusement park.

jifuteria ジフテリア diphtheria
- *Kodomo no toki jifuteria ni kakarimashita.*

I suffered from diphtheria when I was a child.

jiguzagu ジグザグ zigzag
- *Yopparai ga michi o jiguzagu ni aruite imasu.*

A drunken man is walking zigzag down the street.
- *Mae no kuruma ga jiguzagu unten o shite iru no de kininarimasu.*

I'm uneasy because the car in front of me is zigzagging all over the road.

jii-ai ジーアイ GI GI (Government Issue), member of the U.S. armed forces

- *Kono bā wa Amerika no jii-ai ga yoku nomi ni kimasu.*
  American GIs often come to drink at this bar.

jii-enu-pii ジー・エヌ・ピー GNP GNP (gross national product)

- *Konnendo no jii-enu-pii wa yosō gai ni hikui desu.*
  This fiscal year's GNP is lower than we expected.

jii-men ジーメン Gメン [Japanese Usage: G(overnment)-men] G-man, Federal agent, government inspector

- *Mayaku jii-men ni kan suru dokyumentarii o mimashita.*
  I saw a documentary about Federal narcotics agents.
- *Shiwasu ni natte To no shokuhin jii-men ga Tsukiji shijō ya shokuryōhinten no tachiiri kensa o hajimemashita.*
  In December, the Metropolitan Government's food inspection officers began inspecting the sanitary conditions at Tsukiji market and other grocery shops.

jiinzu ジーンズ jeans

- *Kanojo no jiinzu wa taito sugimasu ne.*
  Her jeans are too tight, aren't they?

jii-pan ジーパン Gパン [Japanese Usage: j(eans) pan(ts)] jeans *see* **jiinzu**

- *Jii-pan o haite saikuringu ni ikimasu.*
  I go cycling in jeans.

jiipu ジープ jeep

- *Kare wa chūko no jiipu o unten shite imasu.*
  He is driving a used jeep.

jiizeru enjin ジーゼルエンジン *see* **diizeru enjin**

jimu ジム gym

- *Hiru yasumi ni gakkō no jimu de barēbōru o shimasu.*
  We play volleyball in our school gym during the noon recess.
- *Isshūkan ni ikkai jimu ni torēningu ni itte kenkō iji ni tsutomete imasu.*
  I work out in a gym once a week to keep up my health.

jimunajiumu ジムナジウム *see* **jimu**

jinkusu ジンクス jinx
- *Tsui ni sono jinkusu o yaburu koto ga dekimashita.*
  Finally I was able to break that jinx.

jippā ジッパー zipper
- *Janpā no jippā o hazushimashita.*
  I unzipped my jumper.
- *Senaka no jippā o agete kuremasu ka?*
  Will you zip me up in back?

Jipushii ジプシー Gypsy
- *Kanojo wa Jipushii no yō ni hōrō no isshō o okurimashita.*
  She led a wandering life like a Gypsy.

jirenma ジレンマ dilemma
- *Kanojo wa shigoto to katei no dochira o erabu ka to iu jirenma ni ochiitte imasu.*
  She is in a dilemma and has to choose between her job and her family.

Jisu-māku ジスマーク JISマーク JIS mark (Japanese Industrial Standard)
- *Nippon-kōgyō-kikaku ni gōkaku shita seihin ni Jisu-māku o tsukemasu.*
  A JIS mark is attached to products which meet the Japanese Industrial Standard.

jisutenpā ジステンパー distemper
- *Jisutenpā de koinu ga korori to shinimashita.*
  My puppy died suddenly from distemper.

jogingu ジョギング jogging
- *Kyūjitsu ni wa asa hayaku jogingu ni ikimasu.*
  On holidays I go jogging early in the morning.

jointo ジョイント joint
- *Tasha to no jointo seisan o ikutsuka kikaku shite imasu.*
  We are planning a joint production with other companies.

jointo benchā ジョイントベンチャー joint venture

- *Ryōsha wa jointo benchā setsuritsu no gōi ni tasshimashita.*
  These two firms have agreed to set up a joint venture.

jokki ジョッキ jug, mug
- *Kare wa jokki ippai no biiru o gutto nomihoshimashita.*
  He gulped down a mug of beer in one go.

jōku ジョーク joke
- *Sukoshi sake o nomu to, kare wa jōku o renpatsu shidashimasu.*
  When he drinks a little sake, he cracks one joke after another.

junia ジュニア junior, son, second generation
- *Eigakai de wa sutā no junia ga totemo motete imasu.*
  In the film world, the children of stars are highly sought after.

jūkubokkusu ジュークボックス jukebox
- *Jūkubokkusu ni koin o irete suki na ongaku o kikimasu.*
  I'll put a coin in the jukebox and listen to a song I like.

jūsā ジューサー juicer
- *Kono jūsā wa kotoshi no shinseihin desu.*
  This juicer is a new product this year.

jūsu ジュース juice
- *Jūsu wa ikaga desu ka?*
  Would you care for some juice?

jūsu ジュース deuce
- *Pinpon no shiai wa mata jūsu ni narimashita.*
  The ping-pong game has just gone to deuce again.

K

kā カー car
- *Kā tsuki no dansei ga wakai josei ni yoku motemasu.*

A man with a car is very popular with young women.

kabā カバー cover; **~suru** する to cover
- *Yogorenai yō ni isu ni kabā o kakemasu.*
  I'll put a cover on the chair so that it won't get dirty.
- *Kenkō hoken ga nyūinhi no hotondo o kabā shimashita.*
  My health insurance covered most of my hospital expenses.

kabā chāji カバーチャージ cover charge
- *Kono naitokurabu no kabā chāji wa yoso yori takai desu.*
  This nightclub's cover charge is higher than the others'.

kabā gāru カバーガール cover girl
- *Wakai songuraitā ga shūkanshi no kabā gāru ni narimashita.*
  A young songwriter became a cover girl for a weekly.

kābon カーボン carbon
- *Shorui no kopii o toru tame ni kābonshi o tsukaimasu.*
  Carbon papers are used to make copies of documents.

kābu カーブ curve; **~suru** する to curve
- *kyū na kābu*
  a sharp curve
- *Kuruma ga kōsaten de kābu shimashita.*
  A car curved at the intersection.

kādegan カーデガン *see* **kādigan**

kādigan カーディガン cardigan
- *Kono kādigan wa haha ga ande kuremashita.*
  My mother knitted this cardigan for me.

kādo カード card
- *Ano mise de wa Kurisumasu kādo ya bāsudē kādo nado o utte imasu.*
  That store sells Christmas cards, birthday cards, and so on.

kafē カフェー cafe, coffee shop
- *Sēnu-gawa no hotori no kafē ni tachiyorimashita.*
  We stopped at a cafe by the Seine.

kafein カフェイン [German: *Kaffein*] caffeine

- *Kafein no nai kōhii o nomimasu.*
  I drink decaffeinated coffee.
- *Nihoncha ni mo kafein ga fukumarete imasu.*
  There's caffeine in Japanese tea, too.

kā ferii カーフェリー car ferry

- *Kā ferii wa kuruma o mansai shite shukkō shimashita.*
  The car ferry left port with a full cargo of vehicles.

kafeteria カフェテリア cafeteria

- *Kafeteria no yasui shokuji ni akimashita.*
  I got tired of the cheap food in the cafeteria.
- *Ano hoteru no kafeteria de matteite kudasai.*
  Wait for me in the cafeteria of that hotel.

kafusu カフス cuffs, cuff links.

- *Kare wa kafusu o takushiagete shigoto o shite imasu.*
  He is working with his cuffs rolled up.

kajino カジノ casino

- *Makao ni aru kajino*
  a casino in Macao

kajuaru カジュアル casual

- *Kare wa kajuaru na fukusō ga yoku niaimasu.*
  He looks nice in casual clothes.

kajuaru uea カジュアルウエア casual wear

- *Kanojo wa sūtsu ya pātii doresu yori kajuaru uea ni o-kane o tsukaimasu.*
  She spends more money on casual clothes than on suits and party dresses.

kāki カーキ khaki

- *kāki iro no sētā*
  a khaki sweater

kakuteru カクテル cocktail

- *Yūshoku no mae ni kakuteru o nomimashita.*
  I had a cocktail before supper.

kakuteru pātii カクテルパーティー cocktail party

- *Kakuteru pātii de meishi o kōkan shimashita.*
  We exchanged business cards at a cocktail party.

kamera カメラ camera
- *Mishiranu hito ga watashi ni kamera o mukemashita.*
  A stranger aimed his camera at me.

kameraman カメラマン cameraman, professional photographer
- *Kameraman ga horyo ni natte imashita.*
  A cameraman was held as a prisoner of war.

kamofurāju カモフラージュ *see* **kamufurāju**

kamubakku カムバック comeback; **~suru** する to come back
- *Kanojo no sutēji e no kamubakku wa subarashikatta desu.*
  Her comeback to the stage was brilliant.
- *Kono moderu no uriage wa nii ni kamubakku shimashita.*
  This model's sales went back up to second place.
- *Gonen no buranku ga atta nimo kakawarazu kare wa migoto ni kamubakku shimashita.*
  In spite of his not doing anything for 5 years, he came back brilliantly.

kamufurāju カムフラージュ camouflage; **~suru** する to camouflage, conceal
- *Kare no hatsugen wa kaisha no jitsujō o kamufurāju suru tame no yō na ki ga shimasu.*
  I suspect that he may try to conceal the actual state of the company.

Kanada カナダ Canada
- *Jitensha de Kanada no kokkyō o koemashita.*
  I crossed the Canadian border by bicycle.

kanbakku カンバック *see* **kamubakku**

kanbasu カンバス canvas
- *Kanojo wa kanbasu ni shōzo o kaite imasu.*
  She is painting a portrait on canvas.

kānēshon カーネーション carnation
* *Shiroi kānēshon o miru to, nakunatta haha o omoidashimasu.*
White carnations remind me of my late mother.

kānibaru カーニバル carnival
* *Rio no kānibaru*
the Rio de Janeiro Carnival

kanma カンマ *see* **konma**

kanningu カンニング cheating
* *Kanningu o mitsukatte, sensei ni shikararemashita.*
I got caught cheating and was reprimanded by my teacher.

kanpa カンパ [Russian: *kampaniya*] fund-raising campaign
* *Samui hi ni, gakusei ga gaitō de kanpa o tsunotte imashita.*
On a cold day, students were conducting a fund-raising campaign on the street.

kantorii kurabu カントリークラブ country club
* *Kare wa ichiryū no kantorii kurabu no menbā desu.*
He is a member of an exclusive country club.

kantorii risuku カントリーリスク [Japanese Usage: country risk] country with a high degree of risk
* *Seifu wa kantorii risuku no takai gaikoku e no tōshi ni wa shinchō desu.*
The government is cautious about investments in foreign countries with a high degree of instability.

kanū カヌー canoe
* *Kanū de kyūryū o kudarimashita.*
We shot down the rapids in a canoe.

kāpetto カーペット carpet
* *Kāpetto no iro ga heya o akaruku shite imasu.*
The color of the carpet brightens the room.

kāpōto カーポート carport
* *Kāpōto ni shiroi ōpun kā ga haitte imasu.*

A white convertible is parked in the carport.

kappu カップ cup (with a handle), prize cup
- *Kappu ga tana kara ochite waremashita.*
  A cup fell off the shelf and broke.

kappuru カップル couple
- *o-niai no kappuru*
  a well-matched couple

kapuseru カプセル capsule
- *Kapuseru no kusuri wa nomiyasui desu.*
  Medicine in capsule form is easy to take.

karā カラー collar
- *karā no nai burausu*
  a blouse without a collar

karā カラー color, character
- *Shigotoburi ni kare no karā ga yoku arawarete imasu.*
  His character is revealed well in his work.

karā firumu カラーフィルム color film
- *Kamera ni wa karā firumu ga irete arimasu.*
  There is color film in the camera.

karā fuirumu カラーフイルム *see* **karā firumu**

karafuru カラフル colorful
- *Kanojo wa hachijussai de sono karafuru na jinsei o tojimashita.*
  Her colorful life ended at the age of eighty.

karā terebi カラーテレビ color television
- *Ōgata no karā terebi no ureyuki ga totemo ii desu.*
  Large-sized color television sets sell very well.

karejji ringu カレッジリング college ring
- *Sotsugyō shite kara karejji ringu o moraimashita.*
  We got our college rings at our graduation.

karendā カレンダー calendar
- *Shinshitsu no kabe ni Nihon no karendā ga kakete arimasu.*

A Japanese calendar is hanging on the bedroom wall.

karento topikkusu カレントトピックス current topics

- *Kanojo wa zasshi ni karento topikkusu ni kan suru kiji o kaite imasu.*

She writes articles on current topics for magazines.

karē raisu カレーライス [Japanese Usage: curry rice] curry with rice

- *Yasukute oishii karē raisu wa kono mise no ichiban ninki desu.*

Inexpensive and tasty curry served over rice is this restaurant's best seller.

karikachua カリカチュア caricature

- *Kono shōsetsu ni wa jitsuzai no jinbutsu ga karikachua sarete tōjō shite imasu.*

There are caricatures of real people in this novel.

karikyuramu カリキュラム curriculum

- *Yūzūsei no aru karikyuramu o kumu beki desu.*

We should create a flexible curriculum.

karisuma カリスマ charisma

- *Shinshachō wa jitchoku na jinbutsu desu ga karisuma sei ni kakete imasu.*

Our new company president is a man of integrity but he doesn't have charisma.

karorii カロリー calorie

- *Karorii no ōi tabemono wa sakeru yō ni shite imasu.*

I try to avoid high-calorie foods.

kāru カール curl

- *Kanojo wa nagai kami o kāru ni shite imasu.*

She wears her long hair in curls.

- *Kami ga kirei ni kāru shite imasu ne.*

Your hair curls beautifully.

karuchā カルチャー culture

- *Nippon no karuchā*

Japanese culture

- *Kanojo wa karuchā o takameru tame ni Igirisu no shōsetsu o yonde imasu.*

She reads English novels to cultivate herself.

karuchā sentā カルチャーセンター cultural center

- *Karuchā sentā de Eikaiwa o naratte imasu.*

I am learning English conversation at a cultural center.

karuchā shokku カルチャーショック culture shock

- *Kanojo wa karuchā shokku de shokuyoku mo arimasen.*

Because of culture shock she doesn't even have any appetite.

karuchua カルチュア *see* **karuchā**

karushiumu カルシウム calcium

- *Kore wa dono kurai karushiumu o fukunde imasu ka?*

How much calcium does this contain?

karute カルテ [German: *Karte*] medical chart

- *Isha wa kanja no shōjō o karute ni kakikomimashita.*

The doctor wrote the patient's symptoms on his medical chart.

karutetto カルテット quartet

- *Haidon no Bādo Karutetto o kiita koto ga arimasu ka?*

Have you ever listened to Haydon's Bird Quartet?

karuto カルト cult

- *Kanojo wa kazoku o sutete karuto ni kanyū shimashita.*

She abandoned her family to join the cult.

kashimia カシミア cashmere

- *kashimia no shōru*

a cashmere shawl

kashimiya カシミヤ *see* **kashimia**

Kasorikku カソリック *see* **Katorikku**

katarogu カタログ catalog

- *Go-kibō no kata ni katarogu o o-okuri itashimasu.*

We will send a catalog on request.

katasutorofii カタストロフィー catastrophe
- *Sekai no achikochi de ō-jishin ya dai-kōzui nado no katasutorofii ga okotte imasu.*
 Catastrophes such as earthquakes and floods are happening in several places around the world.

kategorii カテゴリー category
- *Yunyū kanzei wa shinamono no kategorii ni yotte chigaimasu.*
 Import duties differ depending on the category of goods.

kāten カーテン curtain
- *Kāten no semai sukima kara hi no hikari ga sashikonde kimasu.*
 The sunlight comes in through a narrow opening in the curtains.

Katorikku カトリック [Dutch: *Katholiek*] Catholic
- *Kanojo wa shin'yū no kanka o ukete Katorikku ni kaishū shimashita.*
 She became a Catholic due to the influence of her close friend.

katsu カツ cutlet
- *Kanai wa katsu ga tokui desu.*
 My wife is good at cooking cutlets.
- *Tonkatsu mo biifu-katsu mo suki desu.*
 I like both pork and beef cutlets.

katsuretsu カツレツ *see* **katsu**

katto カット cut; **~suru** する to cut
- *Sendenhi no katto ga aru kamo shiremasen.*
 There may be a cut in the advertising expenses.
- *Sono eiga no mondai ni natta bamen wa katto sarete imasu.*
 The controversial scenes in that movie have been cut.

katto gurasu カットグラス cut glass
- *Gōjasu na bara ga katto gurasu ni ikete arimasu.*

Gorgeous roses are arranged in a cut glass vase.

kaubōi カウボーイ cowboy
- *Tekisasu no nōjō de uma ni notta kaubōi o mimashita.*
  I saw a cowboy on horseback at the farm in Texas.

kaunserā カウンセラー counselor
- *Sono koto wa kaunserā ni sōdan shita hō ga ii desu yo.*
  You had better discuss this matter with the counselor.

kaunseringu カウンセリング counseling
- *Ano gakusei wa nando mo kaunseringu o shimashita ga kōka wa arimasen.*
  I counseled the student many times but with no effect.

kauntā カウンター counter
- *Kare wa bā no kauntā de hitori de nonde imasu.*
  He is drinking alone at the counter in a bar.

kaunto カウント count; **~suru** する to count
- *Kaunto wa tsū sutoraiku wan bōru desu.*
  The count is one ball and two strikes.
- *Kono tesuto wa seiseki ni kaunto saremasen.*
  This test won't count toward your grade.

kaunto auto カウントアウト to count out
- *Bokusā ga taoreta mama kaunto auto ni narimashita.*
  The boxer fell down and was counted out.

kāvu カーヴ *see* **kābu**

kea ケア care; **~suru** する to take care of
- *Kono puranto wa tokubetsu na kea ga irimasu.*
  This plant needs special care.
- *Seishin hakujakuji o kea suru koto ni yorokobi o mitsukemashita.*
  I found great satisfaction in taking care of mentally-retarded children.

kebin ケビン *see* **kyabin**

kēburu kā ケーブルカー cable car
- *Kēburu kā de Rokkō-zan ni noborimashita.*

I went up Mount Rokko in a cable car.

kechappu ケチャップ ketchup
- *Ryōri ni yoku kechappu o tsukaimasu.*
  I use a lot of ketchup when I cook.

kēki ケーキ cake
- *Kono kēki wa anata no o-tesei desu ka?*
  Did you bake this cake yourself?

kemikaru shūzu ケミカルシューズ [Japanese Usage: chemical shoes] shoes made of synthetic materials
- *Ame no hi ni wa kanojo wa kemikaru shūzu o hakimasu.*
  On rainy days, she wears synthetic leather shoes.

kēpu ケープ cape
- *Kēpu o kata ni haotte niwa ni demashita.*
  I put a cape over my shoulders and went out to the garden.

kēsu ケース case, box
- *Kēsu ni biiru o tsumete kudasai.*
  Please put these beer bottles in a box.
- *Akibin wa kono kēsu ni irete oite kudasai.*
  Please put the empty bottles in this case.
- *Kare no kēsu wa watashi no kēsu to wa chigaimasu.*
  His case is different from mine.

kēsu bai kēsu ケース・バイ・ケース case by case, case-by-case basis
- *Mondai wa kēsu bai kēsu de shori shimashō.*
  We'll deal with these problems on a case-by-case basis.

kēsu sutadi ケーススタディ case study
- *Kēsu sutadi to shite arukōru chūdoku no mondai ni torikunde imasu.*
  I'm doing a case study on the problem of alcoholism.

kēsu sutadii ケーススタディー *see* **kēsu sutadi**

kii キー key
- *Kuruma no kii o nakushimashita.*
  I lost my car keys.

- *Tokidoki taipuraitā no machigatta kii o tatakimasu.*
  Once in a while I hit the wrong keys on the typewriter.

kiibōdo キーボード keyboard
- *Wāpuro no kiibōdo no tsukaikata o oshiete kudasai.*
  Please teach me how to use a word processor keyboard.

kii horudā キーホルダー [Japanese Usage: key holder] key ring, key case
- *Kono kii horudā wa ryokōsaki de kaimashita.*
  I bought this key ring while traveling.

kii panchā キーパンチャー key puncher, data entry operator
- *Kanojo wa kii panchā no shigoto wa tsumaranai to itte imasu.*
  She says that her job as a key puncher is boring.

kii pointo キーポイント key point
- *Mondai kaiketsu no kii pointo wa ryōsha ga jōho suru ka dōka desu.*
  The key point to solving the problem is knowing whether both parties will make concessions or not.

kii sutēshon キーステーション key station, parent station
- *Kii sutēshon de tsukutta bangumi o chihō kyoku o tsūjite zenkokuteki ni hōsō shimasu.*
  Programs made at the parent station are rebroadcast nation-wide through local stations.

kiiwādo キーワード keyword
- *Kare no keiei kōsō no kiiwādo wa gurōbarizēshon desu.*
  The keyword in his management plan is globalization.

kikku キック kick
- *Kare wa sakkā senshu no naka de kikku ga ichiban umai desu.*
  He is the best kicker among all the soccer players.

kikkuofu キックオフ kickoff
- *Sono shiai wa kikkuofu kara nessen deshita.*
  The game was tough from the kickoff.

kingu キング king
- *Kare wa gakkō no geki de kingu no yaku o enjimasu.*
  He will play the role of a king in his school play.

kingu-saizu キングサイズ king-size
- *kingu-saizu no beddo*
  a king-size bed

kiosuku キオスク *see* **kiyosuku**

Kirisuto キリスト [Portuguese: *Christo*] Christ
- *Iisutā wa Kirisuto no fukkatsu o iwau hi desu.*
  Easter is the day when the resurrection of Christ is celebrated.

kiro キロ kilogram, kilometer
- *Kono kozutsumi wa san kiro desu.*
  This parcel weighs three kilograms.
- *Koko kara eki made go kiro gurai desu.*
  It's about five kilometers from here to the station.

kiruku キルク *see* **koruku**

kirutingu キルティング quilting
- *kirutingu no heyagi*
  a quilted dressing gown

kisu キス kiss; **~suru** する to kiss
- *Kisu wa aijō no hyōgen desu.*
  A kiss is an expression of love.
- *Kūkō de kare ni kisu shite wakaremashita.*
  I kissed him goodbye at the airport.

kitchin キッチン kitchen
- *Kitchin o akarui iro ni nurikaemashita.*
  I had my kitchen painted a bright color.

kiyosuku キヨスク kiosk, station shop
- *Eki no kiyosuku de jūsu to zasshi o kaimashita.*
  I bought a can of juice and a magazine at a station kiosk.

koara コアラ koala
- *Kodomo wa koara no nuigurumi o hoshigatte imasu.*

My child wants a stuffed koala.

kōchi コーチ coach

* *Kōchi no o-kage de yūshō dekita no desu.*

We owe our victory to our coach.

kōdinētā コーディネーター coordinator

* *Ii hōsō bangumi o tsukuru tame ni wa ude no ii kōdinētā ga zettai hitsuyō desu.*

A talented coordinator is a must for good broadcast programs.

kōdinēto suru コーディネートする to coordinate

* *Shinpuru na dezain wa taitei no mono to kōdinēto dekimasu.*

A dress with a simple design can be coordinated with almost anything.

* *Kono jaketto wa shinpuru na dezain nanode kōdinēto shiyasui desu.*

The design of this jacket is simple so it's very easy to wear with almost anything.

kōdo コード cord

* *Kore o enchō kōdo ni tsunaide kudasai.*

Please connect this to an extension cord.

kōdo コード code

* *akusesu kōdo*
  access code

* *Kono hon ni denshin no kōdo ga notte imasu.*

This book has telegraphic codes.

* *Apāto no omote doa ni wa kōdo jikake no mono mo arimasu.*

The main door in an apartment building might have an access code.

kōdoresu hon コードレスホン cordless phone, portable phone

* *Niwa de hataraku toki wa kōdoresu hon o motte ikimasu.*

I take a portable phone with me when I work in the yard.

kōdoresu terehon コードレステレホン *see* **kōdoresu hon**

kōhii コーヒー coffee

- *Kōhii no kaori de me ga samemashita.*
  I woke up to the aroma of coffee.

kōhii burēku コーヒーブレーク coffee break

- *Kanojo wa kōhii burēku ni bōifurendo to denwa de hanashimasu.*
  She talks with her boyfriend on the phone during her coffee break.

kōhii shoppu コーヒーショップ coffee shop

- *Kōhii shoppu de shōsetsu no neta o hiroimasu.*
  I pick up material for my novel at a coffee shop.

koin コイン coin

- *Kodomo no chokinbako ni koin o iremasu.*
  I put coins in my child's piggy bank.

koin randorii コインランドリー [Japanese Usage: coin laundry] coin-operated laundromat

- *Sentakuki o kau made koin randorii o riyō shimasu.*
  I will be using a laundromat until I buy a washing machine.

koin rokkā コインロッカー coin-operated locker

- *Eki no koin rokkā kara taikin ga hakken saremashita.*
  A large amount of money was found in a coin-operated locker at the station.

koketisshu コケティッシュ coquettish

- *koketisshu na furumai*
  coquettish behavior
- *Kanojo wa koketisshu ni karada o kunerasemashita.*
  She twisted her body coquettishly.

kokku コック [Dutch: *kok*] cook

- *Sono resutoran de wa Furansu kara kokku o yatotta bakari desu.*
  The restaurant has just hired a cook from France.

kokoa ココア cocoa, hot chocolate
- *Sobo wa o-cha no jikan ni kokoa o nomimasu.*
My grandmother drinks cocoa at tea time.

kokonattsu ココナッツ coconut
- *Kono kukkii wa kokonattsu ga haitte imasu ne.*
These cookies have coconut in them, don't they?

komāsharu コマーシャル commercial
- *Aru terebi no komāsharu wa ātisutikku desu.*
Some TV commercials are artistic.
- *Kono komāsharu wa omoshirokute inshō ni nokorimasu.*
This commercial is funny and leaves an impression.

komedi コメディ *see* **komedii**

komedii コメディー comedy
- *Sono geki wa kazoku sorotte tanoshimeru komedii desu.*
That play is a comedy that you can enjoy with your whole
family.

komedian コメディアン comedian
- *Oyako sorotte ii komedian desu.*
Both father and son are good comedians.

komentētā コメンテーター commentator
- *Sono komentētā wa wakasa to shinsensa de ninki ga
arimasu.*
That commentator is popular due to his youth and freshness.

komento コメント comment; **~suru** する to comment
- *Gakusei kara sono kōgi ni tsuite omoshiroi komento ga
demashita.*
Students came up with interesting comments on that lec-
ture.
- *Sono teian ni wa dare mo komento shimasen deshita.*
No one commented on that proposal.
- *Mada kōshiki happyō ga arimasen no de komento wa
hikaesasete itadakimasu.*
Since there is no official announcement yet, I refrain from

commenting on it.

komikku コミック comic

- *Kare wa komikku na yaku mawari o jōzu ni konashimashita.*
  He performed the comic role creditably.

- *Densha no naka de wakamono dake de naku sarariiman made mo komikku ni yomifukette imasu.*
  Not only young people but also businessmen are engrossed in reading comics on the train.

kominizumu コミニズム *see* **komyunizumu**

komisshon コミッション commission

- *Ichiwari no komisshon de shigoto o hikiukemashita.*
  I undertook a job on a ten percent commission.

komon sensu コモンセンス common sense

- *Kanojo wa shūsai desu ga komon sensu ni kakete imasu.*
  She is a bright person but has no common sense.

komyunike コミュニケ communiqué

- *Hatten tojō koku e no keizai enjo ni tsuite komyunike ga happyō saremashita.*
  A communiqué was issued about the financial aid to developing countries.

komyunikēshon コミュニケーション communication

- *Shokutaku ga kazoku no komyunikēshon no ba ni natte imasu.*
  The dinner table is a place for communication in our family.

komyunikēto suru コミュニケートする to communicate

- *Mazui Eigo de nantoka Amerika-jin to komyunikēto shimashita.*
  I somehow managed to communicate with the Americans using my poor English.

komyunisuto コミュニスト communist

- *Kare wa subete o sutete komyunisuto ni narimashita.*
  He abandoned everything to become a communist.

komyunitii コミュニティー community
- *Komyunitii katsudō ni wa dekiru dake sanka suru yō ni shite imasu.*
  I try to participate in community activities as much as possible.

komyunizumu コミュニズム communism
- *Sono kuni no kokumin wa imada ni komyunizumu to tatakatte imasu.*
  The people of that country are still struggling against communism.

kōn コーン cone
- *Otoko no ko wa aisu kuriimu kōn o ryōte ni nigitte imasu.*
  A boy is holding ice cream cones in both hands.

kōnā コーナー corner
- *Keshōhin kōnā wa tō depāto no nikai ni utsurimashita.*
  The cosmetics corner was moved to the second floor of this department store.
- *Sentō rannā ga ima kōnā o mawarimashita.*
  The first runner just turned the corner now.

konbain suru コンバインする to combine
- *Kono niwa wa shizenbi to jinkōbi o konbain shite tsukurarete imasu.*
  This garden combines natural beauty and man-made beauty.

konbenshon コンベンション convention
- *Wai-emu-shii-ē wa chikajika konbenshon o hirakimasu.*
  The YMCA will hold a convention in the near future.

konbi コンビ combination *see* **konbinēshon**
- *Ano futari wa kono shigoto ni wa ii konbi deshō.*
  Those two will be a good combination for this task.

konbinēshon コンビネーション combination *see* **konbi**
- *howaito to burū no konbinēshon*
  a combination of white and blue

konbini コンビニ *see* **konbiniensu sutoa**

konbiniensu sutoa コンビニエンスストア convenience
store
- *Shin'ya konbiniensu sutoa ni gōtō ga hairimashita.*
  A burglar broke into a convenience store at midnight.

koncheruto コンチェルト concerto
- *Rajio kara Shopan no yūbi na piano koncheruto ga
  nagarete kimashita.*
  The sound of Chopin's elegant piano concerto flowed from
  the radio.

kondakutā コンダクター conductor (for orchestra, tour)
- *Kare wa Rondon Firuhāmonii Ōkesutora no kondakutā
  deshita.*
  He was the conductor for the London Philharmonic Orchestra.

kondensu miruku コンデンスミルク condensed milk
- *Kōhii ni kondensu miruku o iremasu.*
  I put condensed milk in my coffee.

kondishon コンディション condition
- *Kon shiizun no pitchā no kondishon wa saikō de wa
  arimasen.*
  The pitcher is not in top condition this season.
- *Kare wa saikō no kondishon de kaimakusen o mukae
  mashita.*
  He went into the opening game in perfect condition.

kone コネ connection, pull
- *Kare wa kone de ichiryū mēkā ni saiyō saremashita.*
  He got a job with a top-ranking manufacturer through
  connections.

konekushon コネクション *see* **kone**

konfarensu コンファレンス conference
- *Kyō no konfarensu wa raishū no Suiyōbi ni enki saremasu.*
  Today's conference will be postponed until next Wednes-

day.

konkōsu コンコース concourse

• *Kūkō no konkōsu de keikan ga sūnin mihatte imashita.*
Several policemen were on guard in the airport concourse.

konkuriito コンクリート concrete

• *konkuriito no kabe*
a concrete wall

konkūru コンクール [French: *concours*] contest, competition

• *Kanojo wa kitto piano no konkūru de nyūshō suru to omoimasu.*
I'm sure that she will be successful in the piano contest.

konma コンマ comma

• *Kono kotoba no ato ni konma o utsu to, yomiyasui desu.*
If you put a comma after this word, it is easier to read.

konpa コンパ [Japanese Usage: company] student social gathering

• *Shinnyūsei o kangei suru tame ni konpa ga hirakaremashita.*
We had a social gathering to welcome the new students.

konpakuto コンパクト compact, woman's compact

• *konpakuto na keisanki*
a compact calculator

• *Kono hon ni wa jōhō ga konpakuto ni tsumekomarete imasu.*
Information is squeezed compactly into this book.

• *Imeruda wa daiyamondo o chiribameta konpakuto o motte ita to omoimasu.*
I bet Imelda had a diamond-studded compact.

konpakuto kā コンパクトカー compact car

• *Konpakuto kā wa pākingu ga kantan desu.*
A compact car is easy to park.

konpanion コンパニオン companion, female guide (for a

convention or expo)

- *Eigo no jōzu na kanojo wa bankokuhaku de konpanion o tsutomemashita.*

With her excellent spoken English, she was employed as a guide at the international exposition.

konpasu コンパス drawing compass, legs

- *Konpasu de en o egakimasu.*

I draw a circle with a compass.

- *Kare wa konpasu ga mijikai desu.*

He has short legs.

konpātomento コンパートメント compartment

- *Sono resutoran no naibu wa ikutsu mo no konpātomento ni shikirarete imasu.*

The inside of the restaurant is divided into many smaller rooms.

konpe コンペ competition

- *Kare wa gorufu no konpe de kappu o kakutoku shimashita.*

He won a cup in the golf competition.

konpetishon コンペティション *see* **konpe**

konpurekkusu コンプレックス complex

- *Kare wa supōtsu ni senshin shite konpurekkusu o kokufuku shimashita.*

He overcame his complex by devoting himself to sports.

konpyūta コンピュータ *see* **konpyūtā**

konpyūtā コンピューター computer

- *Imaya konpyūtā no jidai desu.*

This is the age of computers.

konpyūtā gurafikkusu コンピューターグラフィックス computer graphics

- *Konpyūtā gurafikkusu o tsukatte, herikoputā no jiko o fusegu koto ga dekimasu.*

Using computer graphics, you can avoid helicopter accidents.

konsaba コンサバ *see* **konsābatibu**

konsabatibu コンサバティブ *see* **konsābatibu**

konsābatibu コンサーバティブ conservative
- *Konsābatibu na keiei de wa kaisha wa yatte ikemasen.*
  The company will go out of business due to its excessively conservative management.

konsaisu コンサイス concise, small size
- *Kanojo wa itsumo konsaisu gata no jisho o motte aruite imasu.*
  She always carries a pocket-size dictionary with her.

konsarutanto コンサルタント consultant
- *Keiei konsarutanto to keiyaku shimashita.*
  We signed an agreement with a management consultant.

konsāto コンサート concert
- *Kono tsuā ni wa konsāto ga futatsu haitte imasu.*
  This tour includes two concerts.

konsensasu コンセンサス consensus
- *Kaku shōhin no namae wa shanai no konsensasu de kimemasu.*
  The name of each product is determined by consensus within the company.

konsento コンセント concentric plug, electrical outlet
- *Beddo no ushiro ni konsento ga arimasu.*
  There are electrical outlets behind the bed.

konseputo コンセプト concept, viewpoint
- *atarashii konseputo no fasshon bukku*
  a fashion book with new viewpoints

konsome コンソメ consommé
- *Natsu ni wa tsumetai konsome ga ii desu ne.*
  Cold consommé is good in summer, isn't it?

kōn sūpu コーンスープ corn soup
- *Tokidoki ranchi ni insutanto no kōn sūpu o nomimasu.*
  Sometimes I have instant corn soup for lunch.

konsutanto コンスタント constant
- *konsutanto na hanbai kakuchō*
  constant expansion of sales
- *Eigyō seiseki wa konsutanto na nobi o shimeshite imasu.*
  Sales figures show constant increase.
- *Kono shōhin wa konsutanto ni urete imasu.*
  This product sells constantly.

kontakuto コンタクト contact, contact lens; **~suru** する to contact
- *Kono ken ni tsuite wa honsha to kontakuto o totte imasu.*
  We are in contact with our main office about this matter.
- *Kare to kontakuto o toritai no desu ga dōshitara ii deshō?*
  I want to get in touch with him, but how should I do it?
- *Tokidoki yoru kontakuto o me ni ireta mama nemasu.*
  Sometimes at night I sleep with my contact lenses in.

kontakuto renzu コンタクトレンズ *see* **kontakuto**

kontekusuto コンテクスト context
- *Kotoba no imi wa kontekusuto no naka de kangaeru beki desu.*
  The meaning of a word should be taken in context.

kontena コンテナ container
- *Kontena wa kamotsu no yusō ni hiroku riyō sarete imasu.*
  Containers are widely used for transporting freight.

kontenā コンテナー *see* **kontena**

kontesuto コンテスト contest
- *Kare no e wa kontesuto de rakusen shimashita.*
  His painting did not win a prize in the contest.

konto コント [French: *conte*] little story, skit
- *Kono zasshi wa fūshiteki na konto de motte imasu.*
  This magazine is sustained by its satirical stories.
- *Ano bangumi no konto wa itsu mite mo okashii desu ne.*
  That program's skits are always funny, aren't they?

kontorakuto コントラクト contract

- *Sono kaisha to no kontorakuto ga kiremashita.*
  Our contract with that company has expired.

kontorasuto コントラスト contrast
- *Kono futatsu no chōkoku wa ichijirushii kontorasuto o nashite imasu.*
  These two sculptures make a striking contrast.

kontorōru コントロール control; **~suru** する to control
- *Bukka no kontorōru ga hitsuyō ni naru deshō.*
  Price controls will probably become necessary.
- *Daietto o shite taijū o kontorōru shite imasu.*
  I control my body weight by dieting.

kontorōru tawā コントロール・タワー control tower
- *Kontorōru tawā kara ririku no shiji ga hairimashita.*
  We received the signal for takeoff from the control tower.

kontseruto コンツェルト *see* **koncheruto**

kopii コピー copy; **~suru** する to copy
- *Kore wa Hiroshige no hanga no kopii desu.*
  This is a copy of Hiroshige's woodblock print.
- *kopii shokuhin*
  imitation food
- *Kono pēji o kopii shite kudasai.*
  Please copy this page.

kopiiraitā コピーライター copywriter
- *Chōnan mo jinan mo kopiiraitā ni naritagatte imasu.*
  Both my oldest and second sons want to become copywriters.

kōporēto adobataijingu コーポレート・アドバタイジング
corporate advertising
- *Kigyō imēji o takameru tame ni kōporēto adobataijingu ga taisetsu desu.*
  It is important to improve the company's image through corporate advertising.

koppu コップ cup, glass

- *Pikunikku de wa kami koppu o tsukaimasu.*
  Paper cups are used at picnics.
- *Koppu ni yogore ga tsuite imasu.*
  These glasses are dirty.

kōra コーラ cola
- *Doko e itte mo kōra no jidō hanbaiki ga arimasu.*
  Wherever I go, I find vending machines for cola.

koramu コラム filler, column
- *Shinbun no supōtsu ran de omoshiroi koramu o mitsukemashita.*
  In the newspaper I read an interesting column in the sports page.

koramunisuto コラムニスト columnist
- *Kanojo wa chihō shinbun no koramunisuto desu.*
  She is a columnist for a local newspaper.

kōrasu コーラス chorus
- *Kōrasu no sōchō na utagoe ga mada mimi ni nokotte imasu.*
  The solemn singing of the chorus still rings in my ears.

korekushon コレクション collection
- *Kono bijutsukan ni wa aburae no bōdai na korekushon ga arimasu.*
  This art museum has an extensive collection of oil paintings.

korekuto kōru コレクトコール collect (telephone) call;
~suru する to call collect
- *Tōkyō kara korekuto kōru ga haitte orimasu.*
  You have a collect call from Tokyo.

korepon コレポン correspondence
- *Kyōjū ni senpō ni korepon o utte oite kudasai.*
  Please send the letter by the end of the day.
- *Eigo no korepon wa bijinesu sukūru ni kayotte naraimashita.*

I learned how to write letters in English at a business school.

korera コレラ cholera

* *Tasū no hinanmin ga korera de shinimashita.*
A large number of refugees died of cholera.

koresupóndensu コレスポンデンス *see* **korepon**

koresupóndento コレスポンデント correspondent

* *Kare wa koresupondento to shite ima Indo e itte imasu.*
He is now in India as a correspondent.

korokke コロッケ croquette

* *Kare no wakai okusan wa korokke shika tsukuremasen.*
His young wife can cook only croquettes.

* *Ano mise no korokke wa nakanaka oishii desu yo.*
The croquettes at that restaurant are really good.

koronii コロニー colony

* *Koronii ga kokka ni narimashita.*
A colony became a nation.

* *Arasuka wa pengin no koronii desu.*
Alaska is a colony for penguins.

* *Uchū ni koronii o tsukurō to kangaete iru hito mo imasu.*
There are even people who are thinking of building a colony
in space.

Koroseumu コロセウム *see* **Koroshiamu**

Koroshiamu コロシアム the Colosseum

* *Itaria no Koroshiamu de opera ga jōen saremashita.*
An opera was performed at the Colosseum in Italy.

kōru コール call

* *Fan no kōru ni kotaete, saido no ensō ryokō o keikaku
shite imasu.*
In response to our fans' call, we are planning a second
concert tour.

kōrudo gēmu コールドゲーム [Japanese Usage: called
game] called-off game

* *Ame no tame shiai wa kōrudo gēmu to narimashita.*

The game was called off due to rain.

kōrudo kuriimu コールドクリーム cold cream (cosmetic)
- *Te ni kōrudo kuriimu o nutte massāji o shimasu.*
  I put cold cream on my hands and massage it in.

kōru gāru コールガール call girl
- *Ano hoteru ni kōru gāru ga deiri shite iru sō desu.*
  I hear that call girls go in and out of that hotel.

koruku コルク cork
- *koruku no sen*
  a cork stopper

kōsu コース course (for study, dinner, trip), route, trail
- *Haikingu wa dono kōsu ni shimasu ka?*
  Which hiking course should we take?
- *Kyūshu ryokō wa kono kōsu ga yosasō desu ne.*
  This route sounds good for a Kyushu tour, doesn't it?
- *Kanojo wa daigaku de Supein-go no kōsu o totte imasu.*
  She is taking a course in Spanish at college.

kosuchūmu コスチューム costume
- *Opera no gōka na kosuchūmu ni kanshin shimashita.*
  I was impressed by the gorgeous costumes in the opera.

kosumechikku コスメチック cosmetic
- *Kosumechikku wa yunyūhin yori kokusanhin no hō ga ii desu.*
  I prefer domestic cosmetics to imports.

kosumetikku コスメティック *see* **kosumechikku**

kosumoporitan コスモポリタン cosmopolitan (person)
- *Kare wa sekaiteki ni katsuyaku shite iru kosumoporitan desu.*
  He is a cosmopolitan who takes an active part in international affairs.

kosuto コスト cost
- *Kosuto o kirisageru koto ga dekimasu ka?*
  Can you reduce the cost?

kōto コート coat
- *Atatakai kara, kōto wa irimasen.*
  Since it's warm, I don't need a coat.

kōto コート court
- *Tenisu kōto wa hitotsu mo aite imasen.*
  Not one of the tennis courts is open.

kuarutetto クアルテット *see* **karutetto**

kūdeta クーデタ *see* **kūdetā**

kūdetā クーデター coup d'etat
- *Yosō dōri ni kūdetā ga boppatsu shimashita.*
  As we expected, the coup d'etat occurred.

kuesuchon māku クエスチョンマーク question mark
- *Koko ni kuesuchon māku o tsukete kudasai.*
  Please put a question mark here.

kuikku クイック quick
- *matte iru uchi ni dekiru kuikku shūri*
  a quick repair while you wait

kuikku tān クイックターン quick turn
- *Sono suiei senshu wa kuikku tān ga umai desu.*
  That swimmer is very good at doing quick turns.

kuin クイン *see* **kuiin**

kuiin クイーン queen
- *Kanojo wa watashi-tachi no kurasu no kuiin deshita.*
  She was the queen of our class.

kuintetto クインテット quintet
- *Shitsunaigaku de wa Burāmusu no Piano Kuintetto ga suki desu.*
  As for chamber music, I like Brahms' Piano Quintet .

kuizu クイズ quiz
- *Aru kuizu bangumi ni gaijin ga dete imasu.*
  Foreigners appear on some quiz shows.

kukkingu sukūru クッキングスクール cooking school
- *Musume wa kukkingu sukūru ni kayotte imasu.*

My daughter goes to a cooking school.

kukkii クッキー cookie
- *Kore wa watashi no yaita kukkii desu.*

These are the cookies I baked.

kuontitii クオンティティー quantity
- *Kuontitii yori kuoritii ga daiji desu.*

Quality counts more than quantity.

kuoritii クオリティー quality
- *Kono mēkā no seihin wa kuoritii ga ii desu.*

This manufacturer's products are of good quality.

kuōtā クオーター quarter
- *Saisho no kuōtā de waga chiimu wa niten riido shimashita.*

In the first quarter, our team led by two points.

kuōtarii クオータリー quarterly
- *Kuōtarii ni deta kare no tanpen shōsetsu o yomimashita.*

I read his short story that was published in a quarterly.

kuōtsu クオーツ quartz
- *Chikagoro no tokei wa hotondo minna kuōtsu desu.*

These days almost all watches are quartz.

kūpon クーポン coupon
- *Ryokō ni dekakeru toki wa mae motte ressha no shūyū kūpon-ken o katte okimasu.*

When I go on a trip, I buy round-trip train ticket coupons beforehand.

kūrā クーラー cooler, air conditioner
- *Yūbe wa hitobanjū kūrā o tsuketa mama nemashita.*

All last night I slept with the air conditioner on.

kurabu クラブ club
- *Sasowarete shashin kurabu ni hairimashita.*

I was talked into joining a photo club.

kuraianto クライアント client
- *Sono kōkoku dairiten wa ii kuraianto ga tsuite imasu.*

The advertising agency has good clients.

kuraimakkusu クライマックス climax

- *Shiai wa dōten hōmu ran de kuraimakkusu ni tasshimashita.*

The game reached a climax with a game-tying home run.

kurakkā クラッカー cracker

- *Gen'en kurakkā ga sūpā ni dehajimemashita.*

Low salt crackers began to appear in supermarkets.

kurakushon クラクション Klaxon, horn

- *Kuruma ga kurakushon o narashinagara tōrisugimashita.*

A car passed while sounding its horn.

kuranku in クランクイン [Japanese Usage: crank in] to start shooting

- *Kono eiga no kuranku in wa raigetsu nakaba no yotei desu.*

This film is scheduled to start shooting in the middle of next month.

kurashikku クラシック [Japanese Usage: classic] classical music

- *Kare wa kurashikku kara jazu ni tenkō shita pianisuto desu.*

He is a pianist who switched from classical music to jazz.

kurasu クラス class

- *Kanojo no sainō wa kurasu de wa amari medachimasen deshita.*

Her ability didn't show very much in class.

kurasumēto クラスメート classmate

- *Kōkō jidai no kurasumēto ga atsumatte mukashibanashi o shimashita.*

The former high school classmates got together and talked about old times.

kurejitto クレジット credit

- *Kurejitto de eakon o kaimashita.*

I bought an air conditioner on credit.
- *eiga no kurejitto*
movie credits

kurejitto kādo クレジットカード credit card
- *Taitei no baai kurejitto kādo de shiharaimasu.*
In most cases, I pay with a credit card.

kurēmu クレーム claim, complaint
- *Kono kurēmu wa judaku dekimasen.*
We cannot accept this complaint.

kurēn クレーン construction crane
- *Kurēn ga taorete tsūkōnin ga sokushi shimashita.*
A crane fell over and a passerby was killed on the spot.

kurenzā クレンザー cleanser
- *Kurenzā de o-nabe o migakimasu.*
I polish pans with a cleanser.

kureon クレオン *see* **kureyon**

kurēpu クレープ crêpe (cloth, pastry)
- *Shiroi kurēpu no burausu ga suzushisō desu.*
A white crêpe blouse looks cool.
- *Tomodachi no uchi de kurēpu to remon tii ga demashita.*
Crêpes and tea with lemon were served at my friend's house.

kurētā クレーター crater
- *Sono kyodai na kurētā wa masa ni sōkan o teishite imasu.*
The huge crater presents a truly grand spectacle.

kureyon クレヨン crayon
- *Kodomo ga kureyon de nurie o shite imasu.*
Children are coloring with crayons.

kuria クリア clear; **~suru** する to clear
- *kuria na iro*
a clear color
- *Kuria ni setsumei shite arimasu.*
It is explained clearly.

- *Mazu shakkin o kuria shinakereba narimasen.*
  We must clear our debts first.

kuriā クリアー *see* **kuria**

kuriaransu sēru クリアランスセール clearance sale
- *Kuriaransu sēru de wa aru shinamono nado wa hangaku desu.*
  Some things are sold at half price at a clearance sale.

kurieitibu クリエイティブ *see* **kuriētibu**

kurieito クリエイト *see* **kurieto suru**

kuriēshon クリエーション creation
- *Kono dezain wa dare no kuriēshon desu ka?*
  Whose creation is this design?

kuriētibu クリエーティブ creative
- *Kare wa kaisha no naka de kuriētibu na bumon ni zokushite imasu.*
  He belongs to the creative section in the company.

kurieto suru クリエートする to create
- *Kare wa kyodai na abusutorakuto no chōkoku o kurieto shimashita.*
  He created a huge abstract sculpture.

kuriimu クリーム cream (food, cosmetic)
- *Gyūnyū kara kuriimu o torimasu.*
  They skim the cream from milk.
- *Kōhii ni kuriimu o iremasu ka?*
  Shall I pour cream in your coffee?
- *Kao ni kuriimu o nurimasu.*
  I apply cream to my face.

kuriin クリーン clean
- *kuriin na seiji*
  clean politics
- *Kūki o kuriin ni tamotsu beki desu.*
  Air should be kept clean.

kurinikku クリニック clinic

- *Kurinikku de nagai aida matasaremashita.*
  I had to wait a long time at the clinic.

kuriiningu クリーニング dry cleaning; **~suru** する to dry-clean

- *Rēnkōto o kuriiningu ni dashimashita.*
  I sent my raincoat to the dry cleaner's.
- *Sukāto o kuriiningu shite moraimashita.*
  I had my skirt dry-cleaned.

kurippu クリップ clip, paper clip

- *Kono shorui o kurippu de tomete kudasai.*
  Please fasten these papers with a clip.

Kurisuchan クリスチャン Christian

- *Kanojo wa Kurisuchan ni narimashita.*
  She became a Christian.

Kurisumasu クリスマス Christmas

- *Tsugi no Kurisumasu wa Hawai de sugoshitai to omoimasu.*
  We hope to spend our next Christmas in Hawaii.

Kurisumasu ibu クリスマスイブ Christmas Eve

- *Kurisumasu ibu ni hatsuyuki ga furimashita.*
  We had the first snowfall of the season on Christmas Eve.

Kurisumasu kyaroru クリスマスキャロル Christmas carol

- *Kodomo-tachi ga Sandē sukūru de Kurisumasu kyaroru o renshū shite imasu.*
  Children are practicing Christmas carols at Sunday School.

Kurisumasu tsurii クリスマスツリー Christmas tree

- *Kurisumasu tsurii ni aoi raito ga meimetsu shite imasu.*
  Blue lights are twinkling on the Christmas tree.

kurisutaru クリスタル crystal

- *kurisutaru no shokki*
  a crystal dinner set

Kurisuto クリスト *see* **Kirisuto**

kuriyā クリヤー *see* **kuria**

kurōku (rūmu) クローク(ルーム) cloak room
- *Kono nimotsu wa kurōku ni azukemashō.*
  Let's check this baggage in the cloak room.

kurōru クロール crawl stroke (swimming)
- *Kanojo wa kurōru de oyoide imasu.*
  She is doing the crawl stroke.

kurosu クロス cloth
- *kurosu sei no hon*
  a clothbound book

kurōsu クロース *see* **kurosu**

kurosu suru クロスする to cross
- *Nihon no senro ga hankō genba no atari de kurosu shite imasu.*
  Two railroad tracks cross near the scene of the crime.

kurōzu-appu クローズアップ close-up; **~suru** する to be highlighted
- *joyū no kao no kurōzu-appu*
  a close-up of an actress's face
- *Oshoku jiken ga kurōzu-appu saremashita.*
  A bribery scandal was highlighted.

kurōzudo sēru クローズド・セール [Japanese Usage: closed sale] going-out-of business sale
- *Kurōzudo sēru de kakuyasu-hin o horidashimashita.*
  I picked up some bargains at a going-out-of-business sale.

kurōzu suru クローズする to close
- *Jiko no tame ano michi wa kurōzu sarete imasu.*
  That road has been closed due to the accident.

kūru クール cool, calm
- *kūru na taido*
  a calm attitude
- *Kare wa koto no nariyuki o kūru ni mimamotte imasu.*
  He is watching the course of events coolly.

kurū クルー crew

- *Kono hikōki ni wa kurū ga jūnin notte imasu.*
  There are ten crew members on this airplane.

kurūzu クルーズ cruise

- *Kurūzu de kaigairyokō ni dekakeru no ga watashi no yume desu.*
  It is my dream to go traveling abroad on a cruise ship.

kusshon クッション cushion

- *Kare wa kusshon o makura ni shite sofā ni yoko ni natte imasu.*
  He is lying on the sofa using a cushion for a pillow.

kwarutetto クァルテット *see* **karutetto**

kwintetto クィンテット *see* **kuintetto**

kworitii クォリティー *see* **kuoritii**

kwōtā クォーター *see* **kuōtā**

kwōtarii クォータリー *see* **kuōtarii**

kwōtsu クォーツ *see* **kuōtsu**

kyabarē キャバレー cabaret

- *Sono kyabarē no kaji wa hōka deshita.*
  The fire at that cabaret was caused by arson.

kyabin キャビン cabin (ship)

- *Funayoi no tame ichinichijū kyabin ni imashita.*
  I stayed in the cabin all day because of seasickness.

kyabinetto キャビネット cabinet

- *Kyabinetto no kagi wa kakete oita hō ga ii desu yo.*
  You'd better keep the cabinet locked.

kyadii キャディー caddie

- *Kanojo wa kantorii kurabu no kyadii o shite imasu.*
  She works as a caddie at a country club.

kyanbasu キャンバス *see* **kanbasu**

kyandē キャンデー *see* **kyandii**

kyandii キャンディー candy

- *Kono kyandii wa ichigo no aji ga shimasu.*
  This candy has a strawberry taste.

kyandoru キャンドル candle
* *Bāsudē kēki no kyandoru o fukikeshimashita.*
  I blew out the candles on the birthday cake.
kyanpasu キャンパス campus
* *Daigaku no kyanpasu de bōdō ga arimashita.*
  There was a riot on the university campus.
kyanpēn キャンペーン campaign
* *Shinseihin no uridashi kyanpēn wa hajimatta bakari desu.*
  A sales campaign for our new products has just begun.
kyanpingu kā キャンピングカー [Japanese Usage: camping car] camper
* *Kyanpingu kā de Amerika tairiku o ōdan shimashita.*
  We crossed the American continent in a camper.
kyanpu キャンプ camp; **~suru** する to camp
* *Mori no naka ni kyanpu o harimashita.*
  We set up our camp in the woods.
* *nanmin kyanpu*
  refugee camp
kyanpufaia キャンプファイア *see* **kyanpufaiyā**
kyanpufaiyā キャンプファイヤー campfire
* *Kyanpufaiyā ga yozora o kogashite ikioi yoku moete imasu.*
  The campfire is burning vigorously and illuminating the night sky.
kyanseru キャンセル cancel, cancellation; **~suru** する to cancel
* *Kyanseru ga attara, shirasete kudasai.*
  If there is a cancellation, please let me know.
* *Hoteru no yoyaku o kyanseru shimasu.*
  I'll cancel my hotel reservation.
kyapitaru gein キャピタルゲイン capital gain
* *Kyapitaru gein ni wa zeikin ga kakarimasu.*
  Capital gain is taxable.

kyappu キャップ cap
* *Bin no kyappu o totte kudasai.*
Please remove the cap from the bottle.

kyaputen キャプテン captain
* *Kanojo wa barēbōru chiimu no kyaputen o tsutomemashita.*
She captained a volleyball team.

kyaraban キャラバン caravan
* *Koko wa kyaraban no tōtta michi desu.*
This was a caravan route.

kyarakutā キャラクター character
* *Kare wa kyarakutā ga tsuyoi no de, kono yaku ni wa muite imasen.*
He is not fit for that role because he has such a strong character.

kyarameru キャラメル caramel
* *Kodomo ga kyarameru o shaburinagara, ehon o mite imasu.*
A child is looking at a picture book while chewing caramel candy.

kyaria キャリア career
* *Kare wa gaikōkan to shite nijūnen no kyaria ga arimasu.*
He has a twenty-year career as a diplomat.

kyaria ūman キャリアウーマン [Japanese Usage: career woman] working woman, woman with a career
* *Kanojo wa māketingu ni yutaka na keiken o motsu kyaria ūman desu.*
She is a working woman with rich experience in marketing.

kyasshā キャッシャー cashier
* *Kyasshā de o-shiharai kudasai.*
Please pay the cashier.

kyasshingu キャッシング cashing; **~suru** する to withdraw cash

- *Kurejitto kādo o tsukatte kyasshingu shimasu.*
  I withdraw cash with a credit card.

kyasshu キャッシュ cash
- *Kyasshu o kirashite imasu.*
  I am out of cash.

kyasshu kādo キャッシュカード cash card, ATM card
- *Itsumo kyasshu kādo o motte dekakemasu.*
  I always take my ATM card when I go out.

kyasuchingu キャスチング *see* **kyasutingu, kyasutingu bōto**

kyasuchingu bōto キャスチングボート *see* **kyasutingu bōto**

kyasutingu キャスティング casting
- *Sono eiga no kyasutingu wa dōmo patto shimasen ne.*
  The casting for that movie wasn't great, was it?

kyasutingu bōto キャスティングボート casting vote, decisive power, final say
- *Kono ken de wa dare ga kyasutingu bōto o nigitte iru no desu ka?*
  Who has the final say in this matter?

kyasuto キャスト cast
- *Kono eiga no kyasuto wa gōkaban desu ne.*
  The cast in this movie is splendid, isn't it?

kyatchā キャッチャー catcher
- *Kyatchā no erā de rannā ga ichirui ni demashita.*
  The catcher's error allowed a runner to get to first base.

kyatchi キャッチ catch; **~suru** する to catch
- *Kono shigoto ni wa jōhō no subayai kyatchi ga naniyori mo taisetsu desu.*
  For this job, nothing is more important than getting information quickly.
- *Kamera ga kaitei dōbutsu no dōsei o tsubusa ni kyatchi shite imasu.*

The camera clearly catches the movements of seabed creatures.

kyatchi-appu キャッチアップ catch-up; **~suru** する to catch up
* *Ichido okureru to, kyatchi-appu ga taihen desu.*
  Once you get behind, catching up is very difficult.
* *Kare wa sugu hoka no gakusei ni kyatchi-appu shimasu yo.*
  He'll catch up with other students in no time.

kyatchi-bōru キャッチボール [Japanese Usage: catch ball] playing catch; **~suru** する to play catch
* *Kodomo ga kōen de kyatchi-bōru o shite imasu.*
  Children are playing catch in the park.

kyatchi-furēzu キャッチフレーズ catch phrase
* *Shinseihin ni fusawashii kyatchi-furēzu o kangaete imasu.*
  We are thinking up a fitting catch phrase for our new product.

Kyūpiddo キューピッド Cupid
* *Kyūpiddo wa ai no shisha desu.*
  Cupid is the messenger of love.
* *Kanojo wa hakarazumo futari no Kyūpiddo yaku o tsutomete shimaimashita.*
  She unintentionally played a go-between for the two of them.

kyūto キュート cute
* *kyūto na onna no ko*
  a cute girl

L

L see **eru**
LL see **erueru** (*extra large*) or **erueru** (*language laboratory*)

M

M *see* **emu**

M&A *see* **emu-ando-ē**

MMC *see* **emuemushii**

māchi マーチ march
- *Kare wa rajio no māchi ni awasete kuchibue o fuite imasu.*
  He is whistling along with a march on the radio.

machinē マチネー matinee
- *Tomodachi ni shibai no machinē no kippu o moraimashita.*
  I received a theater ticket for a matinee performance from my friend.

madamu マダム [French: *madame*] married woman, proprietress
- *Kono bā no madamu wa wakakute miryokuteki desu.*
  The proprietress of this bar is young and charming.

Madonna マドンナ Madonna
- *Hitori no shōjo ga Madonna no zō o miagete imasu.*
  A young girl is looking up at a statue of the Madonna.

Mafia マフィア [Italian] Mafia
- *Sono seijika no Mafia to no kankei ga akarumi ni demashita.*
  The politician's connection with the Mafia was brought to light.

mafin マフィン muffin
- *Mafin ni batā o tsukemasu.*
  I spread butter on a muffin.

mafurā マフラー muffler, scarf
- *arai kōshi no mafurā*
  a loud, checked scarf

- *Kare no kuruma no mafurā wa hazushite arimasu.*
  His car's muffler is gone.

magajin rakku マガジンラック magazine rack
- *Magajin rakku ni zasshi ga takusan tamatte imasu.*
  Many magazines are stored in the magazine rack.

māgarin マーガリン margarine
- *Kono māgarin wa koresuterōru ga arimasen.*
  This margarine is cholesterol-free.

magunetto マグネット magnet
- *Kono handobaggu no botan wa magunetto ni natte imasu.*
  The clasp on this handbag is magnetic.

magunichūdo マグニチュード magnitude
- *Sono jishin wa magunichūdo go deshita.*
  The earthquake registered a magnitude of five.

mahoganii マホガニー mahogany
- *Kaigishitsu no mahoganii no tēburu wa inshōteki deshita.*
  The mahogany table in the conference room was impressive.

mai hōmu マイホーム [Japanese Usage: my home] one's own home
- *Mai hōmu o motsu koto wa wakamono no yume desu.*
  Young people dream of having their own home.

mai kā マイカー [Japanese Usage: my car] one's own car
- *Shūmatsu ni mai kā de dekakeru hito ga fuemashita.*
  The number of people who go for a drive in their cars on weekends has increased.

maiku マイク *see* **maikurofon**

maikurobasu マイクロバス microbus, van
- *Hoteru no maikurobasu ga eki made mukae ni kite kuremashita.*
  The hotel's shuttle bus came to pick us up at the station.

maikuro-firumu マイクロフィルム microfilm
- *Kore-ra no shiryō wa maikuro-firumu ni hozon shite*

arimasu.

This information is kept on microfilm.

maikurofon マイクロフォン microphone

- *Pātii de amachua kashu ga maikurofon o nigitte utaimasu.*
  At parties, amateur singers sing while holding microphones.

mainasu マイナス minus, disadvantage

- *Kongetsu wa shōbai wa mainasu desu.*
  My business can't make ends meet this month.
- *Sukyandaru ga kaisha no imēji ni ōkina mainasu ni narimashita.*
  The scandal was a big blow to the company's image.
- *Kesa no kion wa sesshi mainasu jūdo deshita.*
  This morning's temperature was minus ten degrees centigrade.

maindo マインド mind, feeling, intention, interest

- *Chikagoro josei no tōshi maindo ga tsuyomatte imasu.*
  The number of women showing an interest in investments has increased recently.

mai pēsu マイペース [Japanese Usage: my pace] one's own pace

- *Chichi wa mai pēsu de jogingu o shite imasu.*
  My father jogs at his own pace.

mairu マイル mile

- *Undō no tame ni mainichi ichi mairu arukimasu.*
  I walk one mile every day for exercise.

mairudo マイルド mild

- *mairudo na aji no kōhii*
  mild coffee, weak coffee
- *Kare no taido wa mairudo ni narimashita.*
  His attitude has become milder.

majikku マジック magic

- *majikku shō*

    magic show
- *Byōki o naosu no ni majikku wa arimasen.*
  There is no magic to cure sickness.

mājin マージン margin
- *Wazuka na mājin de urimashita.*
  We sold it with a slim profit margin.

majoritii マジョリティー majority
- *Kare no gurūpu wa kaigi de wa majoritii o shimete imasu.*
  His group is in the majority at the conference.

makaroni マカロニ [Italian *maccheroni*] macaroni
- *Makaroni sarada o tsukurimashō ka?*
  Shall we make a macaroni salad?

māketingu マーケティング marketing
- *Ima māketingu puran o kentōchū desu.*
  We are examining the marketing plan right now.

mākettingu マーケッティング *see* **māketingu**

māketto マーケット market
- *Māketto de tabetai mono wa nan de mo kaemasu.*
  I can buy anything I want to eat at the market.
- *Amerika wa Nihon no māketto ni norikomō to shite imasu.*
  America is trying to get into the Japanese market.

makishimamu マキシマム maximum
- *Sono gekijō wa makishimamu gohyakunin o shūyō dekimasu.*
  The theater seats up to five hundred people.

māku マーク mark; **~suru** する to mark
- *Shussekisha no namae ni māku o tsukemasu.*
  I put a mark by the names of those present.

makushimamu マクシマム *see* **makishimamu**

mama ママ mama, proprietress
- *Mama ga inai no de, shōjo wa sabishisō desu.*
  The little girl looks lonely because her mama is away.
- *Ginza no bā no mama(-san)*

the proprietress of a bar on the Ginza

māmarēdo マーマレード marmalade
  • *binzume no māmarēdo*
  marmalade in a jar

manā マナー manners
  • *Kare wa manā ga warui desu.*
  He has bad manners.

manē マネー money
  • *Imaya manē bannō no jidai desu.*
  Money is everything nowadays.

manē biru マネービル [Japanese Usage: money building]
  making money
  • *Oi mo wakaki mo manē biru ni yonen ga arimasen.*
  Both young and old are absorbed in making money.

manējā マネージャー manager
  • *Kanojo wa rizōto hoteru no manējā ni ninmei*
  saremashita.
  She was appointed manager of a resort hotel.

manejimento マネジメント *see* **manējimento**

manējimento マネージメント management
  • *Aru Amerika no kaisha wa Nihon shiki manējimento o*
  toriirete imashita.
  Some American companies have adopted a Japanese style
  of management.

manēji suru マネージする to manage
  • *Kare wa mise o umaku manēji shite imasu.*
  He is managing the store well.

manekin マネキン mannequin
  • *Shō-uindō no manekin mo aki no yosooi ni kawarimashita.*
  Even the mannequins in the shop window have been
  changed into autumn outfits.

manē māketto マネーマーケット money market, financial
  circle

- *Kare no kaisha wa manē māketto kara shimedasaremashita.*
  His company was ousted from financial circles.

manhōru マンホール manhole
- *Kodomo ga manhōru ni ochimashita.*
  A child fell into a manhole.

mania マニア mania, fanatic
- *Kare wa mokei-hikōki no mania desu.*
  He is a model airplane fanatic.

manikyua マニキュア manicure
- *Kanojo wa kawaii tsume ni pinku no manikyua o shite imasu.*
  She has a pink manicure on her tiny fingernails.

maniya マニヤ *see* **mania**

manmosu マンモス mammoth, huge
- *Manmosu toshi wa gendai shakai no ichi genshō deshō.*
  Huge cities are a phenomena of modern society.

manneri マンネリ mannerism, stereotype
- *Kare no supiichi wa isasaka manneri no kan ga arimasu ne.*
  His speech is somewhat mannered, isn't it?

mannerizumu マンネリズム *see* **manneri**

manpawā マンパワー manpower
- *Kono shigoto o suru dake no manpawā ga arimasen.*
  We don't have enough manpower to do this job.

manshon マンション [Japanese Usage: mansion] condominium, condo
- *Kanojo wa manshon ni hitori de sunde imasu.*
  She is living alone in a condominium.

mantorupiisu マントルピース mantelpiece
- *Mantorupiisu no ue ni tokei ga arimasu.*
  There is a clock on the mantelpiece.

man-tsū-man マン・ツー・マン man-to-man, frankly, face-to-face

* *Gokai o toku tame ni kare to man-tsū-man de hanashiaimashita.*
  I had a man-to-man talk with him to clear up our misunderstandings.

manukan マヌカン *see* **manekin**

manyuaru マニュアル manual

* *Kono manyuaru ni tsukaikata ga setsumei shite arimasu.*
  This manual explains how to use it.

mappu マップ map

* *Mokutekichi o mappu de shirabemashita.*
  I checked my destination on the map.

mararia マラリア malaria

* *Kare wa tokidoki mararia no hossa o okoshimasu.*
  Once in a while he has an attack of malaria.

marariya マラリヤ *see* **mararia**

marason マラソン marathon

* *Kare wa mainen machi no marason ni sanka shimasu.*
  He participates in the city marathon every year.

marifana マリファナ marijuana

* *Kare wa kōkishin kara marifana o suimashita.*
  He smoked marijuana out of curiosity.

maruchi マルチ multi-, multilevel

* *maruchi na kinō o sonaeta kikai*
  a multi-function machine
* *kenkō shokuhin ya keshōhin o nezumikō shiki ni urikomu maruchi shōhō*
  multilevel marketing plan for pyramid selling of health products and cosmetics

maruchi-tarento マルチタレント [Japanese Usage: multi-talent] person with many talents

* *Kanojo wa uta mo utae, dansu mo deki, piano mo hikeru maruchi-tarento desu.*

She is a multi-talented girl who can sing, dance, and play the piano.

maruchi-tasuku マルチタスク [Japanese Usage: multi-task] multi-tasking, doing more than one task
  • *Kono konpyūtā wa maruchi-tasuku ga kanō desu.*
  This computer can run more than two programs simultaneously.

mashiin マシーン *see* **mashin**

mashin マシン machine, automobile, motorcycle
  • *Atarashii mashin no shindō ga kokochi yokatta desu.*
  The vibrations of my new motorcycle felt great.
  • *Bōdai na dēta o kōsoku mashin de shori dekimasu.*
  A huge amount of data can be processed by a high-speed machine.

massāji マッサージ massage
  • *Kata kara senaka ni kakete massāji shite moraimashita.*
  I had my shoulders and back massaged.

masshu poteto マッシュポテト mashed potatoes
  • *Furenchi furai yori masshu poteto ni shimashō.*
  Let's have mashed potatoes rather than French fries.

masu gēmu マスゲーム [Japanese Usage: mass game] group calisthenics
  • *Shōgakusei ga undōjō de masu gēmu o kurihirogete imasu.*
  The school children are doing group calisthenics in the schoolyard.

masu komi マスコミ [Japanese Usage] mass communication, mass media
  • *Sono jiken wa masu komi ni sawagarete imasu.*
  That incident is receiving a lot of publicity in the press.

masu komyunikēshon マスコミュニケーション *see* **masu komi**

masukotto マスコット mascot, idol

- *Kanojo wa jōkyūsei no masukotto deshita.*
  She was the mascot of the senior students.

masuku マスク mask
- *Haisha wa masuku o kakete imashita.*
  The dentist was wearing a mask.

masu media マスメディア mass media
- *Shinseihin no senden ni masu media o tsukaimasu.*
  The mass media is used to promote new products.

masu puro マスプロ [Japanese Usage] mass production
- *masu puro kyōiku no heigai*
  an ill effect of production-line education
- *masu puro no shinamono*
  mass-produced goods

masu-purodakushon マス プロダクション *see* **masu puro**

masutā マスター master, proprietor; **~suru** する to master
- *bā no masutā*
  the proprietor of a bar
- *Sumisu-san wa Nihongo o masutā shimashita.*
  Ms. Smith mastered the Japanese language.

masutādo マスタード mustard
- *Hottodoggu ni wa kechappu yori masutādo no hō ga oishii desu.*
  A hot dog tastes better with mustard than ketchup.

masutā kii マスターキー master key
- *Masutā kii o karite doa o akemashita.*
  I borrowed the master key and opened the door.

masutā kōsu マスターコース Master's degree, Master's program
- *Kanojo wa daigaku no masutā kōsu de benkyo shite imasu.*
  She is studying for her Master's at the university.

masuto マスト mast
- *Sono fune wa masuto ga sanbon arimasu.*
  That ship has three masts.

matchi マッチ match; **~suru** する to match
- *Matchi o sutte kyandoru ni hi o tsukemashita.*
  I struck a match and lit a candle.
- *Kono sukāto wa sētā ni matchi shite imasen.*
  This skirt doesn't match my sweater.
- *hebii-kyū taitoru matchi*
  a heavyweight title match

matto マット mat
- *Apāto no iriguchi ni midori no matto ga shiite arimasu.*
  A green mat is placed in front of the apartment entrance.

mattoresu マットレス mattress
- *Kono mattoresu wa yawaraka sugimasu.*
  This mattress is too soft.

maundo マウンド mound
- *Pitchā wa maundo ni tatte imasu.*
  The pitcher is on the mound.

mausu マウス mouse
- *Sono jikken ni wa mausu ga tsukawaremashita.*
  Mice were used for that experiment.
- *Konpyūtā gurafikkusu wa mausu o tsukatte zukei o egakimasu.*
  With computer graphics you use a mouse to draw diagrams.

mayonēzu マヨネーズ mayonnaise
- *Sarada ni mayonēzu o kakemasu.*
  I put mayonnaise on the salad.

mazā マザー mother
- *Kanojo wa kojiin de mazā no yaku o shite imasu.*
  She is playing the role of a mother at an orphanage.

medarisuto メダリスト medalist
- *Kare wa Orinpikku de kin-medarisuto no hitori deshita.*
  He was one of the gold medalists in the Olympics.

medaru メダル medal
- *Kanojo wa medaru o kakutoku suru tame ni besuto o*

tsukushimashita.
She tried her best to win a medal.

Mēdē メーデー May Day
• *Mēdē no demo kōshin ga chōdo tōtte imasu.*
The May Day demonstration march is just passing by.

media メディア media
• *Gendai shakai ni okeru media no yakuwari wa jūdai desu.*
The media plays a significant role in modern society.

mēdo メード maid
• *Shinbun ni kōkoku o shite mēdo o boshū shimasu.*
We'll advertise for a maid in the newspaper.

mēdo in Japan メード・イン・ジャパン made in Japan
• *Mēdo in Japan no seihin ga kaigai de takaku hyōka sarete imasu.*
Products made in Japan are rated highly in foreign countries.

medorē メドレー medley
• *Kono tēpu ni Burāmusu no medorē ga haitte imasu.*
This tape has a Brahms' medley on it.

megahon メガホン megaphone; **~o toru** をとる to direct a movie
• *Kōchi wa megahon de gakusei ni hanashite imasu.*
The coach is speaking to the students through a megaphone.
• *Kare wa hajimete megahon o torimashita.*
He directed a movie for the first time.

meikyappu メイキャップ *see* **meiku**

meiku メイク make-up
• *Kanojo no meiku wa kitsusugimasu.*
She uses too much make-up.

meiku-appu メイクアップ *see* **meiku**

mein メイン main
• *Kore no riyōsha wa wakai josei ga mein desu.*
The main users of this are young women.

- *Kyō no mein no ryōri wa nan desu ka?*
  What is today's main dish?

mein banku メインバンク [Japanese Usage: main bank]
bank one mainly deals with
- *Mein banku kara kore ijō no yūshi wa kitai dekimasen.*
  We can't expect further financing from our usual bank.

mein ebento メインエベント main event
- *Ashita no bokushingu no mein ebento wa dare to dare no shiai desu ka?*
  Who will the boxers be in tomorrow's main event?

mein sutoriito メインストリート main street
- *Sono depāto wa mein sutoriito ni arimasu.*
  That department store is on the main street.

meintenansu メインテナンス *see* **mentenansu**

meiru メイル *see* **mēru**

mejā メジャー major
- *mejā na kigyō*
  a major company

meka メカ mechanics
- *Meka ni yowai no de, kanojo wa konpyūtā ni kyōmi o shimeshimasen.*
  Not being good with machines, she shows no interest in computers.

mēkā メーカー manufacturer
- *Ano mise wa ichiryū mēkā no mono shika atsukatte imasen.*
  That store handles only top manufacturers' products.

mekanikusu メカニクス *see* **meka**

mekanizumu メカニズム mechanism, structure
- *Keizai no mekanizumu wa kiwamete fukuzatsu desu.*
  The economic mechanisms are highly complex.

Mekishiko メキシコ Mexico
- *Mekishiko ni Amerika no shitauke kōjō ga takusan*

arimasu.

There are many American subcontractor factories in Mexico.

mekka メッカ mecca

- *Wiin wa ongaku aikōka no mekka desu.*

  Vienna is a mecca for music lovers.

mēku メーク *see* **meiku**

mēku-appu メークアップ *see* **meiku**

mēkyappu メーキャップ *see* **meiku**

memo メモ memorandum

- *Yamada-kyōju no kōgi no memo o torimashita.*

  I took notes during Professor Yamada's lecture.

mēn メーン *see* **mein**

menbā メンバー member

- *Yūjin no suisen de Rōtarii Kurabu no menbā ni narimashita.*

  I became a member of the Rotary Club at the recommendation of my friend.

mēn banku メーンバンク *see* **mein banku**

mēn ebento メーンエベント *see* **mein ebento**

mēn ibento メーンイベント *see* **mein ebento**

mēn sutoriito メーンストリート *see* **mein sutoriito**

mentaritii メンタリティー mentality, intelligence

- *Kare no mentaritii wa toshi no wari ni hikui desu.*

  His intelligence is lower than usual for his age.

mentaru メンタル mental

- *Gorufu wa iroiro na supōtsu no naka de watashi no shitteiru kagiri mottomo mentaru na kyōgi desu.*

  Among various sports, golf is the most mental game I know.

mentenansu メンテナンス maintenance

- *Apāto no mentenansu wa kanrinin ni makasete arimasu.*

  I leave the maintenance of the apartment to the building manager.

menyū メニュー menu
- *Menyū o misete kudasai.*
 Please show me a menu.

menzu uea メンズウエア men's wear
- *Menzu uea wa ano esukarētā no mukōgawa ni gozaimasu.*
 Men's wear is on the other side of that escalator.

merankorii メランコリー melancholy
- *merankorii ni michita sakuhin*
 a work full of melancholy
- *Kanojo wa hitori de iru to, merankorii na kimochi ni narimasu.*
 When she is alone, she feels melancholy.

merankorikku メランコリック melancholic, gloomy
- *merankorikku na kibun*
 a melancholic mood

merii-gō-raundo メリーゴーラウンド merry-go-round
- *Merii-gō-raundo ga keikai na ongaku ni notte mawatte imasu.*
 The merry-go-round is playing cheerful music as it turns.

meritto メリット merit, advantage
- *Kono shinamono wa kantan ni araeru to iu meritto ga arimasu.*
 This product has the advantage of being easily cleaned up.

meriyasu メリヤス [Spanish: medias] knitted goods
- *Sono meriyasu kōjō wa sengetsu heisa saremashita.*
 The factory for knitted goods was closed last month.

merodii メロディー melody
- *Utsukushii merodii ni kikihoremashita.*
 We were enraptured by the beautiful melody.

merodorama メロドラマ melodrama
- *Kanojo no shōgai wa masa ni merodorama sonomono deshita.*
 Her life was truly melodrama itself.

meron メロン melon
- *Reizōko ni meron ga hiyashite arimasu.*
  A melon is chilling in the refrigerator.

mēru メール mail
- *Denshi mēru de chūmon shimashita.*
  I placed an order by electronic mail.

mēru ōdā メールオーダー mail order
- *Kanojo wa mēru ōdā no mise o hajimemashita.*
  She started a mail-order house.

messēji メッセージ message
- *Messēji o o-negai dekimasu ka?*
  May I leave a message?

messenjā メッセンジャー messenger
- *Messenjā ga kore o todokete kuremashita.*
  A messenger delivered this for me.

mesu メス [Dutch: *mes*] surgical knife, scalpel
- *Kensatsu wa oshoku jiken ni sōsa no mesu o iremashita.*
  The Public Prosecutor's Office began investigating the corruption case.

mētā メーター meter
- *Takushii no mētā ga niman en ijō ni agarimashita.*
  The taxi's meter read more than ¥20,000.
- *Kore wa ichi mētā ikura desu ka?*
  How much is one meter?

metarikku メタリック metallic
- *Garasu bari no yane ga metarikku ni kagayaite imasu.*
  The glazed rooftops are shining with a metallic hue.
- *metarikku burū no kuruma*
  a metallic blue car

metaru メタル *see* **medaru**

metaru メタル metal
- *Kono bubun wa metaru de dekite imasu.*
  This part is made of metal.

metaru furēmu メタルフレーム [Japanese Usage: metal frame] metal frames
- *Metaru furēmu no megane o kaketa otoko ga watashi o mitsumete imashita.*
  A man with metal-frame glasses was staring at me.

metoroporisu メトロポリス metropolis
- *Metoroporisu no kōtsū jigoku wa akka suru ippō desu.*
  Traffic jams in the metropolis are getting worse and worse.

mētoru メートル meter, metric
- *Nihon de wa mētoru hō ga saiyō sarete imasu.*
  The metric system has been adopted in Japan.

mezo-sopurano メゾソプラノ mezzo-soprano
- *Sono mezo-sopurano kashu wa hanabanashiku debyū shimashita.*
  That mezzo-soprano made a splendid debut.

midiamu ミディアム medium
- *Sutēki wa midiamu de onegai shimasu.*
  I want my steak medium.

midoru eiji ミドルエイジ middle age
- *Kanojo wa midoru eiji kara haiku o kakihajimemashita.*
  She took up writing haiku in her middle age.

midoru kurasu ミドルクラス middle class
- *Midoru kurasu ga kokka no keizai o sasaete imasu.*
  The middle class supports the nation's economy.

miitingu ミーティング meeting
- *Miitingu wa mō hajimatte imasu.*
  The meeting has already started.

miito shoppu ミートショップ [Japanese Usage: meat shop] butcher shop
- *Sukiyaki no niku o kai ni miito shoppu ni yorimashita.*
  I stopped by a butcher shop to buy meat for sukiyaki.

mikisā ミキサー mixer, blender
- *Mikisā de kudamono ya yasai no jūsu o tsukurimasu.*

I make fruit and vegetable juice with a blender.

mikkusu suru ミックスする *to mix*
* *Shiriaru ni furūtsu o mikkusu shimasu.*
  I mix fruit with cereal.

mineraru ミネラル *mineral*
* *Mineraru wa jintai ni hitsuyō na eiyōso desu.*
  Minerals are vital nutrients for the human body.

mineraru uōtā ミネラルウオーター *mineral water*
* *Mineraru uōtā wa hito bin de utte imasu.*
  Mineral water is sold by the bottle.

mini ミニ *mini-skirt*
* *mini o haita shōjo-tachi*
  mini-skirted girls

miniachua ミニアチュア *see* **minichua**

minichua ミニチュア *miniature*
* *O-miyage ni Tōkyō-tawā no minichua o kaimashita.*
  I bought a miniature model of Tokyo Tower as a souvenir.

mini-kā ミニカー *minicar, miniature car*
* *Ano shokudō de wa mini-kā de demae o shimasu.*
  That restaurant delivers in a minicar.
* *Osanai musuko wa heya de hitori mini kā de asonde imasu.*
  My little son is playing with a miniature car alone in his room.

minimamu ミニマム *minimum*
* *Kare wa minimamu no doryoku shika shimasen.*
  He does everything with a minimum of effort.

mini pato ミニパト [Japanese Usage: mini pat(rol car)] small-sized police car
* *Fujin keikan ga keisatsusho no mae de mini pato o orimashita.*
  A policewoman got out of the small-sized patrol car in front of the police station.

mini patorōru kā ミニパトロールカー　*see* **mini pato**
mini-sukāto ミニスカート　*see* **mini**
minku ミンク　mink
- *minku no kōto o kita fujin*
  a lady in a mink coat
miri ミリ　milli-, millimeter
- *go miri(-guramu)*
  five milligrams
- *roku miri(-mētoru)*
  six millimeters
mirionea ミリオネア　millionaire
- *Kanojo wa hansamu na mirionea to kekkon shimashita.*
  She married a handsome millionaire.
mirioneā ミリオネアー　*see* **mirionea**
mirion serā ミリオンセラー　million seller
- *Mirion serā ni naru rekōdo wa goku wazuka desu.*
  Only a few records become million sellers.
miritarizumu ミリタリズム　militarism
- *Miritarizumu ga sono kuni o sensō ni karitatemashita.*
  Militarism drove the country to war.
miruku ミルク　milk, cream
- *Ichinichi ni miruku o nihai nomimasu.*
  I drink two glasses of milk a day.
- *Kōcha ni miruku o iremasu.*
  I put cream in my tea.
mirukusēki ミルクセーキ　milkshake
- *Kissaten de mirukusēki o nominagara kare o machimashita.*
  I waited for him while drinking a milkshake in a coffee shop.
miruku tii ミルクティー　[Japanese Usage: milk tea] tea with milk
- *Dezāto no kawari ni miruku tii o nomimashita.*

I had tea with milk instead of dessert.

misa ミサ [Latin: *missa*] mass (Catholic)
- *Ōzei no hito ga Kurisumasu no misa ni sanretsu shimashita.*

Many people attended Christmas mass.

misairu ミサイル missile
- *Tekikoku ni misairu o hassha shimashita.*

They launched missiles into the enemy country.

misesu ミセス Mrs., married woman
- *Misesu Buraun*

Mrs. Brown
- *misesu no tame no yosooi*

outfits for married ladies

mishin ミシン sewing machine
- *Kono mishin wa hen na oto ga shimasu.*

This sewing machine is making funny noises.

misshon ミッション mission
- *Seifu wa gaikoku e yushutsu sokushin no tame misshon o haken shimashita.*

The government sent missions to foreign countries to promote exports.

misshon sukūru ミッションスクール mission school
- *Kanojo wa misshon sukūru no de na node, Eigo ga tokui desu.*

Being a graduate from a mission school, she speaks excellent English.

misu ミス Miss, unmarried woman
- *Kanojo wa Misu Nippon ni erabaremashita.*

She was chosen to be Miss Japan.
- *Ane wa mada misu desu.*

My older sister is still single.

misu ミス miss, error, mistake, typo
- *Sono jiko wa jin'iteki na misu de okotta sō desu.*

I hear that the accident was caused by human error.

• *Kare no shigoto ni wa misu wa hotondo arimasen.*
There are almost no mistakes in his work.

misukyasuto ミスキャスト miscast

• *Kare ni shuyaku o yaraseru no wa misukyasuto desu.*
He is miscast in the leading role.

misupurinto ミスプリント misprint, typo

• *Kono pēji no misupurinto o naoshite kudasai.*
Please correct the typos on this page.

misuriidingu ミスリーディング misleading

• *Kono midashi wa kiji to chiguhagu nano de misuriidingu desu.*
This headline has little to do with the article and is misleading.

misuriido ミスリード *see* **misuriidingu**

misutā ミスター Mister, Mr.

• *Kare wa Misutā Bēsubōru to iwareta mei senshu deshita.*
He was a talented player known as "Mr. Baseball."

misuteiku ミステイク *see* **misu**

misutēku ミステーク *see* **misu**

misuteriasu ミステリアス mysterious

• *misuteriasu na jinbutsu*
a mysterious character

• *Watashi ni wa misuteriasu na kare no kimochi wa mattaku wakarimasen.*
I don't understand my mysterious boyfriend's feelings at all.

misuterii ミステリー mystery

• *Kanojo no shissō wa imada ni misuterii desu.*
Her disappearance is still a mystery to this very day.

• *Hikōki no naka de wa taitei misuterii o yomimasu.*
I usually read mystery stories on airplanes.

mitto ミット mitt

- *Kore wa ani ga tsukatte ita mitto desu.*
  This is a mitt my older brother used to use.

mochibēshon モチベーション motivation
- *Kono hōhō wa gakusei no mochibēshon o takameru no ni yakudatsu deshō.*
  This method will help improve students' motivation.

mochiifu モチーフ motif
- *Kore wa yūjō o mochiifu ni shita shōsetsu desu.*
  This is a novel with friendship as its motif.

modan モダン modern
- *modan na kenchiku*
  modern architecture

modān モダーン *see* **modan**

moderu モデル model
- *Kono shōzōga no moderu wa gaka no aijin desu.*
  The model for this portrait is the artist's lover.

moderu chenji モデルチェンジ [Japanese Usage: model change] restyling, face-lift
- *Tokidoki suchuwādesu no seifuku no moderu chenji ga arimasu.*
  Once in a while the stewardesses' uniforms are restyled.

mōningu モーニング morning coat
- *Chichi wa watashi no kekkon shiki ni mōningu o kimashita.*
  My father wore a morning coat at my wedding.

mōningu kōru モーニングコール wakeup call
- *Mōningu kōru no beru de me ga samemashita.*
  The wakeup call woke me up.

monitā モニター monitor; ~**suru** する to monitor
- *Kono seihin ni tsuite monitā no iken o kikimashita.*
  We listened to the monitors' opinions about this product.
- *Kikai no chōshi o monitā shimasu.*
  We monitor the condition of the machine.

monkii モンキー monkey
- *Kanojo wa petto ni monkii o katte imasu.*
  She keeps a monkey as a pet.

monorēru モノレール monorail
- *Kūkō kara toshin made monorēru ga tsūjite imasu.*
  A monorail runs from the airport to the heart of the city.

monorōgu モノローグ monologue
- *Sono geki wa hajime kara owari made monorōgu desu.*
  The play is a monologue from start to end.

monsūn モンスーン monsoon
- *Natsu no monsūn ga tairyō no ame o motarashimasu.*
  The summer monsoon brings large quantities of rain.

monsutā モンスター monster
- *Usugurai mori no naka ni taiboku ga monsutā no yō ni tatte imasu.*
  In the dusky forest, gigantic trees stand like monsters.

montāju モンタージュ montage
- *Kore wa hannin no montāju shashin desu.*
  This is the criminal's montage.

monyumentaru モニュメンタル monumental
- *monyumentaru na jiin*
  a monumental temple

monyumento モニュメント monument
- *Kono sakuhin wa kare no monyumento desu.*
  This work is his monument.
- *Washinton-dii-shii de iroiro na monyumento o otozuremashita.*
  We visited various monuments in Washington, D.C.

moppu モップ mop
- *Moppu de daidokoro no yuka o fukimashita.*
  I wiped the kitchen floor with a mop.

morarisuto モラリスト moralist
- *Kanojo wa morarisuto butte imasu.*

She acts as if she were a moralist.

moraru モラル morals, ethics

- *Tabi no moraru o wasureta ryokōsha ga ōi desu.*
  There are many tourists who have forgotten about good conduct while traveling.

moraru モラル morale

- *Jin'in seiri no uwasa ga shain no moraru ni eikyō shimashita.*
  A rumor about a personnel cut affected employee morale.

morufin モルフィン *see* **moruhine**

moruhine モルヒネ morphine

- *Moruhine wa chintsūzai ni tsukawaremasu.*
  Morphine is used as a painkiller.

morumotto モルモット [Dutch: *mormot*] guinea pig

- *Dōbutsu jikken de morumotto ga tsukawaremashita.*
  Guinea pigs were used in the animal experiments.
- *Gakusei ga atarashii karikyuramu no morumotto ni natte imasu.*
  Students are being used as guinea pigs for the new curriculum.

mōshon モーション motion; **~ o kakeru** をかける to make a pass at

- *Kare wa kissaten no uētoresu ni mōshon o kakete imasu.*
  He is making a pass at a waitress in the coffee shop.

mōtā モーター motor

- *Sono mōtā o tomete kudasai.*
  Please shut off that motor.

mōtābaiku モーターバイク motorbike

- *Shōnen wa mōtābaiku de o-tsukai ni ikimasu.*
  The boy goes on errands on a motorbike.

motiifu モティーフ *see* **mochiifu**

mottō モットー motto

- *Kare wa hayane-hayaoki o mottō ni shite imasu.*

He makes 'early to bed, early to rise' his motto.

mūbii kamera ムービーカメラ movie camera
- *Mūbii kamera ga chiisaku natte mochihakobi ni benri desu.*
  Movie cameras have become smaller and easier to carry around.

mūbumento ムーブメント movement
- *Aru kuni de wa seifu ni hantai no mūbumento ga okotte imasu.*
  Anti-government movements are taking place in certain countries.

mūdo ムード mood, atmosphere
- *romanchikku na mūdo no heya*
  a room with a romantic atmosphere

mūdo myūjikku ムードミュージック mood music
- *Chero ga mūdo myūjikku o kanadete imasu.*
  A cello is playing mood music.

mūsu ムース mousse
- *Ano mise no mūsu wa hijō ni oishii desu.*
  The mousse at that restaurant is very tasty.

myūjiamu ミュージアム museum
- *Furansu de myūjiamu meguri o shimashita.*
  I made a tour of museums in France.

myūjikaru ミュージカル musical
- *Sono myūjikaru no saishūbi ni wa gekijō wa chō-man'in deshita.*
  On the last day of the musical, the theater was completely full.

N

nābasu ナーバス nervous
- *nābasu na hito*
  a nervous person
- *Intabyū no toki, nābasu ni narimashita.*
  When I went for the interview, I was nervous.

Nachi ナチ *see* **Nachisu**

Nachisu ナチス [German: *Nazis*] the Nazis, Nazi
- *Sono tatemono wa Nachisu jidai no ibutsu desu.*
  The building is a remnant from the Nazi era.

nachurarisuto ナチュラリスト naturalist, nature lover
- *Kanojo wa yasei shokubutsu ni kanshin o motsu nachurarisuto desu.*
  She is a nature lover who has an interest in wild plants.

nachurarizumu ナチュラリズム naturalism
- *Bungaku ni nachurarizumu ga mebaemashita.*
  Naturalism developed in literature.

nachuraru ナチュラル natural
- *nachuraru na utaikata*
  natural singing
- *Kono tegami ni wa kanojo no kimochi ga nachuraru ni arawarete imasu.*
  Her feelings are naturally expressed in this letter.

naichingēru ナイチンゲール nightingale
- *Yogoto naichingēru no utagoe o kikimashita.*
  Every night I heard the song of a nightingale.

nafukin ナフキン *see* **napukin**

naifu ナイフ knife
- *Naifu de yubi o kirimashita.*
  I cut my finger with a knife.

naiibu ナイーブ naive
- *naiibu na shōjo*
  an innocent virgin

nain ナイン nine, members of a baseball team
- *Nain ga tsuyoku danketsu shite yoku tatakaimashita.*
  The baseball team was strongly united and played well.

nairon ナイロン nylon
- *nairon no kutsushita*
  nylon socks

naisu ナイス nice
- *naisu na heasutairu*
  a nice hairstyle

naitā ナイター [Japanese Usage: nighter] night (baseball) game
- *Yūbe no naitā wa tsumaranakatta desu.*
  Last night's baseball game was boring.

naito ナイト knight, guardian, escort
- *Kare wa joō kara naito no kurai o sazukeraremashita.*
  He was knighted by the Queen.

naitogaun ナイトガウン nightgown
- *Naitogaun ni kigaemashita.*
  I changed into a nightgown.

naitokurabu ナイトクラブ nightclub
- *Sono naitokurabu wa eigyōteishi o meijiraremashita.*
  The nightclub was shut down.

naitokyappu ナイトキャップ nightcap
- *Kare wa naitokyappu o kabutte nemasu.*
  He sleeps with a nightcap on.
- *Neru mae ni naitokyappu o nomimasu.*
  Before going to bed, I have a nightcap.

naito tēburu ナイトテーブル night table
- *Naito tēburu no ue no mezamashidokei ga narimashita.*
  The alarm clock on the night table went off.

nanbā ナンバー number
- *Gentei-bon ni wa minna nanbā ga utte arimasu.*
  All the limited-edition books are numbered.

nanbā purēto ナンバープレート [Japanese Usage: number plate] license plate
- *Ano kuruma no nanbā purēto wa Ōsaka desu ka?*
  Does that car have an Osaka license plate?

numbā wan ナンバーワン number one
- *Watashi-tachi no naka de wa gorufu wa kare ga osoraku nanbā wan deshō.*
  He is probably the best golf player among us.

nansensu ナンセンス nonsense
- *Nansensu na giron wa mō yame ni shimashō.*
  Let's stop the nonsensical arguments already.
- *Sore wa mattaku nansensu desu.*
  It's utter nonsense.

napukin ナプキン napkin
- *Fudan wa kami no napukin o tsukaimasu.*
  I usually use paper napkins.

narēshon ナレーション narration
- *Sono eiga no narēshon wa totemo kōkateki deshita.*
  The narration in that movie was very effective.

narētā ナレーター narrator
- *Sono dokyumentarii no narētā wa rōren na haiyū desu.*
  The narrator of that documentary is an experienced actor.

nashonarisuto ナショナリスト nationalist
- *Nashonarisuto wa kokuminsei no hozon o ōi ni kyōchō shite imasu.*
  A nationalist puts great emphasis on the preservation of national characteristics.

nashonarizumu ナショナリズム nationalism
- *Aru hito wa nashonarizumu no fukkatsu o osorete imasu.*
  Some people are afraid of the rebirth of nationalism.

Nashonaru-torasuto ナショナルトラスト National Trust
  environmental movement
  • *Shizen kankyō o hogo suru tame ni shimin no aida kara
  Nashonaru-torasuto undō ga okorimashita.*
  The National Trust movement arose among the citizenry
  who wanted to protect the environment.
nāsu ナース nurse
  • *Kanojo wa Sekijūji byōin no nāsu desu.*
  She is a nurse at a Red Cross hospital.
nattsu ナッツ nuts
  • *Aru Chūgoku ryōri ni wa nattsu ga tsukawarete imasu.*
  Nuts are used in some Chinese dishes.
nau ナウ now, new, fresh
  • *nau na rizumu no ongaku*
  music with contemporary rhythms
nēbii burū ネービーブルー navy blue
  • *nēbii burū no unifōmu*
  a navy blue uniform
nega ネガ negative (photo)
  • *Nega karā firumu wa arimasu ka?*
  Do you have any negative color film?
negatibu ネガティブ negative
  • *Kare wa negatibu na senkyo undō o okonaimashita.*
  He carried out a negative election campaign.
  • *Kanojo wa monogoto o negatibu ni torimasu.*
  She takes things negatively.
negoshiēshon ネゴシエーション negotiation
  • *Yamada-eigyōbuchō wa negoshiēshon ni tsuyoi hito desu.*
  Mr. Yamada, the head of the sales department, is good at
  negotiating.
negurije ネグリジェ negligee
  • *sukitōru yō na usui negurije*
  a sheer see-through negligee

neguro ネグロ　*see* **niguro**

nekkachiifu ネッカチーフ　neckerchief
- *hana moyō no nekkachiifu*
  a neckerchief with a floral pattern

nekku ネック　neck, bottleneck
- *Kūkō e no akusesu ga nekku ni natte imasu.*
  The access into the airport is bottlenecked.
- *Kare ga buchō to shite sonzai shite iru koto ga saidai no nekku ni natte imasu.*
  His being a department manager is the biggest block.

nekkurain ネックライン　neckline
- *Ano kata no doresu wa nekkurain ga utsukushii desu ne.*
  That lady's dress has a beautiful neckline, hasn't it?

nekkuresu ネックレス　necklace
- *hōseki o chiribameta gōka na nekkuresu*
  a gorgeous necklace studded with gems

nekutai ネクタイ　necktie
- *shima no nekutai*
  a striped necktie

nēmingu ネーミング　naming, name
- *Sono kōsui wa ekizochikku na nēmingu de ninki o yobimashita.*
  The perfume became popular because of its exotic name.

nēmu ネーム　name
- *Sūtsu no mikaeshi ni watashi no nēmu ga shishū shite arimasu.*
  My name is embroidered on the inside of my suit.

nēmu baryū ネームバリュー　name value, good reputation
- *nēmu baryū no aru shashinka*
  a photographer with an established reputation

neon ネオン　neon lights
- *Machi wa neon de kagayaite imasu.*
  The street is lit with neon lights.

neon sain ネオンサイン neon sign
* *Iro toridori no neon sain ga tsuitari kietari shite imasu.*
  Multi-colored neon signs are flashing on and off.

netto ネット net
* *Kyūjō no netto ura kara shiai o kansen shimashita.*
  I watched the game from behind the backstop net in the stadium.

nettowāku ネットワーク network
* *Tōsha wa hanbai no nettowāku o hirogeru keikaku desu.*
  Our company plans to expand our sales network.

nia misu ニアミス near miss
* *Sora no kōtsūryō ga fueta tame ni nia misu mo fuemashita.*
  Since air traffic has increased, the number of near-miss accidents has also increased.

niguro ニグロ black (person)
* *Kare wa niguro no rekishi o kenkyū shite imasu.*
  He is doing research on black history.

nihirisuto ニヒリスト nihilist
* *Kare wa nihirisuto da kara, kami o shinjite imasen.*
  Being a nihilist, he does not believe in God.

nihiru ニヒル nihil, nihilistic
* *nihiru na warai*
  a nihilistic laugh

niito ニート neat, cool
* *Shō uindō ni niito na sangurasu ga kazatte arimasu.*
  Cool sunglasses are displayed in the shop window.
* *Kare wa shiroi sūtsu o niito ni kite imasu.*
  He looks neat in a white suit.

niizu ニーズ needs
* *O-kyaku sama no niizu ni atta shōhin no kaihatsu ni tsutomete imasu.*
  We are trying to produce goods which satisfy our customers' needs.

nikkunēmu ニックネーム nickname
- *Kare wa itsumo nikkunēmu de yobarete imasu.*
  He is always called by his nickname.

nikochin ニコチン nicotine
- *Kare wa nikochin no nai tabako o sutte imasu.*
  He smokes nicotine-free cigarettes.

ninfu ニンフ nymph
- *Mukashi mukashi Girisha no aru mori ni utsukushii ninfu ga sunde imashita.*
  Once upon a time, beautiful nymphs lived in the woods in Greece.

nitto ニット knit
- *Karukute kigokochi ga yokute, nitto no sūtsu wa ichiban desu.*
  Knit suits are best because they are light and comfortable.

nittouea ニットウエア knitwear
- *Nittouea no sēru wa nankai desu ka?*
  On which floor is the knitwear sale?

nō ノー no
- *Kare-ra no yōkyū ni taishite wa nō to wa iemasen ne.*
  We can't say no to their request, can we?

nobu ノブ knob
- *Doa no nobu o atarashii no ni torikaemashita.*
  I replaced the doorknob with a new one.

nōburu ノーブル noble
- *Hitobito wa kare no nōburu na yōbō o homesoyashimashita.*
  People greatly admired his noble looks.

nō-hau ノーハウ *see* **nou-hau**

noirōze ノイローゼ [German: *Neurose*] neurosis, nervous breakdown
- *Kanojo wa narenai kankyō de noirōze ni natte nayande imasu.*

In unfamiliar environments, she suffers from neuroses.

noizu ノイズ noise
- *Kono rekōdo wa noizu ga haitte imasu.*
  This record has noises on it.

nō katto ノーカット [Japanese Usage: no cut] uncut
- *Sono eiga wa nō katto de jōei saremashita.*
  That movie was shown in its uncut version.

nō kaunto ノーカウント [Japanese Usage: no count] not counted
- *Kore wa nō kaunto ni shimasu.*
  I won't count this.

nokku ノック knock, knocking; **~suru** する to knock
- *Doa no nokku no oto ga kikoemasen ka?*
  Can't you hear a knock at the door?
- *Nan-do mo nokku shimashita ga henji ga arimasen deshita.*
  I knocked many times but there was no answer.

nokkuauto ノックアウト knockout; **~suru** する to knock out
- *Bokusā wa nokkuauto de kachimashita.*
  The boxer won by knockout.
- *Reisai kigyō wa hageshii kyōsō de nokkuauto sareru deshō.*
  Small businesses will be knocked out due to severe competition.

nokkudaun ノックダウン knockdown; **~suru** する to knock down
- *Kare no nokkudaun de kankyaku ga ōini wakimashita.*
  His being knocked down excited the spectators.
- *Kare wa kao ni panchi o ukete nokkudaun shimashita.*
  He got punched in the face and was knocked down.

nō komento ノーコメント no comment
- *Sono seimei ni kanshite wa nō komento desu.*

I have no comment to make on that statement.

nokutān ノクターン nocturne
- *Efuemu hōsō ga nokutān de shūryō shimashita.*
  The FM broadcast ended with a nocturne.

nōmaru ノーマル normal
- *Kare ni wa nōmaru na kōdō wa kitai dekinai desu yo.*
  We can't expect normal behavior from him.
- *Tenkō wa nōmaru ni modorimashita.*
  The weather returned to normal conditions.

nō meiku ノーメイク [Japanese Usage: no make] without make-up
- *Kanojo no nō meiku no kao wa igai to wakaku ikiiki to shite imasu.*
  Even without make-up, her face looks surprisingly young and fresh.

nō mēku ノーメーク *see* **nō meiku**

nominēto suru ノミネートする to nominate
- *Sono eiga wa Akademii shō ni nominēto saremashita.*
  That movie was nominated for an Academy Award.

nonbanku (banku) ノンバンク(バンク) [Japanese Usage: nonbank bank] credit agency (other than banks)
- *Kare wa ginkō ni kotowararete, nonbanku (banku) kara kōri de kane o karimashita.*
  Refused by the bank, he borrowed money from a credit agency at a high rate of interest.

nonfikushon ノンフィクション nonfiction
- *Kare no jijoden wa nonfikushon bumon de besuto serā desu.*
  His autobiography is one of best sellers in nonfiction.

nonpori ノンポリ [Japanese Usage] nonpolitical
- *Kare wa seijika no musuko desu ga mattaku nonpori desu.*
  Although he is a politician's son, he is very nonpolitical.

nonpuro ノンプロ nonprofessional, amateur

- *Kodomo-tachi o nonpuro yakyū ni tsurete ikimashita.*
  I took my children to an amateur ball game.
- *Dorafuto de kakutoku sarenakereba nonpuro e iku tsumori desu.*
  If I am not picked up in the draft, I'll go to the amateur league.

nonsensu ノンセンス *see* **nansensu**

nonsutoppu ノンストップ nonstop
- *Kono furaito wa Nyū-yōku made nonsutoppu de tobimasu.*
  This flight is nonstop to New York.

nō sumōkingu ノースモーキング no smoking
- *Shanai wa nō sumōkingu ni natte imasu.*
  Smoking is not permitted in the train.

nosutarujia ノスタルジア nostalgia
- *Kanojo wa Pari no seikatsu ni nosutarujia o kanjite shōga arimasen.*
  She feels nostalgia for her life in Paris, but there's nothing she can do about it.

nosutarujikku ノスタルジック nostalgic
- *nosutarujikku na machinami*
  a nostalgic row of stores and houses on a street

nō tatchi ノータッチ [Japanese Usage: no touch] not touch
- *Kankatsugai no dekigoto ni wa nō tatchi desu.*
  We don't touch matters outside our jurisdiction.

nōto ノート note, notebook; **~suru** する to note, take notes
- *Anata no nōto o utsusasete moratte mo ii desu ka?*
  May I copy your notes?
- *Kanojo no nokoshita nōto wa ai no shi de umatte imashita.*
  The notebook that she had left behind was filled with love poems.
- *Kyō no kōgi wa nōto shimasen deshita.*
  I didn't take any notes on today's lecture.

nōtobukku ノートブック *see* **nōto**

nou-hau ノウハウ know-how
 • *Kabushiki tōshi no nou-hau o setsumei shita hon o shōkai shite kudasai.*
   Please recommend to me a book which explains the ins and outs of stock speculation.

nūdo ヌード nude
 • *Kono shashin zasshi ni wa nūdo shashin ga ippai desu.*
   This photography magazine is full of nude photos.

nūdoru ヌードル noodle
 • *Chikin sūpu ni nūdoru o kuwaemashita.*
   I added some noodles to the chicken soup.

nyū ニュー new
 • *Kanojo wa o-nyū no sētā o kite imasu.*
   She is wearing a new sweater.

nyuansu ニュアンス nuance
 • *Kore wa bimyō na nyuansu no aru ii bunshō desu ne.*
   This is good writing with delicate nuances.

nyūfēsu ニューフェース [Japanese Usage: new face] newcomer
 • *Kanojo wa nyūsha shita bakari no nyūfēsu desu.*
   She is a newcomer to the company.

nyū media ニューメディア new media, new information technologies
 • *Jōhō sangyō no hatten ni tomonai, nyū media ga jidai no sutā ni narimashita.*
   With the development of the information industry, new media has become a star of the age.

nyū mōdo ニューモード [Japanese Usage: new mode] new fashion
 • *Pari kara no fuyu no nyū mōdo*
   the new winter fashions from Paris

nyū rukku ニュールック new look (in clothes)
 • *Kanojo wa atama kara tsumasaki made nyū rukku desu.*

From head to foot, she has a new look in fashion.

nyūsu ニュース news

• *Daitōryō no byōki ga ōkina nyūsu ni narimashita.*
The president's illness was big news.

nyūsu anarisuto ニュースアナリスト news analyst, news commentator

• *Sono nyūsu anarisuto no kaisetsu wa fukami ga arimasen.*
That news analyst's commentary lacks depth.

nyūsu baryū ニュースバリュー [Japanese Usage: news value] newsworthy

• *Kisha wa nyūsu baryū no aru neta o asatte imasu.*
Reporters hunt for material that is newsworthy.

nyūsukyasutā ニュースキャスター newscaster

• *Kanojo wa saiki to bibō de nyūsukyasutā ni batteki saremashita.*
She was selected as a newscaster for her talent and good looks.

nyūsu sōsu ニュースソース news source

• *Watashi-tachi wa nyūsu sōsu o akasu wake ni wa ikimasen.*
We cannot disclose the source of this story.

nyūtoraru ニュートラル neutral

• *Shingō machi de gia o nyūtoraru ni iremashita.*
I put the car into neutral while waiting for the light to change.

nyū taun ニュータウン new town

• *Ōku no nyū taun ga daitoshi no kinkō ni kaihatsu saremashita.*
Many new towns were developed in the areas surrounding big cities.

nyūzu ニューズ *see* **nyūsu**

O

OA *see* **ōē**
ODA *see* **ō-dii-ē**
OHP *see* **ōbāheddo purojekutā**
OK *see* **ōkē**
OL *see* **ōeru**
OPEC *see* **Opekku**

oashisu オアシス oasis
  • *Biya hōru wa natsu no atsusa o wasuresasete kureru oashisu desu.*
  A beer hall is an oasis where you can forget the summer heat.

ōbā オーバー over; **~suru** する to exceed
  • *Tenrankai no nyūjōsha wa sennin o ōbā shimashita.*
  The attendance at the exhibition exceeded one thousand people.
  • *Kare wa jiken o ōbā ni hanashimashita.*
  He exaggerated the situation.

ōbā オーバー overcoat
  • *Ōbā o shinchō shimashita.*
  I had a new overcoat made.

ōbāburausu オーバーブラウス overblouse
  • *beruto tsuki no ōbāburausu*
  an overblouse with a belt

ōbāfurō suru オーバーフローする to overflow
  • *Rajiētā ga reikyakusui de ōbāfurō shite imasu.*
  Cooling water is overflowing out of the radiator.

ōbāheddo purojekutā オーバーヘッドプロジェクター
  overhead projector
  • *Kaku kyōshitsu ni ōbāheddo purojekutā ga arimasu.*

arimasu.
Each classroom has an overhead projector.

ōbāhōru オーバーホール　overhaul; **~suru** する　to have a checkup
- *Kono kuruma wa ōbāhōru ga hitsuyō desu.*
  This car needs an overhaul.
- *Nen ni ichido byōin de ōbāhōru shimasu.*
  I have a checkup once a year at the hospital.

ōbā-kōto オーバーコート　*see* **ōbā** (*overcoat*)

ōbāran suru オーバーランする　to overrun
- *Rannā wa sekando o ōbāran shimashita.*
  The runner overran second base.

ōbārappu suru オーバーラップする　to overlap
- *Eiga no naka no futatsu no shiin ga ōbārappu shimashita.*
  The two scenes of the movie overlapped.

ōbātaimu オーバータイム　overtime
- *Getsumatsu ni wa ōbātaimu o shimasu.*
  We work overtime toward the end of the month.

ōbāwāku オーバーワーク　overwork
- *Kanojo wa ōbāwāku no tame byōki ni narimashita.*
  She became sick from working too hard.

obuje オブジェ　objet d'art
- *metaru to garasu de shitateta obuje*
  an objet d'art made with metal and glass

ōbun オーブン　oven
- *Ōbun ni poteto o futatsu iremashita.*
  I put two potatoes in the oven.

obuzābā オブザーバー　observer
- *Ōbuzābā to shite kaigi ni shusseki shimashita.*
  I attended the conference as an observer.

ōdā オーダー　order; **~suru** する　to order
- *Ōdā o torikeshimashita.*
  We cancelled the order.

* *Kono seihin o ōdā shitai no desu.*
We'd like to order this product.

ōdā-mēdo オーダーメード [Japanese Usage: order-made] custom-made

* *Saikin sūtsu no ōdā-mēdo wa shitabi ni narimashita.*
Recently custom-made suits have gone out of vogue.

ōdekoron オーデコロン eau de cologne

* *Yokattara kono ōdekoron o tsukatte kudasai.*
Please use this eau de cologne if you wish.

ō-dii-ē オーディーエー ODA ODA, official development aid

* *Nihon wa hatten tojōkoku ya kokusai kikan ni ō-dii-ē o teikyō shite imasu.*
Japan gives ODA to developing countries and international agencies.

ōdio bijuaru オーディオ・ビジュアル audio-visual

* *Atarashii ōdio bijuaru kiki o mi ni iku tokoro desu.*
We are going to take a look at the new audio-visual equipment.

ōdishon オーディション audition

* *Sono koyaku wa ōdishon de erabaremashita.*
That child actor was chosen from the audition.

ōdoburu オードブル hors d'oeuvre

* *Ashita no pātii ni dare ga ōdoburu o motte kimasu ka?*
Who is bringing the hors d'oeuvres for tomorrow's party?

ōē オーエー OA OA, office automation

* *Ōē no okage de jimu-shori ga supidii ni narimashita.*
OA has made office work quicker.

ōeru オーエル OL [Japanese Usage: OL, office lady] female office worker

* *Kanojo wa ōeru seikatsu jūnen me desu.*
She is a ten-year veteran of office work.

ofā オファー offer; **~suru** する to offer, make an offer

- *Sono ofā o kotowarimashita.*
  We declined that offer.
- *Sono kikai o ichiman doru de kaō to ofā shimashita.*
  We made an offer to buy that machine for $10,000.

ofisharu オフィシャル official

- *Kono heya wa ofisharu na kaigō ni tsukawaremasu.*
  This room is used for official meetings.
- *Kare no ninmei wa chikajika ofisharu ni naru deshō.*
  His appointment will soon become official.

ofisu オフィス office

- *Watashi no ofisu wa biru no sangai desu.*
  My office is on the third floor of the building.

ofisu awā オフィスアワー office hours

- *Doyōbi wa ofisu awā wa jūji kara ichiji made desu.*
  Our office hours are from ten to one o'clock on Saturdays.

ofisu redii オフィスレディー *see* **ōeru**

ofu オフ off

- *Suitchi wa ofu desu ka?*
  Is the switch off?
- *Ofu no hi ni wa tsuri ni dekakemasu.*
  I go fishing on my days off.

ofu-howaito オフホワイト off-white

- *ofu-howaito no sukāto*
  an off-white skirt

ofureko オフレコ [Japanese Usage] off the record

- *Sono ekonomisuto wa ofureko de keiki no mitōshi ni tsuite katarimashita.*
  The economist talked off the record about the economic outlook.

ofu-rimitto オフリミット off-limits

- *Koko wa ofu-rimitto da kara, hairemasen.*
  We can't enter here, because it's off-limits.

ofu-shiizun オフシーズン off-season

- *Tozan wa ima ofu-shiizun desu.*
  It's the off-season for mountain climbing now.

ōganaizā オーガナイザー organizer
- *Kono bijutsuten no ōganaizā wa dare desu ka?*
  Who is the organizer of this art exhibition?

ōganizēshon オーガニゼーション organization
- *Kono chāto wa kigyō no ōganizēshon o shimeshita mono desu.*
  This chart shows the organization of the enterprise.

ō-etchi-pii オーエッチピー OHP *see* **ōbāheddo purojekutā**

oiru オイル oil, petroleum
- *Ryōri ni sarada oiru o tsukaimasu.*
  We use salad oil for cooking.
- *Nippon wa tairyō no oiru o yunyū shite imasu.*
  Japan imports large quantities of petroleum.

oiru shokku オイルショック [Japanese Usage: oil shock] oil crisis
- *Mata oiru shokku ga aru kamo shiremasen.*
  We might have another oil crisis.

oisutā sōsu オイスターソース oyster sauce
- *Chūgoku ryōri ni oisutā sōsu o tsukaimasu.*
  Oyster sauce is used in Chinese cooking.

ōkē オーケー OK OK; **~suru** する to approve, accept
- *Shitsu wa ōkē desu ga nedan ga ki ni irimasen.*
  The quality is OK but we don't like the price.
- *Sono teian wa ōkē saremashita.*
  The proposal has been accepted.

okkē オッケー *see* **ōkē**

ōkesutora オーケストラ orchestra
- *Kare wa machi no ōkesutora de baiorin o hiite imasu.*
  He plays the violin in his town orchestra.

ōkushon オークション auction
- *Sono e wa ōkushon de takane de uremashita.*

That painting was sold at a high price at the auction.

omitto suru オミットする to omit
- *Gogo no renshū wa omitto shimasu.*
  We'll skip the afternoon practice.

omunibasu オムニバス omnibus film
- *Kono omunibasu eiga wa kitto ataru deshō.*
  I'm sure this omnibus film will be a hit.

omuretsu オムレツ omelet
- *Tamago mittsu de omuretsu o tsukurimashita.*
  I made an omelet with three eggs.

ōnā オーナー owner
- *Kono mise no ōnā wa dare da ka shirimasen.*
  I don't know who the owner of this shop is.

on ea オンエア on the air, being broadcast
- *Genzai sono bangumi wa on ea sarete imasu.*
  That program is currently on the air.

on-ofu オンオフ on and off
- *Kono reibō sōchi wa jidōteki ni on-ofu shimasu.*
  This air conditioner turns on and off automatically.

on parēdo オンパレード [Japanese Usage: on parade] on display
- *Shōrūmu no erekutoronikusu no on parēdo ga hitome o hikimashita.*
  The electronics on display in the showroom attracted people's attention.

on-rain shisutemu オンラインシステム on-line system
- *on-rain shisutemu no konpyūtā*
  a computer in an on-line system

onsu オンス ounce
- *Sono kōsui wa go onsu desu.*
  That perfume weighs five ounces.

onzarokku オンザロック on the rocks
- *Uisukii o onzarokku de nomimasu.*

I drink whisky on the rocks.

opāru オパール opal
- *Tanjōbi no pātii ni opāru no iyaringu o tsukemashita.*
  I put on opal earrings for my birthday party.

Opekku オペック OPEC OPEC, Organization of Petroleum
Exporting Countries
- *Gen'yu no yushutsu kakaku wa Opekku ni kontorōru
  sarete imasu.*
  The export price for petroleum is controlled by OPEC.

opera オペラ [Italian] opera
- *Terebi de opera no nama hōsō ga arimashita.*
  An opera was telecast live.

opera gurasu オペラグラス opera glasses
- *Oba ni opera gurasu o karite opera ni ikimashita.*
  I borrowed opera glasses from my aunt and went to the
  opera.

operētā オペレーター operator
- *denwa no operētā*
  a telephone operator
- *kikai no operētā*
  a machine operator

operetta オペレッタ operetta
- *Wakai hito ni wa opera yori mo operetta no hō ga ninki ga
  aru yō desu.*
  Operetta seems to be more popular than opera among young
  people.

opinion riidā オピニオンリーダー opinion leader
- *Kare wa atarashii opinion riidā to shite chūmoku sarete
  imasu.*
  He is considered to be a new opinion leader.

opochunitii オポチュニティー opportunity
- *Kore wa ii opochunitii desu.*
  This is a good opportunity.

- *Kare wa "rando obu opochunitii" no Amerika de seikō shimashita.*
  He achieved success in America, "the land of opportunity."

opuchimisuto オプチミスト optimist
- *Kanojo wa umaretsuki opuchimisuto desu.*
  She is an optimist by nature.

opuchimizumu オプチミズム optimism
- *Kare wa sono mochimae no opuchimizumu de ōku no konnan o kirinuketa no desu.*
  His inherent optimism helped him overcome many difficulties.

ōpun オープン open, opening; **~suru** する to open
- *ōpun na taido*
  an open attitude
- *Atarashii shiten no ōpun o iwaimashita.*
  We celebrated the opening of our new branch store.
- *Kare wa sushiya o ōpun shimashita.*
  He opened a sushi shop.

ōpuningu オープニング opening
- *Sono shō no ōpuningu ni wa rēzā kōsen o tsukatta atorakushon ga arimashita.*
  At the opening for the show there was an attraction in which lasers were used.

ōpun kā オープンカー open car, convertible
- *Shiroi ōpun kā ga shissō shite ikimashita.*
  A white convertible drove by at full speed.

ōpun setto オープンセット [Japanese Usage: open set] outdoor set
- *Kono mori wa jidai geki no ōpun setto ni tsukawaremashita.*
  This forest was used as an outdoor set for period adventure films.

oputimisuto オプティミスト *see* **opuchimisuto**

oputimizumu オプティミズム *see* **opuchimizumu**

ōrai オーライ all right, it's mine (when catching a ball)
- *Basu gaido ga "ōrai, ōrai," to iinagara, bakku suru basu o yūdō shimashita.*
  Saying, "all right, all right," the bus guide directed the bus as it backed up.

Oranda オランダ [Portuguese: *Olanda*] the Netherlands, Holland
- *Kono e wa Oranda no den'en fūkei o egaita mono desu.*
  This painting depicts a rural landscape in Holland.

ōraru オーラル oral
- *Ashita no tesuto wa ōraru desu.*
  Tomorrow's test will be an oral one.

orenji オレンジ orange
- *Akutenkō de orenji ga sukkari dame ni narimashita.*
  The poor weather destroyed all the oranges.

orenji jūsu オレンジジュース orange juice
- *Kono orenji jūsu wa amasugimasu ne.*
  This orange juice is too sweet, isn't it?

oriibu オリーブ olive
- *Asoko ni oriibu no ki ga uete arimasu.*
  Olive trees are planted over there.

Orientaru オリエンタル Oriental
- *Buraun-san wa Orientaru bijutsu ni kyōmi o motte imasu.*
  Mr. Brown has an interest in Oriental fine arts.

orientēshon オリエンテーション orientation
- *Shinnyūsei no tame ni orientēshon ga okonawaremasu.*
  An orientation session will be held for the new students.

orijinaritii オリジナリティー originality
- *Kono sakuhin no tsuyomi wa sono orijinaritii ni arimasu.*
  The strength of this work lies in its originality.

orijinaru オリジナル original
- *Kono hanga wa Hiroshige no orijinaru desu.*

This woodblock print is an original work by Hiroshige.

Orinpikku オリンピック Olympic
- *Nagano ga Tōki Orinpikku kaisai toshi ni erabaremashita.*
  Nagano was chosen to be a Winter Olympic city.

ōru オール all, 100%
- *ōru nairon no kutsushita*
  100% nylon socks

ōru オール oar
- *Kare wa chikara ippai ōru o kogimashita.*
  He rowed with all his might.

ōrudo-fasshon オールドファッション old-fashioned
- *Kanojo no yōfuku wa ōrudo-fasshon desu.*
  Her dresses are old-fashioned.

orugan オルガン organ
- *Orugan o hiite iru no wa Abe-san desu.*
  The one who is playing the organ is Miss Abe.

orugōru オルゴール [Dutch: *orgel*] music box
- *Kono orugōru wa watashi no suki na merodii o kanademasu.*
  This music box plays a melody I love.

ōrumaitii オールマイティー almighty
- *Kare wa ōrumaitii desu. Nan de mo kanpeki ni shimasu.*
  He is supreme. He does everything perfectly.

ōru-naito オールナイト all night
- *Ano resutoran wa ōru-naito de eigyō shite imasu.*
  That restaurant is open all night.

ōru-sutā オールスター all-star (game, player)
- *Puro yakyū no ōru-sutā purēyā ni erabareru koto wa taihen ni meiyo na koto desu.*
  It's a great honor to be chosen as a pro baseball all-star.

ōru-sutā kyasuto オールスターキャスト all-star cast
- *ōru-sutā kyasuto no eiga*
  a movie with an all-star cast

ōru-uezā オールウエザー all-weather
- *Ano tenisu kōto wa ōru-uezā desu.*
  That is an all-weather tennis court.

ōsentikku オーセンティック authentic
- *ōsentikku na kon no burezā*
  an authentic navy blue blazer

ōshan オーシャン ocean
- *Samā doresu ni ōshan burū wa ikaga?*
  How about ocean blue for your summer dress?

ōsodokkusu オーソドックス orthodox
- *Kare wa ōsodokkusu na sakkyokuka desu.*
  He is an orthodox composer.

ōsoraizu suru オーソライズする to authorize
- *Shinseihin no sendenhi wa kaigi de ōsoraizu saremashita.*
  The expenses for publicizing the new products were authorized at the meeting.

ōsoritii オーソリティー authority
- *Kare wa kindai kenchiku no ōsoritii desu.*
  He is an authority on modern architecture.

Ōsutoraria オーストラリア Australia
- *Ōsutoraria ni wa mezurashii dōbutsu ga ippai seisoku shite imasu.*
  Many rare animals live in Australia.

ōtobai オートバイ [Japanese Usage: auto bicycle] motorcycle
- *Kodomo ga ōtobai ni haneraremashita.*
  A child was hit by a motorcycle.

ōto-kuchūru オートクチュール [French: *haute couture*] high-fashion clothing shop
- *Pari no ōto-kuchūru de kōka na doresu o takusan mimashita.*
  I saw many expensive dresses in a high-class clothing shop in Paris.

ōtomachikku オートマチック automatic
- *Hoteru no doa wa hotondo minna ōtomachikku desu.*
  Almost all doors at hotels are automatic.
- *Ōtomachikku sha no jiko ga fuete imasu.*
  The accidents involving automatic cars are increasing.

ōtome オートメ *see* **ōtomēshon**

ōtomēshon オートメーション automation
- *Atarashii kōjō wa subete ōtomēshonka sarete imasu.*
  New factories are all automated.

ōtomiiru オートミール oatmeal
- *Kenkō no tame ni ōtomiiru o aiyō shite imasu.*
  I eat oatmeal regularly for my health.

ōto rēsu オートレース [Japanese Usage: auto race] motorcycle race
- *Kinō no ōto rēsu wa ekisaitingu deshita.*
  Yesterday's motorcycle race was exciting.

ōtorokku オートロック [Japanese Usage: autolock] automatic door lock
- *Kono doa wa ōtorokku desu.*
  This is a self-locking door.

P

PR *see* **piiāru**

pabirion パビリオン pavilion
- *Bankoku haku de pabirion o mite mawarimashita.*
  We went around looking at the pavilions at the World's Fair.

pabu パブ pub
- *Shidonii no sono pabu wa yoru osoku made wakamono de nigiwatte imashita.*

The pub in Sydney was hopping with young people until late at night.

paburikku opinion パブリックオピニオン public opinion
- *Paburikku opinion o orikonde terebi bangumi o seisaku shimasu.*

  We produce TV programs after taking public opinion into consideration.

paburishiti パブリシティ *see* **puburishitii**

paburishitii パブリシティー publicity
- *Sono ibento wa kaisha no ii paburishitii ni narimasu.*

  That event is good publicity for our company.

pāfekuto パーフェクト perfect
- *Sono Kabuki yakusha wa pāfekuto na engi o misemashita.*

  That Kabuki actor gave a perfect performance.
- *Gakusei wa shitsumon ni pāfekuto ni kotaemashita.*

  The student answered the questions perfectly.

pafōmansu パフォーマンス performance
- *Sore wa odori to mo shibai to mo tsukanai mattaku atarashii pafōmansu deshita.*

  It was indeed a new performance that could be called neither a dance nor a play.
- *Wakate giin wa sono hade na pafōmansu de ichiyaku yūmei ni narimashita.*

  Due to his spectacular performance, the young assembly-man suddenly leaped into fame.

pagoda パゴダ pagoda
- *Tai de wa pagoda no mae de kinen shashin o torimashita.*

  We took a souvenir photograph in front of a pagoda in Thailand.

pai パイ pie
- *Iroiro na kudamono de pai o tsukurimasu.*

  I make pies with various kinds of fruit.

painappuru パイナップル pineapple

- *Hawai de furesshu na painappuru o tanno shimashita.*
  I had more than enough fresh pineapples in Hawaii.

paionia パイオニア pioneer
- *Kare-ra wa kono shintenchi o kaitaku shita paionia desu.*
  They are the pioneers who opened up this new world.

paipu パイプ pipe *see* **paipurain**
- *Kare wa paipu ni hi o tsukemashita.*
  He lit his pipe.

paipu orugan パイプオルガン pipe organ
- *Kare wa sekai kusshi no paipu orugan sōsha desu.*
  He is one of the leading pipe organ players in the world.

paipurain パイプライン pipe, pipeline
- *Paipurain de Arasuka kara sekiyu o okurimasu.*
  Oil is piped in from Alaska.

pairotto パイロット pilot
- *Pairotto wa hijō na jukuren o yōshimasu.*
  Pilots require a great deal of skill.

pajama パジャマ pajamas
- *Kare wa pajama no mama de asagohan o tabemashita.*
  He ate breakfast in his pajamas.

pāji パージ purge
- *Sengo ōku no fuhai shita kanri ga pāji ni hikkakarimashita.*
  After the war there was a purge of corrupt government officials.

pāka パーカ parka
- *Kaze no fuku samui hi ni wa pāka o kite dekakemasu.*
  On cold, windy days I go out wearing a parka.

pākā パーカー *see* **pāka**

pākingu mētā パーキングメーター parking meter
- *Pākingu mētā ni koin o iremashita.*
  I put a coin in the parking meter.

pākingu suru パーキングする to park

- *Kono tōri ni pākingu shite mo ii desu ka?*
  May I park on this street?

pakkēji パッケージ package
- *Ano mise wa iroiro na mono o pakkēji ni shite utte imasu.*
  That store sells various things as packages.

pakkēji tsuā パッケージツアー package tour
- *Pakkēji tsuā de Nyū-jiirando e itte kimashita.*
  We went to New Zealand on a package tour.

pakkin パッキン *see* **pakkingu**

pakkingu パッキング packing
- *Shukka no mae ni minna de pakkingu o tetsudaimashita.*
  Before the shipment, we all helped out with packing.

pakku パック pack; **~suru** する to pack
- *pakku ryokō=pakkēji tsuā*
  a package tour
- *gyūnyū no pakku*
  a carton of milk
- *Shokuhin ga purasuchikku yōki ni pakku shite arimasu.*
  Food is packed in plastic containers.
- *Shū ni ichido kao o pakku shimasu.*
  I apply a facial pack once a week.

pākorētā パーコレーター percolator
- *Tomodachi no kekkon no o-iwai ni pākorētā o agemashita.*
  I gave my friend a percolator as a wedding gift.

pāma パーマ perm, permanent wave
- *Hoteru no biyōin de pāma o kakemashita.*
  I got a perm at a beauty salon in the hotel.

pāmanento パーマネント permanent
- *Kono kisoku wa pāmanento na mono desu.*
  This rule is a permanent one.

pan パン [Portuguese: *pão*] bread
- *yakitate no pan*
  freshly baked bread

panchi パンチ punch
- *Panchi de fairu yō no ana o akemashita.*
  Using a hole punch, I made holes for filing.
- *Ago ni panchi o kuraimashita.*
  I got punched in the jaw.
- *Oishii panchi o nomimashita.*
  I drank some delicious punch.
- *panchi no kiita supiichi*
  a speech that has punch

panda パンダ panda
- *Panda ni akachan ga umaremashita.*
  The panda had a baby.

paneru パネル panel
- *Tenjikai de omoshiroi paneru shashin o mimashita.*
  I saw interesting photos displayed on panels at the exhibition.

paneru disukasshon パネルディスカッション panel discussion
- *Paneru disukasshon de kappatsu na iken no kōkan ga arimashita.*
  A lively exchange of opinions took place during the panel discussion.

panfuretto パンフレット pamphlet
- *Kono panfuretto wa Eigo to Nihongo de kaite arimasu.*
  This pamphlet is written in English and Japanese.

panikku パニック panic
- *Kabuka no bōraku de kabushiki shijō wa panikku jōtai ni ochiirimashita.*
  A slump in the stock market caused a panic.

pankēki パンケーキ pancake
- *Watashi wa pankēki ni wa shiroppu o takusan kakete tabemasu.*
  I eat pancakes with lots of syrup.

panku suru パンクする to puncture, burst
 • *Watashi no kuruma no taiya ga panku shimashita.*
   One of my car's tires was punctured.
 • *Sono shi no zaisei wa imanimo panku shisō desu.*
   It seems that the city's finances are going to burst at any
   moment.

panorama パノラマ panorama
 • *Oka no ue kara shi-zentai no panorama o
   mioroshimashita.*
   From the hilltop we overlooked a panorama of the whole
   city.

pantii sutokkingu パンティーストッキング [Japanese
   Usage: panty stocking] pantyhose
 • *Ano sūpā de pantii sutokkingu o hangaku de utte imasu.*
   Pantyhose are being sold at half price in that supermarket.

pantsu パンツ pants, underpants
 • *Tii-shatsu ni pantsu o haite pātii ni ikimashita.*
   I went to the party wearing a T-shirt and pants.
 • *Ano ko wa mada hitori de pantsu ga hakemasen.*
   That child can't put on his underpants by himself yet.

papa パパ papa
 • *Papa to imōto to issho ni dōbutsuen e ikimashita.*
   I went to the zoo with my dad and little sister.

paradaisu パラダイス paradise
 • *Kono shima wa tori ya dōbutsu no paradaisu desu.*
   This island is a paradise for birds and animals.

paradokkusu パラドックス paradox
 • *Kono hon no paradokkusu wa jinsei no igi o fukaku
   kangaesasemasu.*
   The paradoxes in this book make us think more deeply
   about the meaning of life.

parafin パラフィン paraffin
 • *Kukkii ya kēki o tsutsumu no ni parafin shi o tsukaimasu.*

Wax paper is used for wrapping cookies and cakes.

parareru パラレル parallel

- *Furui michi to parareru ni atarashii michi o tsukurimasu.*

They will build a new road parallel to the old one.

parashūto パラシュート parachute

- *Parashūto de shokuryō o tōka shimashita.*

They dropped food by parachute.

parasoru パラソル parasol

- *Parasoru o sashite natsu no hizashi o sakemasu.*

I use a parasol to avoid the summer sun.

parēdo パレード parade

- *O-matsuri ni parēdo wa tsukimono desu.*

There are no festivals without parades.

pāru パール pearl

- *Tōchi de wa pāru no yōshoku ga sakan desu.*

Pearl culture flourishes in this area.

parupu パルプ pulp

- *Kami wa parupu kara tsukuraremasu.*

Paper is made from pulp.

pāsā パーサー purser

- *Kanojo wa suchuwādesu kara pāsā ni shōkaku shimashita.*

She was promoted from a stewardess to a purser.

pāsentēji パーセンテージ percentage, ratio

- *Kono daigaku no joshi gakusei no pāsentēji wa hikui desu.*

The percentage of female students in this university is small.

pāsento パーセント percent *see* **pāsentēji**

- *Riritsu ga ichi pāsento agarimashita.*

The interest rate went up one percent.

paseri パセリ parsley

- *Paseri o soeru to ryōri ga hikitachimasu.*

A dish becomes more attractive when parsley is added.

pasokon パソコン [Japanese Usage] personal computer, PC

- *Pasokon wa ōku no gakkō ni dōnyū sarete imasu.*

  Personal computers have been introduced at many schools.

pasonaru konpyūtā パーソナルコンピューター *see*
pasokon

pāsonaritii パーソナリティー personality

- *Kare wa dokutoku no pāsonaritii de Osero no yaku o konashimashita.*

  His unique personality enabled him to sustain the role of Othello.

- *Kare wa ninki no aru rajio no shin'ya bangumi no pāsonaritii desu.*

  He is a popular radio personality on late-night radio programs.

passhon パッション passion

- *Kanojo wa saigo made ongaku ni taisuru passhon o ushinaimasen deshita.*

  Right to the end, she never lost her passion for music.

pasu パス pass, free ticket; **~suru** する to pass, skip

- *Chikatetsu no pasu o motte imasu.*

  I have a pass for the subway.

- *Kanojo wa gaikōkan shiken ni pasu shimashita.*

  She passed the Diplomatic Service Examination.

- *Gogo no jugyō o pasu shimashita.*

  I skipped the afternoon classes.

pasupōto パスポート passport

- *Pasupōto o shinsei shimashita.*

  I applied for a passport.

- *Kono hon wa kokusaijin e no pasupōto desu.*

  This book is a passport for people who aspire to be international citizens.

pasuteru パステル pastel

- *Kore wa ane no kaita pasuteru-ga desu.*

  This is a pastel drawing done by my older sister.

patān パターン pattern
- *Burausu no patān o torimasu.*
  I cut out a pattern for a blouse.
- *Kare no ijō na kōi wa onaji patān de kurikaesarete imasu.*
  His abnormal behavior has a repetitive pattern.

patento パテント patent
- *Kare wa sono hatsumei de patento o torimashita.*
  He got a patent for his invention.

pātii パーティー party
- *Nenmatsu made pātii tsuzuki desu.*
  We'll have one party after another toward the end of the year.

pāto パート part, part-time, part-timer
- *jūyō na pāto*
  an important part
- *sopurano no pāto*
  the soprano part
- *Ōzei no pāto o kaiko shimashita.*
  They dismissed many part-timers.

pato-kā パトカー patrol car
- *Pato-kā ga sairen o narashinagara kuruma o tsuiseki shite imasu.*
  A patrol car, with sirens wailing, is chasing a car.

pātonā パートナー partner
- *Kare wa shigoto no ue no pātonā desu.*
  He is my partner at work.

patoron パトロン patron
- *Kono bā no madamu ni wa kanemochi no patoron ga tsuite imasu.*
  The proprietress of this bar has a rich patron.

patorōru パトロール patrol; ~**suru** する to patrol
- *Junsa wa ima patorōru ni dete imasu.*
  The policeman is now out on patrol.

- *Engan keibitai ga sono kaiiki o patorōru shite imasu.*
  The coast guard is patrolling that area of the sea.

patorōru kā パトロールカー *see* **pato-kā**

pāto-taimā パートタイマー part-timer *see* **pāto**

- *Kono mise no ten'in no sanbun no ichi wa pāto-taimā desu.*
  One-third of the clerks in this store are part-timers.

pāto-taimu パートタイム part-time *see* **pāto**

- *Kanojo wa ginkō de pāto-taimu de hataraite imasu.*
  She works part-time at a bank.

pātsu パーツ parts

- *jidōsha no pātsu*
  automobile parts

pawā パワー power

- *Kondo no kuruma wa mae no yori pawā ga arimasu.*
  This car has more power than the old one.
- *Jūmin pawā no hantai de, kōjō kensetsu keikaku wa tekkai saremashita.*
  The plan for constructing the factory has been cancelled because of strong opposition by the local residents.

pawafuru パワフル powerful

- *Aite chiimu wa waga chiimu no pawafuru na kōgeki ni hirumimashita.*
  The opponents shrank from our team's powerful attack.

pazuru パズル puzzle

- *Sono otoko no ko wa sakki wa pazuru o shite imashita.*
  The boy was doing a puzzle a while ago.

pea ペア pair

- *Kono yunomi wa pea ni natte imasu.*
  These teacups make a pair.

pechikōto ペチコート petticoat

- *Pechikōto ga sukāto no suso kara nozoite imasu.*
  Her petticoat is showing from underneath her skirt.

pedanchikku ペダンチック *see* **pedantikku**

pedantikku ペダンティック pedantic
- *pedantikku na hito*
  a pedantic person
- *Kanojo wa kantan na koto o pedantikku ni setsumei shimashita.*
  She explained the simple matters pedantically.

pei ペイ pay
- *Kono kaisha wa pei ga ii desu.*
  This company pays well.

peinto suru ペイントする to paint
- *Doa o shiroku peinto shimashita.*
  I painted the door white.

peipā ペイパー *see* **pēpā doraibā**

pējento ページェント pageant
- *Sono shukujitsu wa hanayaka na pējento o motte maku o tojimashita.*
  The gala day ended with a gorgeous pageant.

pēji ページ page
- *Kono hon wa san pēji rakuchō ga arimasu.*
  This book has three pages missing.

pen ペン pen
- *Pen de kaite kudasai.*
  Please write in pen.

penanto ペナント pennant
- *Kono ryō chiimu ga hageshii penanto arasoi o kurihirogeru koto deshō.*
  These two teams will compete fiercely for the pennant.
- *Kare no heya ni wa daigaku jidai no penanto ga mada kazatte arimasu.*
  In his room, he still displays a pennant from his college days.

penarutii ペナルティー penalty

- *Sono senshu wa jūman en no penarutii o harawasaremashita.*

  The player was made to pay a penalty of ¥100,000.

penarutii kikku ペナルティーキック penalty kick

- *Aite chiimu no hansoku de penarutii kikku o moraimashita.*

  We got a penalty kick when the opposing team violated the rule.

pendanto ペンダント pendant

- *daiyamondo no pendanto*

  a diamond pendant

pen furendo ペンフレンド *see* **pen paru**

pengin ペンギン penguin

- *Pengin-tachi ga furokku kōto o kita shinshi no yō ni tatte imasu.*

  Penguins are standing like gentlemen in frock coats.

penishirin ペニシリン penicillin

- *Byōin de penishirin o chūsha shite moraimashita.*

  I received a shot of penicillin at the hospital.

penki ペンキ [Dutch: *pek*] paint

- *Penki nuritate*

  Wet Paint

pen nēmu ペンネーム pen name

- *Kanojo wa pen nēmu de shōsetsu o kaite imasu.*

  She is writing novels under a pen name.

pen paru ペンパル pen pal

- *Nihon ni kite hajimete pen paru ni aimashita.*

  I came to Japan and met my pen pal for the first time.

penshon ペンション pension (hotel)

- *Sono yama no penshon ni gaikokujin ga sūnin tomatte imashita.*

  Several foreigners were staying at the pension in the mountains.

pēpā doraibā ペーパードライバー [Japanese Usage: paper driver] non-driver with a driving license
- *Kanojo wa ninen mae ni menkyo o totta noni, mada pēpā doraibā desu.*
  Although she got a driving license two years ago, she hasn't driven yet.

pēpā kanpanii ペーパーカンパニー [Japanese Usage: paper company] bogus company
- *Kanojo wa damasarete pēpā kanpanii no kabu o kaimashita.*
  She was tricked into buying stocks in a bogus company.

pepāminto ペパーミント peppermint
- *pepāminto no aisu kuriimu*
  peppermint ice cream

pēpā naifu ペーパーナイフ paper knife
- *Kono pēpā naifu wa amari yoku kiremasen ne.*
  This paper knife doesn't cut very well, does it?

pēpāresu ペーパーレス paperless
- *Shōken-gaisha to pēpāresu no torihiki ga dekimasu.*
  You can do paperless trading with an investment firm.

pēpā tesuto ペーパーテスト [Japanese Usage: paper test] written test
- *Konogoro no gakkō wa pēpā tesuto ga ōsugimasu ne.*
  Schools these days give too many written tests, don't they?

peshimisuto ペシミスト pessimist
- *Kare wa peshimisuto mitai na kurai kao o shite imasu.*
  He has the gloomy face of a pessimist.

pēsosu ペーソス pathos
- *Kono sakuhin wa yūmoa to pēsosu ga takumi ni orikomarete imasu.*
  Humor and pathos are skillfully woven into this work.

pēsu ペース pace
- *Kōshō wa junchō na pēsu de shinkō shite imasu.*

The negotiation is progressing at a proper pace.

petto ペット pet
- *Koko ni wa petto o tsurete haitte wa ikemasen.*
  Pets are not allowed here.

pianisuto ピアニスト pianist
- *Watashi no yume wa pianisuto ni naru koto deshita.*
  My dream was to become a pianist.

piano ピアノ piano
- *Watashi no piano no sensei wa totemo kibishikatta desu.*
  My piano teacher was very strict.

piero ピエロ [French: *pierrot*] clown
- *Piero wa sākasu no ninki-mono desu.*
  A clown is a favorite in the circus.
- *Jinsei ni oite tokiori piero o enjisaserareru koto ga arimasu.*
  In our lives there are times when we are forced to play the clown.

piiāru ピーアール PR PR, public relations
- *Kare wa kaisha no piiāru gakari desu.*
  He's a PR man in the company.

piiku ピーク peak
- *Keiki wa ima ga piiku deshō.*
  Business is probably at its peak now.

piinatsu ピーナツ *see* **piinattsu**

piinattsu ピーナッツ peanut
- *Kankōkyaku ga risu ni piinattsu o yatte imasu.*
  Tourists are feeding the squirrels peanuts.

pike ピケ picket, picket line
- *Kōjō no mon no mae de pike o hatte imasu.*
  They are establishing a picket line in front of the factory gate.

pike ピケ piqué
- *Pike de kodomo ni doresu o tsukutte yarimashita.*

I made a dress with piqué for my child.

piketto ピケット *see* **pike** (picket)

pikkuappu ピックアップ pickup, select; **~suru** する to pick up, select

* *Chōsa taishō no pikkuappu wa watashi ni sasete kudasai.*
  Let me do the selection of people for the survey.
* *Kaeri ni toshokan de kodomo o pikkuappu shimasu.*
  On my way back, I'll pick up my child at the library.

pikkurusu ピックルス *see* **pikurusu**

pikunikku ピクニック picnic

* *Ashita no pikunikku no tame ni kaimono o shinakereba narimasen.*
  I must shop for tomorrow's picnic.

pikurusu ピクルス pickles

* *Kyūri o pikurusu ni shimasu.*
  I make pickles out of cucumbers.

pin ピン pin

* *Kabe ni posutā ga pin de tomete arimasu.*
  A poster is pinned on the wall.

pinchi ピンチ pinch

* *Tōsha wa zaisei pinchi ni ochiitte imasu.*
  Our company is in a financial pinch.

pinchi hittā ピンチヒッター pinch hitter

* *Kyūkai no ura de tsui ni pinchi hittā o okuridashimashita.*
  They finally sent out a pinch hitter in the second half of the ninth inning.

pinku ピンク pink

* *pinku no kānēshon*
  pink carnations

pinto ピント [Dutch: *brandpunt*] focus, point

* *Kono shashin wa pinto ga atte imasen ne.*
  This picture is out of focus, isn't it?
* *Sono kotae wa pinto hazure desu.*

That answer is beside the point.

pirafu ピラフ pilaf
- *Umibe no shiifūdo resutoran de oishii pirafu o tabemashita.*

  We had a delicious pilaf at a seafood restaurant near the ocean.

piramiddo ピラミッド pyramid
- *Ejiputo ni wa kyodai na piramiddo ga nokotte imasu.*

  Huge pyramids remain in Egypt.
- *piramiddo gata no soshiki*

  a pyramid organization

piriodo ピリオド period, stop
- *Kare wa sanjūni sai de dokushin seikatsu ni piriodo o uchimashita.*

  He ended his bachelor lifestyle at age 32.

pisutoru ピストル pistol, revolver, gun
- *Pisutoru de utaremashita.*

  I was shot by a pistol.

pitchā ピッチャー pitcher
- *Kare wa hidarikiki no pitchā desu.*

  He is a left-handed pitcher.

pitchi ピッチ pitch, speed
- *Deddorain ni maniau yō ni kyū-pitchi de shigoto o susumete imasu.*

  They are working at high speed in order to meet the deadline.

pitchingu ピッチング pitching (baseball)
- *Kare no pitchingu wa jitsu ni subarashikatta desu.*

  His pitching was just great.

pittsa ピッツァ *see* **piza**

piza ピザ pizza
- *Oyatsu ni piza o tabemashita.*

  I had a pizza as a snack.

pōchi ポーチ porch
- *Neko ga pōchi de hinatabokko o shite imasu.*
  A cat is basking in the sun on the porch.

pōchido eggu ポーチド・エッグ poached egg
- *Pōchido eggu wa metta ni tabemasen.*
  I seldom eat poached eggs.

pointo ポイント point, score
- *Gēmu no hajime de pointo o takusan kasegimashita.*
  We got a lot of points at the beginning of the game.
- *Kare no hanashi wa pointo ga zurete imashita.*
  His talk missed the point.

poji ポジ positive (photo)
- *Poji firumu o nihon kudasai.*
  Please give me two rolls of positive film.

pojishon ポジション position
- *Kare wa takai pojishon no hito to sessuru kikai ga ōi desu.*
  He has many opportunities to receive people in high positions.
- *Nihon ga ima sekai no naka de dō iu pojishon ni aruka o kangaenakute wa ikemasen.*
  We have to think about what position Japan occupies in the world today.

pojitibu ポジティブ positive
- *pojitibu na taido*
  a positive attitude
- *Kare wa sono mondai o pojitibu ni uketotte imasu.*
  He takes that matter positively.

pōkā feisu ポーカーフェイス *see* **pōkā fēsu**

pōkā fēsu ポーカーフェース poker face
- *Nani ga okotte mo kare wa pōkā fēsu desu.*
  No matter what happens, he keeps his poker face.

pokettaburu ポケッタブル pocketable, pocket-sized
- *pokettaburu na keisanki*

a pocket calculator

poketto ポケット pocket

• *Kono poketto wa ana ga aite imasu.*
There's a hole in this pocket.

poketto manē ポケットマネー pocket money

• *Kanojo no poketto manē de wa sonna mono o kau yoyū wa arimasen.*
She cannot afford such a thing with her pocket money.

pōku ポーク pork

• *Pōku wa yoku yakanakereba narimasen.*
You must cook pork well.

pomādo ポマード pomade

• *Kami ni pomādo o tsuketa dansei wa sukunai desu.*
There are not many men who apply pomade to their hair.

poppusu ポップス pops

• *Poppusu konsāto de hitto-kyoku o takusan ensō shimashita.*
They played many hit tunes at the pops concert.

popyurā ポピュラー popular

• *Hanbāgā ya supagetti wa popyurā na ryōri desu.*
Hamburgers and spaghetti are popular dishes.

pori ポリ polyethylene

• *pori yōki*
polyethylene containers

poriechiren ポリエチレン see **pori**

poriesuteru ポリエステル polyester

• *Poriesuteru no mono wa airon ga irimasen.*
Things made of polyester don't need ironing.

poripu ポリプ polyp

• *I no poripu o totte moraimashita.*
I had the polyps in my stomach removed.

porishii ポリシー policy

• *Kaisha wa atarashii porishii o tatemashita.*

The company made a new policy.

poronēzu ポロネーズ polonaise
- *Dansu hōru kara ka chikarazuyoi poronēzu ga kikoete kimasu.*

A powerful polonaise can be heard coming perhaps from the dance hall.

poroshatsu ポロシャツ polo shirt
- *Poroshatsu o kite gorufu o shimasu.*

I play golf wearing a polo shirt.

poruno ポルノ pornography, pornographic
- *Saikin poruno zasshi ga hanran shite imasu.*

There is a flood of pornographic magazines recently.

porunogurafii ポルノグラフィー *see* **poruno**

posutā ポスター poster
- *Posutā de shinkansho o senden shimasu.*

They advertise new books with posters.

posuto ポスト post, mailbox
- *Kanojo wa ginkō de ii posuto ni tsuite imasu.*

She has a good post at the bank.
- *Kono tegami o kado no posuto ni irete kudasai.*

Please drop this letter in the mailbox at the corner.

pōtaburu ポータブル portable
- *pōtaburu no wāpuro*

a portable word processor

potāju ポタージュ potage
- *Samui kisetsu ni wa atatakai potāju ga oishii desu.*

Hot potage tastes good in a cold season.

potensharu ポテンシャル potential
- *Kanojo ni wa pianisuto no potensharu wa nasasō desu.*

She seems to have no potential as a pianist.

poteto chippu(su) ポテトチップ(ス) potato chip(s)
- *Poteto chippu wa tabehajimeru to yameraremasen.*

Once you start eating potato chips, you can't quit.

pōtoforio ポートフォリオ portfolio
- *Pōtoforio no ikkan to shite kin o kaimashita.*
  I bought gold as a part of my portfolio.

pōtorēto ポートレート portrait
- *Kore wa Amerika no shodai daitōryō no pōtorēto desu.*
  This is the portrait of the first President of the United States.

potto ポット pot, vacuum bottle
- *Potto ni kōhii o ippai iremashita.*
  I filled the pot with coffee.

pōzu ポーズ pause
- *Sorezore no kotoba no ato ni pōzu o oite yonde kudasai.*
  Please read with a pause after each word.

pōzu ポーズ pose
- *Moderu ga shashin o toru tame ni pōzu o totte imasu.*
  The model is posing for a photograph.

puchiburu プチブル [French: *petit bourgeois*] lower middle class
- *Kono hon wa puchiburu ni taisuru karui fūshi desu.*
  This book is a satire lightly mocking the lower middle class.

pudingu プディング pudding
- *Dezāto ni pudingu wa ikaga desu ka?*
  How about some pudding for dessert?

purachina プラチナ [Spanish: *platina*] platinum
- *purachina no kekkon yubiwa*
  a platinum wedding ring

puragu プラグ plug
- *Puragu o sashikonde kudasai.*
  Please plug it in.

puraibashii プライバシー privacy
- *Koko wa puraibashii ga tamote nai kara, koshitsu ni utsuritai no desu ga.*
  We'd like to go to a private room, because there's no privacy here.

puraibēto プライベート private
- *Kore wa puraibēto na mondai desu kara hottoite kudasai.*
  This is a private matter, so leave me alone.
- *Puraibēto ni o-hanashi shitai koto ga arimasu.*
  I have something I'd like to speak with you about privately.

puraido プライド pride
- *Kare wa jibun no shigoto ni puraido o motte imasu.*
  He takes pride in his work.

puraioritii プライオリティー priority
- *Takusan aru naka de mo sono purojekuto ni puraioritii o okimashita.*
  We gave priority to that project above many others.

puraisu プライス price
- *Kōto no puraisu ga juppāsento sagarimashita.*
  The price of the coat was reduced ten percent.

purakādo プラカード placard
- *Kare-ra wa purakādo o motte demokōshin o shimashita.*
  They demonstrated in a march while holding placards.

puran プラン plan; **~suru** する to plan
- *Ryokō no puran o tatemashita.*
  I made plans for my trip.
- *Shiten o dasu koto o puran shite imasu.*
  We are planning to open a new branch.

puraningu プラニング *see* **puranningu**

purankuton プランクトン plankton
- *Aru sakana wa purankuton o esa ni shite imasu.*
  Some fish feed on plankton.

puranningu プランニング planning
- *Kono purojekuto wa mada puranningu no dankai desu.*
  This project is still in the planning stage.

puranto プラント plant, factory
- *Sono jidōsha-gaisha wa gaikoku ni gōben de puranto o kensetsu shimashita.*

The automobile company built a plant under a joint venture in a foreign country.

purasu プラス plus; **~suru** する to add
- *Jinji-idō wa kaisha no keiei ni purasu ni naru deshō.*
  The change in staff will be a plus for the company's management.
- *Kono tensū ni wa kare no doryoku ga purasu sarete imasu.*
  He gets additional marks for effort.

purasuchikku プラスチック plastic
- *purasuchikku no koppu*
  a plastic cup

purasutikku プラスティック *see* **purasuchikku**

puratonikku プラトニック platonic
- *Kare to wa puratonikku na kankei desu.*
  I have a platonic relationship with him.

puratonikku rabu プラトニックラブ platonic love
- *Kanojo wa mada puratonikku rabu o shinjite iru yō desu.*
  She seems to still believe in platonic love.

purattohōmu プラットホーム platform
- *Ressha ga purattohōmu ni haitte kita tokoro desu.*
  A train has just arrived on the platform.

purē プレー play; **~suru** する to play
- *Kare-ra wa sakkā no shiai de umai purē o misemashita.*
  They exhibited a fine play in the soccer game.
- *Kinō wa ichinichijū gorufu o purē shimashita.*
  I played golf all day long yesterday.

purēbōi プレーボーイ playboy
- *Kare wa nadai no purēbōi desu.*
  He is a notorious playboy.

purē gaido プレーガイド [Japanese Usage: play guide] ticket agency
- *Purē gaido de myūjikaru no maeuriken o kaimashita.*

I bought an advance ticket for the musical at the ticket agency.

pureibōi プレイボーイ *see* **purēbōi**

purei gaido プレイガイド *see* **purē gaido**

purein プレイン *see* **purēn**

pureiyā プレイヤー *see* **purēyā**

puremia プレミア *see* **puremiamu**

puremiamu プレミアム premium, additional charge
* *Kono kippu wa juppāsento no puremiamu ga tsuite imasu.*
  This ticket has a premium of ten percent.

purēn プレーン plain
* *purēn na dezain*
  a plain design

pureryūdo プレリュード prelude
* *Ima hiite iru no wa dare no pureryūdo desu ka?*
  Whose prelude is being played now?

puresshā プレッシャー pressure
* *Hayaku kono shigoto o oeru yō puresshā o kakerarete imasu.*
  I am under pressure to finish this work fast.

puresu suru プレスする to press
* *Airon de zubon o puresu shimasu.*
  I press my trousers with an iron.

puresutēji プレステージ prestige
* *puresutēji no aru daigaku*
  a prestigious university

pureta-porute プレタポルテ prête-à-porter, ready-to-wear clothing
* *Kaku depāto ni pureta-porute no kōnā ga arimasu.*
  Each department store has a section for ready-to-wear clothing.

purēyā プレーヤー player
* *Ano ōkesutora wa ichiryū no purēyā ga atsumatte imasu.*

That orchestra boasts the finest gathering of musicians.

purezentēshon プレゼンテーション presentation
- *Kare no shinkikaku ni tsuite no purezentēshon wa hakkiri shite imashita.*
  His presentation of the new plans was clear.

purezento プレゼント present; **~suru** する to present
- *Kore wa imōto e no purezento desu.*
  This is a present for my younger sister.
- *Kare ni nekutai o purezento shimasu.*
  I'll give him a necktie.

purima donna プリマドンナ prima donna (opera)
- *Kanojo wa sekaiteki ni yūmei na purima donna desu.*
  She is a prima donna of global fame.

purimitibu プリミティブ primitive
- *purimitibu na seikatsu*
  a primitive lifestyle

purin プリン *see* **pudingu**

purinsesu プリンセス princess
- *Shinderera wa purinsesu ni narimashita.*
  Cinderella became a princess.

purinshipuru プリンシプル principle
- *Kare wa jiko no purinshipuru ni chūjitsu desu.*
  He is true to his principles.

purinsu プリンス prince
- *Kare wa supōtsukai no purinsu desu.*
  He is a prince of the sporting world.

purinto プリント print; **~suru** する to print
- *hana moyō no purinto no sukāto*
  a print skirt with a floral pattern
- *Sensei ga gakusei ni purinto o kubarimashita.*
  The teacher distributed printed copies to students.
- *Konpyūtā no dēta o purinto shite kudasai.*
  Please print out the computer data.

puro プロ professional
- *Kare wa gorufu ga jōzu desu ga puro de wa arimasen.*
  He is good at golf but not professional.
- *puro yakyū*
  professional baseball

purodakushon プロダクション production
- *Kare wa terebi kyoku o yamete, bangumi purodakushon gaisha o tsukurimashita.*
  After leaving the TV station, he started a program production company.
- *Tamura-san ga purodakushon bumon ni haizoku sarete kara, shoseki no seisaku ga sumūzu ni narimashita.*
  Since Mr. Tamura has been transfered to the production department, the book production process has been smooth.

purodyūsā プロデューサー producer
- *Sono purodyūsā no eiga wa ninki ga ochite kimashita.*
  That producer's movies have lost popularity.

purodyūsu suru プロデュースする to produce
- *Kare wa dokyumentarii mo prodyūsu shimasu.*
  He also produces documentaries.

purofesshonaru プロフェッショナル *see* **puro**

purofiru プロフィル *see* **purofiiru**

purofiiru プロフィール profile
- *Shinbun ni shinshin sakka no shashin to purofiiru ga notte imashita.*
  The photo and profile of a rising novelist appeared in the newspaper.

purofitto プロフィット profit
- *Kono sēru de ōki na purofitto o kitai shite imasu.*
  We expect a large profit from this sale.

puroguramingu プログラミング programming
- *Pasokon no puroguramingu o naraitai desu.*
  I'd like to learn computer programming.

puroguramu プログラム program, schedule
- *Iriguchi de happyōkai no puroguramu o moraimashita.*
  I got a program for the recital at the entrance.
- *Gogo no puroguramu ni sukoshi henkō ga arimasu.*
  There is a slight change in the afternoon schedule.

puroguresshibu プログレッシブ progressive
- *Kare wa puroguresshibu na kyōikusha desu.*
  He is a progressive educator.

purojekuto プロジェクト project
- *Sono purojekuto wa mokka kentōchū desu.*
  That project is being considered right now.

puromōshon プロモーション sales promotion
- *Shin-seihin no puromōshon wa raishū kara hajimarimasu.*
  The sales promotion for the new products will start next week.

puromōtā プロモーター promoter
- *Kare wa bunka kōryū no promōtā to shite katsuyaku shite imasu.*
  He is active as a cultural exchange promoter.

puromunādo プロムナード promenade
- *Kono puromunādo wa shoppingu mōru ni tsūjite imasu.*
  This promenade leads to the shopping mall.

puropaganda プロパガンダ propaganda
- *Puropaganda no posutā o kabe ichimen ni harimashita.*
  I covered the wall with propaganda posters.

puropera プロペラ propeller
- *Puropera ki de Hawai no shimameguri o shimashita.*
  We made a tour of the Hawaiian Islands in a propeller-driven plane.

puropōshon プロポーション proportion
- *Kanojo wa batsugun no puropōshon o shite imasu.*
  Her body is well-proportioned.

puropōzu プロポーズ proposal; **~suru** する to propose

- *Kanojo wa kare no puropōzu o kotowarimashita.*
  She declined his proposal.
- *Kare wa hoshizora no moto de kanojo ni puropōzu shimashita.*
  He proposed to her under the starry sky.

puroretaria プロレタリア [German: *Proletarier*] proletarian
- *Kanojo wa puroretaria sakka desu.*
  She is a proletarian writer.

purorōgu プロローグ prologue
- *Sono jiken ga kare no rakusen e no purorōgu ni narimashita.*
  That incident became a prologue to his defeat in the election.

purosesu プロセス process
- *Kome kara sake o tsukuru purosesu o mimashita.*
  We saw the process of making sake from rice.

purotekuto プロテクト protection
- *Kono sofuto ni wa kopii dekinai yō ni purotekuto ga kakerarete imasu.*
  This software is copy protected.

Purotesutanto プロテスタント Protestant
- *Kare wa Purotesutanto no kyōkai no bokushi desu.*
  He is a minister of a Protestant church.

purotto プロット plot
- *Ima tsugi no shōsetsu no purotto o nette iru tokoro desu.*
  I am working on the plot of my next novel now.

pūru プール swimming pool, pooled capital; **~suru** する to pool
- *Pūru de oyogimasu.*
  I swim in the pool.
- *Sendenhi no tame no pūru ga naku narimashita.*
  The pool of advertising capital ran out.
- *Sono riekikin wa kaihatsu shikin to shite pūru sarete*

imasu.
The profit is pooled as a development fund.

pusshu hon プッシュホン [Japanese Usage: push phone]
push-button phone
- *Sono ofisu no kaku desuku ni pusshu hon ga arimasu.*
  Each desk in the office has a push-button phone.

pusshu suru プッシュする to push
- *Diirā wa kono burando o pusshu shite imasu.*
  Dealers are pushing this brand.

R

rabā ラバー rubber
- *Kono bubun wa rabā de dekite imasu.*
  This part is made of rubber.

rabendā ラベンダー lavender
- *rabendā iro no sētā*
  a lavender sweater

raberu ラベル label
- *Kono wain no raberu ni seisanchi ga kaite arimasu.*
  The place where this wine was made is written on the label.

rabo ラボ (processing) lab *see* **erueru**
- *Kono rabo wa puro no shashinka ga yoku tsukatte imasu.*
  This lab is often used by professional photographers.

raburetā ラブレター love letter
- *Ichū no hito kara raburetā o moraimashita.*
  I received a love letter from my secret crush.

rabu shiin ラブシーン love scene
- *rabu shiin no nai eiga*
  a movie without love scenes

rabu sutōrii ラブストーリー love story
- *Kanashii toki ni wa rabu sutōrii o yomimasu.*

I read love stories when I'm sad.

radikaru ラディカル *see* **rajikaru**

rafu ラフ rough, coarse, casual
- *rafu na fukusō*
  a casual outfit

raguran ラグラン raglan
- *raguran-sode no kōto*
  a raglan-sleeved coat

raibaru ライバル rival
- *Kanojo wa ōzei no raibaru ni kakomarete imasu.*
  She is surrounded by many rivals.

raifuru ライフル rifle
- *Raifuru de tori o uchiotoshimashita.*
  I shot a bird with a rifle.

raifu saikuru ライフサイクル life cycle
- *Hageshii kyōsō no tame shōhin no raifu saikuru ga chijimarimashita.*
  The life cycle of products has shortened because of stiff competition.

raifuwāku ライフワーク lifework
- *Kare wa raifuwāku to shite tōshindai no chōkoku ni torikunde imasu.*
  He is working hard on a life-size sculpture as a symbol of his lifework.

rain ライン line
- *Enpitsu de rain o hikimasu.*
  I draw a line with a pencil.

rainā ライナー line drive
- *Pinchi hittā ga rainā o tobashimashita.*
  A pinch hitter hit a line drive.

rainnappu ラインナップ lineup
- *Kono katarogu ni shinsha no rainnappu ga dete imasu.*
  This catalogue has the lineup of new cars.

raion ライオン lion
- *Raion wa hyakujū no ō to yobarete imasu.*
  The lion is said to be the king of beasts.

raisensu ライセンス license
- *Kare wa kaigyōi no raisensu o motte imasu.*
  He has a medical practitioner's license.

raisu ライス rice
- *Yōshoku ni wa raisu yori pan no hō ga ii desu.*
  I prefer bread to rice with Western dishes.

raisu karē ライスカレー *see* **karē raisu**

raitā ライター writer
- *Kare wa mada kakedashi no raitā desu.*
  He is still a fledgling writer.

raitā ライター lighter
- *Raitā de tabako ni hi o tsukemashita.*
  I lit a cigarette with a lighter.

raito ライト light
- *Kuruma no raito ga tsuite imasu.*
  The car's lights are on.

raito ライト right
- *Battā wa raito ni furai o agemashita.*
  The batter hit a fly ball to right field.

raito-appu suru ライトアップする to light up
- *Shoppingu-mōru no Kurisumasu tsurii ga utsukushiku raito-appu sarete imasu.*
  The Christmas tree at the shopping mall is lit up beautifully.

rajiētā ラジエーター radiator
- *Rajiētā ga hotondo kara ni natte imasu.*
  The radiator is almost empty.

rajikaru ラジカル radical
- *Sono kaigi de rajikaru na giron ga tenkai saremashita.*
  Radical arguments developed in that meeting.

rajio ラジオ radio

• *Rajio no shin'ya hōsō o kikinagara nete shimaimashita.*
I fell asleep while listening to the late-night radio broadcast.

rajio dorama ラジオドラマ radio drama
• *Wakai koro wa rajio dorama ga suki deshita.*
When I was young, I enjoyed radio dramas.

raketto ラケット racket
• *Kore wa josei yō no karui raketto desu.*
This is a light racket for women.

rakkii ラッキー lucky
• *Subete ga umaku yuki honto ni rakkii deshita.*
Everything went well and I was truly lucky.

rakkii sebun ラッキーセブン lucky seventh (inning)
• *Rakkii sebun no hōmu ran ga shiai no nagare o kaemashita.*
The home run in the lucky seventh turned the tide in the game.

ranchi ランチ lunch
• *Ranchi taimu ni wa resutoran wa doko mo konde imasu.*
All the restaurants are crowded at lunchtime.

randebū ランデブー rendezvous, docking; **~suru** する to have a rendezvous, dock
• *Futatsu no uchūsen wa uchū de randebū shimashita.*
The two spaceships rendezvoused in space.

randomāku ランドマーク landmark
• *Kono kinenhi wa tōchi no randomāku desu.*
The monument is a landmark in this area.

randoseru ランドセル [Dutch: *ransel*] satchel
• *Otoko no ko ga randoseru o shotte imasu.*
A boy is carrying a satchel on his back.

rangēji raboratorii ランゲージ・ラボラトリー *see* **erueru**

rankingu ランキング ranking
• *Sono ginkō wa kyonen no rankingu de goi ni ochimashita.*
That bank fell to fifth position in last year's rankings.

ranku ランク rank; **~suru** する to rank
- *Kare wa ranku no hikui shōkō desu.*
  He is a low-ranking officer.
- *Sono chiimu wa tsune ni takaku ranku sarete imasu.*
  That team is always ranked high.

rannā ランナー runner, jogger
- *Maiasa rannā ga uchi no mae o tōrimasu.*
  Every morning some runners pass in front of our house.

ranningu suru ランニングする to go running
- *Gakkō no ato de ichijikan ranningu shimasu.*
  I ran for an hour after school.

ranningu shatsu ランニングシャツ running shirts
- *Rannā wa minna ranningu shatsu o kite imasu.*
  The runners are all in their running shirts.

ranpu ランプ lamp
- *Shinshitsu no kabe ni ranpu o toritsukemashita.*
  I fixed a lamp to my bedroom wall.

ranpu ランプ ramp
- *Jiko no tame ichiji heisa sareteita ranpu ga kaitsū shimashita.*
  The ramp, temporarily closed due to the accident, was reopened.

rapusodii ラプソディー rhapsody
- *Risuto no rapusodii ga konsāto no puroguramu ni haitte imasu.*
  Liszt's rhapsody is in the concert program.

rasshu ラッシュ rush
- *Chūmon no rasshu ni harikitte imasu.*
  Due to a rush of orders, we are working hard.

rasshu (awā) ラッシュ(アワー) rush hour
- *Asaban no rasshu awā wa taihen desu.*
  The morning and evening rush hours are terrible.

rasuto ラスト last

  • *Kare-ra wa rasuto made yoku ganbarimashita.*
  They held on strong to the end.

rasuto shiin ラストシーン last scene
  • *Sono eiga no rasuto shiin wa hakuryoku ga arimashita.*
  The last scene of that movie was powerful.

rasuto supāto ラストスパート last spurt
  • *Sono kōhosha wa senkyo undō ni rasuto supāto o kakete imasu.*
  The candidate is putting the final burst of energy into his election campaign.

Raten ラテン Latin
  • *Shingakkō de Raten-go o benkyō shimashita.*
  I studied Latin at the seminary.

raundo ラウンド round
  • *Sono bokusā wa daini raundo de nokkuauto saremashita.*
  The boxer was knocked out in the second round.

raunji ラウンジ lounge
  • *Hoteru no raunji de shōdan o shimashita.*
  We conducted business talks in the hotel lounge.

rea レア rare
  • *Sutēki wa rea ga ii desu.*
  I want my steak rare.

rebā レバー liver
  • *Rebā wa tetsubun ga ōi desu.*
  Liver is high in iron.

reberu レベル level
  • *Kono tekisuto wa watashi ni wa reberu ga takasugimasu.*
  This book's level is too high for me.

rēberu レーベル *see* **raberu**

rēdā レーダー radar
  • *Kuruma no sokudo o chekku suru no ni rēdā o mochiimasu.*
  Radar is used to check the speed of cars.

redii レディー lady
- *redii rashii furumai*
  ladylike behavior

redii fāsuto レディーファースト ladies first
- *Kare wa mada Amerika no redii fāsuto no shūkan ni narete imasen.*
  He hasn't gotten used to the American custom of ladies going first yet.
- *Kyō no supiichi wa redii fāsuto de ikimashō ka?*
  As for the speeches today, shall we have ladies before gentlemen?

redii-mēdo レディーメード ready-made
- *redii-mēdo no sūtsu*
  a ready-made suit

refuto レフト left
- *Refuto ga hashitte bōru o torimashita.*
  The left fielder ran to catch the ball.

regyurā レギュラー regular
- *Ano senshu wa tsui ni regyurā ni naremasen deshita.*
  He could not become a regular player after all.

regyurā menbā レギュラーメンバー regular member
- *Kanojo wa sono bangumi no regyurā menbā desu.*
  She is a regular member of that program.

rei レイ lei
- *Kare wa kubi ni rei o kakete imasu.*
  He has a lei around his neck.

reiauto レイアウト layout
- *Kono zasshi no reiauto wa dokusōteki desu.*
  This magazine has a creative layout.

reinkōto レインコート raincoat
- *Reinkōto o motte kite yokatta desu.*
  I'm glad I brought my raincoat.

reiofu レイオフ layoff

- *Amerika de wa saikin no fukyō ni tomonai reiofu ga hinpan ni okonawarete imasu.*
  In America frequent layoffs have accompanied the recent recession.

rejā レジャー leisure, leisure-time amusement
- *Rejā būmu de rizōto hoteru wa minna man'in desu.*
  Due to a boom in leisure activities, resort hotels are all full.

reji レジ cash register, checkout, cashier
- *Sūpā no reji de matasaremashita.*
  I had to wait at the supermarket checkout.

rejisutansu レジスタンス [French: *résistance*] resistance movement
- *Kare wa Furansu no rejisutansu no ikinokori desu.*
  He is a survivor from the French Resistance.

rejume レジュメ résumé, summary
- *Kare no ronbun no rejume o yomimashita.*
  I read a summary of his thesis.

rekōdingu レコーディング recording
- *Kono sutajio de rekōdingu ga okonawarete imasu.*
  A recording is being made in this studio.

rekōdo レコード record, disk
- *Bētōben no daigo shinfonii no rekōdo*
  a record of Beethoven's fifth symphony

rekuiemu レクイエム requiem
- *Kono shishū wa kanojo no naki otto e no rekuiemu no yō desu.*
  This collection of poems appears to be a requiem for her late husband.

rekuriēshon レクリエーション recreation
- *Kono hen ni wa rekuriēshon ni tekitō na ba ga arimasen.*
  There's no suitable area for recreation around here.

remon レモン lemon
- *Kōcha ni wagiri no remon o iremasu.*

I put a slice of lemon in my tea.

remon tii レモンティー [Japanese Usage: lemon tea] tea with lemon
- *Remon tii wa ikaga desu ka?*
  Would you care for some tea with lemon?

renji レンジ range (for cooking), extent
- *Watashi wa imademo gasu renji de gohan o takimasu.*
  I still cook rice on the gas range.

rēnkōto レーンコート *see* **reinkōto**

renta-kā レンタカー rent-a-car
- *Shutchōchū wa renta-kā o tsukaimashita.*
  I used a rented car during my business trip.

rentaru レンタル rental
- *Kono ofisu no naka no mono wa hotondo minna rentaru desu.*
  Almost everything in this office is rented.

rentogen レントゲン [German: *Röntgen*] X-ray
- *Mune no rentogen o torimashita.*
  I had my chest X-rayed.

renzu レンズ lens
- *Kono megane no renzu ga kumotte imasu.*
  The lenses of these eyeglasses are clouded.

repātorii レパートリー repertory
- *Kanojo no ryōri no repātorii wa amari hiroku arimasen.*
  Her cooking repertory is not very large.

repōtā レポーター reporter
- *terebi bangumi no repōtā*
  a reporter for a TV program

repōto レポート report; **~suru** する to report
- *Kenshū ryokō no repōto o kaite imasu.*
  I am writing a report on the study tour.
- *Jikken no kekka o repōto shimasu.*
  We'll report the results of our experiment.

reriifu レリーフ relief
- *Ishizukuri no tatemono no achikochi ni utsukushii reriifu ga arimasu.*
There are beautiful carvings in relief all over the stone building.

rēru レール rail
- *Densha no sharin ga rēru kara hazuremashita.*
The train's wheels jumped the track.

resepushon レセプション reception
- *Resepushon de supiichi o suru yō ni tanomaremashita.*
I was asked to give a speech at the reception.

reshiito レシート receipt
- *Henpin no sai wa reshiito ga hitsuyō ni narimasu.*
You need the receipt when returning goods.

rēshingu kā レーシングカー racing car
- *Kore wa rēshingu kā no mokei desu.*
This is a model racing car.

reshipi レシピ recipe
- *Kono kukkii no reshipi wa himitsu desu.*
The recipe for these cookies is a secret.

ressun レッスン lesson
- *piano no ressun*
piano lesson

rēsu レース race
- *Ano rēsu wa sessen deshita ne.*
It was a close race, wasn't it?

rēsu レース lace
- *Rēsu no kāten ga kakatte imasu.*
Lace curtains are being hung.

resubian レスビアン lesbian
- *Kinō sūsennin no hito ga resubian no kenri no tame ni Washinton de demo kōshin shimashita.*
Thousands of people marched for lesbian rights in Wash-

ington yesterday.

resukyū レスキュー rescue
- *Resukyū tai ga genba ni shutsudō shimashita.*
  The rescue party was sent to the scene.

resuringu レスリング wrestling
- *Resuringu no shiai o mita koto ga arimasen.*
  I haven't seen a wrestling match.

resutoran レストラン restaurant
- *Ano resutoran wa shizuka na node dēto ni ii desu yo.*
  That restaurant is quiet and good for a date.

retasu レタス lettuce
- *Retasu to tomato de sarada o tsukurimashita.*
  I made a salad with lettuce and tomatoes.

rēto レート rate
- *Ichi doru hyakujū en no rēto de en o kaimashita.*
  I bought yen at a rate of ¥110 to the U.S. dollar.

retorikku レトリック rhetoric
- *Kare no supiichi wa retorikku bakari de naiyō wa taishita
  koto wa arimasen.*
  His speech is full of rhetoric but its content is not great.

retoruto レトルト [French: *retorte*] canned food, pre-cooked
food in a heat-sealed package
- *Reitō shokuhin ya retoruto shokuhin no shitsu ga kōjō
  shimashita.*
  The quality of frozen food and pre-cooked food in heat-
  sealed packages has improved.

retteru レッテル [Dutch: *letter*] label, sticker *see* **raberu**
- *Bin ni sorezore chigatta retteru ga hatte arimasu.*
  Each bottle has a different label.
- *Kare wa okubyōmono to iu retteru o hararete imashita.*
  He was labeled a coward.

rēyon レーヨン rayon
- *Rēyon ga shiruku ni tottekawarimashita.*

Rayon has replaced silk.

rezā レザー leather, imitation leather

- *rezā no handobaggu*
  a leather handbag

rēzā レーザー laser

- *Rēzā wa tsūshin ya iryō nado tahōmen de tsukawarete imasu.*
  Lasers are used in various fields such as communications and medical treatment.

rezu レズ *see* **resubian**

rēzun レーズン raisin

- *rēzun iri no pan*
  raisin bread

riakushon リアクション reaction

- *Kare no kotoba ni chōshū no riakushon wa hotondo arimasen deshita.*
  The audience showed little reaction to his remarks.

riarisutikku リアリスティック realistic

- *Kono teian wa riaristikku de wa arimasen.*
  This proposal is not realistic.

riarisuto リアリスト realist

- *Kanojo wa ne wa romanchisuto ja nakute riarisuto desu.*
  At heart she is not a romantic but a realist.

riaritii リアリティー reality

- *Riaritii no nai hanashi ni wa kyōmi ga arimasen.*
  I have no interest in talk that is divorced from reality.

riarizumu リアリズム realism

- *Kono shashin no mukidashi no riarizumu wa fukaikan o ataemasu.*
  The blunt realism of this photo is offensive.

riaru リアル real

- *Kono hon wa mayaku jōyōsha no seitai o riaru ni egaite imasu.*

This book depicts the real facts about drug addicts.

riaru taimu リアルタイム real time, simultaneous

- *Nyū-yōku Tōkyō kan wa riaru taimu de jōhō kōkan ga dekimasu.*

  We can exchange information simultaneously between New York and Tokyo.

ribaibaru リバイバル revival

- *Rajio de mo terebi de mo mukashi no uta no ribaibaru ga ōi desu.*

  On the radio and TV there are many revivals of old songs.

riberarisuto リベラリスト liberalist

- *Kare no uketa Suparuta kyōiku ga kare o riberarisuto ni shitatemashita.*

  The Spartan education that he had received made him a liberalist.

riberaru リベラル liberal

- *Kare no riberaru na kangaekata ga jōshi no ikari o kaimashita.*

  His liberal thinking angered his superior.

ribēto リベート rebate

- *Mēkā kara diirā e no ribēto ga kōgakuka shite imasu.*

  The rebate from the manufacturer to the dealer is getting bigger.

- *Sono yakunin wa mēkā ni tokubetsu no onkei o ataete tagaku no ribēto o uketorimashita.*

  The public official received a huge "rebate" for his special favor to the manufacturer.

ribingu kitchin リビングキッチン [Japanese Usage: living kitchen] combined living room, dining area, and kitchen

- *Sono semai ribingu kitchin wa benri ni dekite imasu.*

  That small combination living-dining-kitchen is set up conveniently.

ribingu rūmu リビングルーム living room

- *Uchi no ribingu rūmu kara tōku no umi ga miemasu.*
  The ocean can be seen in the distance from my living room.

ribon リボン ribbon
- *Shōjo wa nagai kami o ribon de musunde imasu.*
  The girl's long hair is tied with a ribbon.

rifōmu suru リフォームする to reform, alter
- *Ofisu o rifōmu shite atarashii kagu ya kikai o iremashita.*
  I rearranged the office and put in new furniture and machines.

rifurein リフレイン *see* **rifurēn**

rifurēn リフレーン refrain
- *Sono rifurēn o motto chikarazuyoku uttate mite kudasai.*
  Sing the refrains more forcefully.

rifuresshu suru リフレッシュする to refresh
- *Kyanpu ni itte shinshin tomo rifuresshu shite kimashita.*
  We went camping to refresh our minds and bodies.

rifuto リフト lift
- *Kōji genba no rifuto de ue ni agarimashita.*
  At the construction site, we took an elevator up.

rihabiri リハビリ *see* **rihabiritēshon**

rihabiritēshon リハビリテーション rehabilitation
- *Rihabiritēshon no okage de ude ga ugoku yō ni narimashita.*
  Thanks to rehabilitation I can move my arm now.

rihāsaru リハーサル rehearsal
- *Bangumi no rihāsaru ga chōdo owatta tokoro desu.*
  The rehearsal for the program has just finished.

riidā リーダー reader
- *Nihongo no shokyū no riidā o sagashite iru no desu ga.*
  I am looking for a Japanese reader for beginners.

riidā リーダー leader
- *Kare wa sono hantai demo no riidā no hitori deshita.*
  He was one of the leaders of that protest march.

riidāshippu リーダーシップ leadership
- *Kare wa shuwanka desu ga riidāshippu ni kakete imasu.*
  He is an able man but he lacks leadership qualities.

riido リード lead; **~suru** する to lead
- *Waga chiimu wa gokai no ura de riido o ubawaremashita.*
  Our team lost the lead in the second half of the fifth inning.
- *Kashu no ninki tōhyō de wa dare ga riido shite imasu ka?*
  Who leads in the popularity contest for singers?

riigu リーグ league
- *Kare wa dai-riigu no senshu desu.*
  He is a major league player.

riiku suru リークする to leak, disclose
- *Himitsu no jōhō ga riiku saremashita.*
  The secret information leaked out.
- *Kare wa naimitsu no kotogara o riiku shimashita.*
  He disclosed the confidential matter.

riisu リース lease; **~suru** する to lease
- *Kono kopii-ki wa raigetsu riisu ga kiremasu.*
  The lease of this copier will expire next month.
- *Kono konpyūtā wa ichinen keiyaku de riisu shimashita.*
  We leased out this computer on a one-year contract.

rikōru リコール recall; **~suru** する to recall, remove from office
- *Shichō ga rikōru saremashita.*
  The mayor was removed from office.
- *Saikin kuruma no rikōru ga yoku arimasu.*
  Lately there have been many recalled cars.
- *Kaisha wa kekkan shōhin o rikōru shimashita.*
  The company recalled the defective goods.

rikuesuto リクエスト request; **~suru** する to request
- *Kono uta wa rajio no chōshusha kara ōku no rikuesuto ga arimashita.*
  The radio audience made many requests for this song.

rikurainingu shiito リクライニングシート reclining seat
- *Kinai no rikurainingu shiito de yoku nemuremashita.*
  I slept well in the reclining seat in the airplane.

rikuriēshon リクリエーション *see* **rekuriēshon**

rikurūto リクルート recruitment
- *Sono kaisha wa kenkyūin no rikurūto o hajimemashita.*
  That company has started recruiting research workers.

rikurūto sūtsu リクルートスーツ [Japanese Usage: recruit suit] suit worn for job interviews
- *Daigakusei ga rikurūto sūtsu de kaisha mawari o shite imasu.*
  University students wearing "recruit suits" are visiting companies one after another.

rimitto リミット limit
- *Kono repōto wa asatte no rimitto made ni shiagemasu.*
  I'll finish this report by the deadline, the day after tomorrow.

rimokon リモコン remote control
- *Terebi no channeru wa rimokon de kirikaeraremasu.*
  You can change the TV channels with the remote control.

rimōto kontorōru リモートコントロール *see* **rimokon**

rimujin (basu) リムジン(バス) [Japanese Usage: limousine bus] airport express bus
- *Kūkō yuki no rimujin basu wa koko kara jūgofun oki ni demasu.*
  Express buses bound for the airport leave here every fifteen minutes.

rinchi リンチ beating; **~suru** する to punish, beat up
- *Rinchi jiken de giseisha ga futari demashita.*
  There were two victims in the beating.

ringu リング ring
- *Kanojo wa daiya no engēji ringu o hamete imasu.*
  She wears a diamond engagement ring.

- *Sono bokusā wa ringu de taoreta mama shibō shimashita.*
  That boxer fell and died in the ring.

rinku リンク *see* **sukēto rinku**

rinsu リンス rinse
- *Kono rinsu o tameshite mitara dō desu ka?*
  Why don't you try this rinse?

ripōtā リポーター *see* **repōtā**

ripōto リポート *see* **repōto**

rirakkusu suru リラックスする to relax
- *Onsen de nisannichi rirakkusu shitai desu.*
  I'd like to relax for a few days at a hot spring.

rirē リレー relay; **~suru** する to relay, pass
- *Rirē de itchaku ni narimashita.*
  We came in first place in the relay.

ririifu リリーフ relief, substitute
- *Nihon shiriizu de wa ryō-chiimu no kantoku ga ririifu o ikani umaku tsukau ka ga pointo desu.*
  The question in the Japan Series is how well the managers of both teams can use their relief pitchers.

risāchi リサーチ research
- *Kare wa sono shōhin no kaihatsu no tame ni sūnen no risāchi o shimashita.*
  He spent several years of research developing that product.

risaikuru リサイクル recycling; **~suru** する to recycle
- *shimin ni yoru risaikuru undō*
  a recycling campaign by the citizens
- *Risaikuru shita kami o tsukatte imasu.*
  We are using recycled paper.

risaitaru リサイタル recital
- *Kinō no risaitaru wa Shopan zukume deshita.*
  Yesterday's recital was entirely Chopin's work.

risuku リスク risk
- *Tōshi ni risuku wa tsukimono desu.*

We cannot invest without risks.

risuto リスト list; **~suru** する to list

- *Zaikohin no risuto o misete kudasai.*
  Please show me a list of the inventory in stock.
- *Sono kaisha no namae wa koko ni wa risuto sarete imasen.*
  That company's name is not listed here.

ritaia suru リタイアする to retire, drop out

- *Kare wa sono marason rēsu de zenhan wa kōchō ni tobashite imashita ga sanjukkiro chiten o sugita tokoro de fukutsū no tame ritaia shimashita.*
  He was running smoothly in the first half of the marathon, but after the 30 kilometer point he dropped out due to a stomachache.

ritchi リッチ rich, extravagant

- *Minna de ritchi na Yōroppa ryokō o keikaku shite imasu.*
  We are planning an extravagant trip to Europe.

rittoru リットル [French: *litre*] liter

- *Kono mahōbin ni wa ichi rittoru hairimasu.*
  This thermos can hold one liter.

rizabēshon リザベーション reservation

- *Hoteru no rizabēshon wa ryokōsha ni yatte moraimasu.*
  I'll get a travel agency to make the hotel reservations.

rizābu suru リザーブする to reserve, make a reservation

- *Sono resutoran wa mikka mae ni rizābu shimashita.*
  I made a reservation for the restaurant three days ago.

rizōto リゾート resort

- *Umibe no rizōto ni gōka na manshon ga taterarete imasu.*
  A gorgeous condominium has been built in the coastal resort area.

rizōto uea リゾートウエア resort wear

- *Depāto ni karafuru na rizōto uea ga hanran shite imasu.*
  There is a flood of colorful resort wear in the department

store.

rizumikaru リズミカル rhythmical
- *Sono e no rizumikaru na utsukushisa ni miryō saremashita.*
  I was fascinated by the rhythmical beauty of that painting.

rizumu リズム rhythm
- *Gakudan wa hayai rizumu de ensō shite imasu.*
  The band is playing with a quick rhythm.

robii ロビー lobby, lounge
- *Gekijō no robii ni ekizochikku na kabekake ga kakatte imasu.*
  An exotic tapestry is hanging in the theater lobby.

robotto ロボット robot, figurehead
- *Sangyō yō robotto wa kindai sangyō no kage no tateyakusha desu.*
  Industrial robots are center stage in modern industry.
- *Kare wa jibun no ishi de wa nani mo dekinai tannaru robotto ni sugimasen.*
  He can't do anything of his own volition and is really only a figurehead.

rōdo mappu ロードマップ road map
- *Kare wa rōdo mappu o minagara unten shite imasu.*
  He is driving while looking at a road map.

rōdo rēsu ロードレース road race
- *Hajimete rōdo rēsu de hashirimashita.*
  I ran a road race for the first time.

rōdo shō ロードショー road show
- *Sono eiga nara, rōdo shō (gekijō) de mimashita.*
  I saw that movie at a theater showing first-run movies.

rogu hausu ログハウス log cabin
- *Natsu wa kōgen no rogu hausu de genkō o kakimasu.*
  In summer I write manuscripts in a log cabin on the plateau.

rojikaru ロジカル logical

- *Kanojo to wa rojikaru na giron wa dekimasen.*
  One can't have logical arguments with her.

rojikku ロジック logic
- *Kare no itte iru koto wa rojikku ni aimasen.*
  There is no logic in what he is saying.

rojji ロッジ lodge, mountain hut
- *Tozansha wa asa hayaku rojji o demashita.*
  The mountain climbers left the lodge early in the morning.

rōkaru ローカル local
- *Shinbun no rōkaru ban ni me o tōshimashita.*
  I looked through the local section of the newspaper.

rōkaru karā ローカルカラー local color
- *Kono zasshi wa rōkaru karā ga tsuyosugiru to omoimasu.*
  I think that this magazine has too much local color.

roke ロケ location, location for filming
- *Kare-ra wa Hawai ni roke ni dekakemasu.*
  They will go to do on-location filming in Hawaii.

rokēshon ロケーション *see* **roke**

roketto ロケット locket
- *Kanojo wa roketto no naka ni naki fianse no shashin o irete imasu.*
  She has a photo of her dead fiancé in a locket.

roketto ロケット rocket
- *Roketto de tsuki no sekai e tonde itta yume o mimashita.*
  I dreamt that I flew to the moon in a rocket.

rokkā ロッカー locker
- *Rokkā ni kagi o kakemashita.*
  I locked the locker.

rokkingu chea ロッキングチェア rocking chair
- *Sobo wa rokkingu chea de inemuri o shite imasu.*
  My grandmother is sleeping in the rocking chair.

rokku ロック rock (music)
- *Rokku ga kaijō ni narihibikimashita.*

The rock music resounded throughout the hall.

rokku suru ロックする to lock
* *Doa o rokku shite kudasai.*
  Please lock the door.

rokkuauto ロックアウト lockout; **~suru** する to lock out
* *Sono kōjō no rokkuauto wa tsuzukisō desu.*
  The lockout at that factory seems like it will continue.

rokkun rōru ロックンロール rock 'n' roll
* *Wakai koro ni wa yoku rokkun rōru o odotta mono desu.*
  When we were young, we often danced to rock 'n' roll.

Rōma ローマ [Latin: *Roma*] Rome
* *Rōma no kyūjitsu o tanoshimi ni shite imasu.*
  I look forward to the holiday in Rome.

roman ロマン [French: *roman*] spirit of adventure
* *Umi wa otoko no roman o kakitatemasu.*
  The ocean awakes man's spirit of adventure.

romanchikku ロマンチック romantic
* *Kono sakuhin wa romanchikku na mūdo o tadayowasete imasu.*
  This work is permeated with romantic feeling.

romanchishizumu ロマンチシズム romanticism
* *Bētōben wa ongaku ni okeru romanchishizumu no senkusha desu.*
  Beethoven was the herald of romanticism in music.

romanchisuto ロマンチスト romanticist
* *Romanchisuto no kare wa tsune ni seishun no yume o oimotomemashita.*
  Being a romanticist, he constantly pursued dreams of youth.

romansu ロマンス romance, love affair.
* *Futari no aida ni romansu ga mebaemashita.*
  A romance blossomed between them.

rōn ローン loan
* *Ginkō no rōn de mai hōmu o tatemashita.*

I built my home with a bank loan.

Rondon ロンドン London

- *Rondon wa kiri ni tozasarete imashita.*

London was enveloped in fog.

rongu ran ロングラン long run

- *Sono shō wa sannen mo rongu ran o tsuzukemashita.*

The show had a run of three years.

rongu serā ロングセラー [Japanese Usage: long seller] longtime seller

- *Kono sankōsho wa nijūnen no rongu serā desu.*

This reference book is a longtime seller of twenty years.

rōpu ロープ rope

- *Toranku ni wa genjū ni rōpu o kakete arimashita.*

A rope was tied securely to the trunk.

rōpuuē ロープウエー ropeway

- *Rōpuuē de sanchō made noborimashita.*

We went up to the top of the mountain by ropeway.

rōrā kōsutā ローラーコースター roller coaster *see* **jetto kōsutā**

- *Rōrā kōsutā ni notte suriru o ajiwaimashita.*

It was a thrill to ride the roller coaster.

rōrā sukēto ローラースケート roller skate

- *Akai sētā no shōjo ga rōrā sukēto de subette imasu.*

A girl in a red sweater is on roller skates.

rōringu ローリング rolling

- *Fune wa nijikan ijō rōringu o tsuzukemashita.*

The ship kept rolling for more than two hours.

Roshia ロシア Russia

- *Watashi no barē no sensei wa Roshia-jin desu.*

My ballet teacher is Russian.

rōshon ローション lotion

- *Areta te ni rōshon o tsukemashita.*

I applied lotion to my rough hands.

rosu ロス loss
* *Kaisha wa sono buhin de ōki na rosu o dashimashita.*
  The company suffered a big loss on those parts.

rōsu ロース roast, loin (sirloin, pork loin)
* *Sūpā de gyū rōsu o gohyaku guramu katte kite kudasai.*
  Please buy 500 grams of sirloin beef at the supermarket.

rōsuto biifu ロストビーフ roast beef
* *Ano mise wa rōsuto biifu o suraisu shite utte imasu.*
  That store sells sliced roast beef.

rōtēshon ローテーション rotation
* *Rōtēshon de yakin o shimasu.*
  We have night duty by rotation.

rō-tiin ローティーン [Japanese Usage: low teens] early teens
* *rō-tiin no shōnen shōjo*
  boys and girls in their early teens

rozario ロザリオ [Portuguese: *rosario*] rosary
* *Katorikku kyōkai no hon'ya de kono rozario o kaimashita.*
  I bought this rosary at the Catholic Church's bookstore.

rubii ルビー ruby
* *rubii iro no wain*
  ruby-colored wine

rūju ルージュ rouge
* *ussuri to rūju o nutta kuchibiru*
  slightly rouged lips

rukkusu ルックス looks
* *Kanojo wa kare no rukkusu ni hikarete kekkon shimashita.*
  She married him for his looks.

rūmu kūrā ルームクーラー [Japanese Usage: room cooler] air conditioner
* *Suzushii natsu datta no de rūmu kūrā o tsukawazu ni sumimashita.*
  Due to the cool summer I managed without using the air

conditioner.

rūmu sābisu ルームサービス room service
- *Hoteru de rūmu sābisu no shokuji o chūmon shimashita.*
  At the hotel, we ordered a meal from room service.

runba ルンバ rumba
- *Wakamono ga muchū ni natte runba o odotte imasu.*
  Young people are dancing the rumba wildly.

Runesansu ルネサンス Renaissance
- *Runesansu wa jūyon seiki no Itaria de okorimashita.*
  The Renaissance originated in Italy in the fourteenth century.

Runessansu ルネッサンス *see* **Runesansu**

runpen ルンペン [German: *lumpen*] loafer, tramp
- *Runpen ga kono machi kara sugata o keshimashita.*
  Tramps have disappeared from this town.

rupo ルポ *see* **ruporutāju**

ruporaitā ルポライター [Japanese Usage: reportage writer] a reporter
- *Kare wa sekaijū o kakemawatte iru enerugisshu na ruporaitā desu.*
  He is an energetic reporter who often travels around the world.

ruporutāju ルポルタージュ reportage
- *Kono bangumi wa Taiheiyō Sensō no shūketsu no urabanashi o ruporutāju-fū ni matometa mono desu.*
  This program tells the inside story of the conclusion of the Pacific War in a journalistic manner.

rūpu ループ loop
- *Sentōki ga rūpu o egaite tonde ikimasu.*
  The fighter plane draws circles as it flies.

rūretto ルーレット roulette, roulette wheel
- *Kajino de rūretto ga taema naku mawatte imasu.*
  Roulette wheels turn incessantly in the casino.

rūru ルール rule
- *Rūru ni hanshita te o tsukatte wa ikemasen.*
  You shouldn't do things against the rules.
- *Sore wa rūru ihan desu.*
  It's against the rules.

rūto ルート route, channel
- *Sanchō e wa iroiro na rūto ga arimasu.*
  There are many different routes to the summit of the mountain.
- *Kono shinamono wa seiki no rūto o tōtte haitta mono de wa arimasen.*
  These goods didn't come through a legitimate channel.

rūtsu ルーツ roots, ancestry, origin
- *Nippon-jin no rūtsu*
  the ancestry of Japanese people
- *Kare wa kome no rūtsu o kenkyū shite imasu.*
  He is doing research on the origin of rice.

rūzu ルーズ loose
- *Kare no rūzu na seikatsu ni wa gaman dekimasen.*
  I can't stand his slovenly lifestyle.

ryukkusakku リュックサック rucksack, knapsack
- *Chikagoro no daigakusei wa ryukkusakku o seotte gakkō e kimasu.*
  University students come to school with knapsacks recently.
- *Wasuremono ga nai yōni ryukkusakku no nakami o mō ichido tenken shimashita.*
  To make sure that I hadn't forgotten anything, I checked the contents of my knapsack one more time.

ryūmachi リューマチ rheumatism
- *Tokidoki ryūmachi ga okorimasu.*
  Sometimes I have attacks of rheumatism.

S

S *see* **esu**

SF *see* **esuefu**

SOS *see* **esu-ō-esu**

sābā サーバー server
- *Sābā no sābu ga tsuyosugite bōru ga endorain o koemashita.*

  The server served too hard and the ball went out of bounds.

sabaibaru サバイバル survival
- *Jin'in seiri wa kaisha no sabaibaru no tame shikata ga nai no desu.*

  It can't be helped; we must cut some personnel for the company's survival.

sābisu サービス service, free of charge *see* **sābu**
- *Ano ryokan wa totemo sābisu ga ii desu.*

  The service at that Japanese inn is very good.
- *Kono tii-shatsu wa sābisu desu.*

  This T-shirt is free of charge.

sābisu eria サービスエリア service area
- *Sābisu eria ni chūsha shite keishoku o torimashita.*

  We parked in the service area and had a snack.

sābisu sutēshon サービスステーション service station
- *Ano sābisu sutēshon wa yoku hayatte imasu.*

  That service station is doing good business.

sābu サーブ serve (tennis)
- *seikaku na sābu*

  an accurate serve

sabotāju サボタージュ [French: *sabotage*] work slowdown
- *Rōdōsha wa sabotāju o yaru kamo shiremasen.*

  The workers might stage a work slowdown.

sabu サブ sub-, assistant
- *Kare wa manējā no sabu, iwayuru sabumane desu.*
He works under the manager, in other words, he's an assistant manager.

sabutaitoru サブタイトル subtitle
- *Sono hon ni omoshiroi sabutaitoru ga tsuite imasu.*
That book has an interesting subtitle.

sāchiraito サーチライト searchlight
- *Yukuefumei-sha o sagasu tame ni sāchiraito de suimen o terashite imasu.*
They are shining a searchlight on the surface of the water, looking for the missing person.

sadisuto サディスト sadist
- *Sono hankō wa sadisuto ni yotte okonawaremashita.*
The crime was committed by a sadist.

sadizumu サディズム sadism
- *Kanojo wa otto no sadizumu o riyū to shite rikon o seikyū shite imasu.*
She is asking for a divorce on grounds of her husband's sadism.

sado サド *see* **sadisuto, sadizumu**

sādo サード third base, third baseman
- *Rannā wa sādo ni tasshimashita.*
The runner advanced to third base.

sadoru サドル saddle
- *Uma ni sadoru o okimasu.*
I put a saddle on the horse.

sāfā サーファー surfer
- *Hawai wa sāfā no paradaisu desu.*
Hawaii is a paradise for surfers.

safaia サファイア sapphire
- *Kono ishi wa safaia no yō ni aoku hikarimasu.*
This stone shines blue like a sapphire.

safaiya サファイヤ *see* **safaia**

safari サファリ safari
- *Afurika e safari tai ga haken saremashita.*
  A safari was sent to Africa.

safari pāku サファリパーク safari park
- *Kankō basu de safari pāku o mite mawarimashita.*
  We went around the safari park in a sightseeing bus.

sāfin サーフィン surfing
- *Biichi ni yokotawatte, sāfin o mimashita.*
  Lying on the beach, I watched them surfing.

saidā サイダー cider, soda pop
- *Nihon no saidā wa appuru jūsu de wa naku sōda no isshu desu.*
  Japanese cider is not apple juice but a kind of soda pop.

saido サイド side
- *Shōhisha no saido kara mireba, shōhizei wa mattaku arigatakunai mono desu.*
  From the consumers' side, the consumption tax is totally unwelcome.

saido bijinesu サイドビジネス [Japanese Usage: side business] side job
- *Shashin wa kare no saido bijinesu desu.*
  Photography is his side job.

saidokā サイドカー sidecar
- *Ano ōtobai no saidokā ni wa dare mo notte imasen deshita.*
  No one was riding in the sidecar of that motorcycle.

saidorain サイドライン sideline
- *Tategaki no bun no jūyō na kotoba ni saidorain o hikimasu.*
  I draw lines alongside the important words in vertically written sentences.
- *Bōru ga saidorain o demashita.*

A ball went over the sideline.
* *Rarii no ōshū no sue bōru ga tsui ni saidorain o warimashita.*
The ball that was hit back and forth finally went out of bounds to end the rally.

saido tēburu サイドテーブル side table
* *Saido tēburu no ue no denki sutando ga tsuite imasu.*
The reading lamp on the side table is on.

saiensu サイエンス science
* *Saiensu wa jinrui ni shiawase mo fushiawase mo motarashimasu.*
Science brings both happiness and unhappiness to humankind.

saiensu fikushon サイエンスフィクション science fiction
* *Kare wa saiensu fikushon no sekai o hōkō shite imasu.*
He is roaming about in a world of science fiction.

saikorojii サイコロジー psychology
* *Daigaku de kenkyū shita saikorojii ga ima no shigoto ni yakudatte imasu.*
The psychology I learned in college is useful in my present job.

saikuringu サイクリング cycling
* *Tenki ga yoku nattara, saikuringu ni dekakemashō.*
If the weather improves, let's go cycling.

saikuru サイクル cycle
* *Keiki no saikuru kara miru to, ima ga tōshi no jiki desu.*
From the standpoint of business cycles, now is the time for investment.

sain サイン sign, signature, autograph; **~suru** する to sign
* *Kono shorui ni wa buchō no sain ga irimasu.*
This paper requires the general manager's signature.
* *Kin'en no sain ga kiemashita.*
The No Smoking sign was turned off.

- *Koko ni sain shite kudasai.*
  Please sign here.

sairen サイレン siren
- *O-hiru no sairen de minna shigoto o chūdan shimashita.*
  At the noon siren, everybody stopped working.

sairento サイレント silent
- *Kanojo wa sairento eiga de katsuyaku shita joyū desu.*
  She was an actress who was active in silent films.

sairento majoritii サイレント・マジョリティー silent majority
- *Sairento majoritii to shite todomarazu, dondon iu beki desu.*
  We shouldn't remain a silent majority; we must speak out.

sairo サイロ silo
- *Hokkaidō no nōjo ni sairo ga miraremasu.*
  Silos can be seen on farms in Hokkaido.

saizu サイズ size
- *Kono kutsu wa saizu ga aimasen.*
  These shoes are not the right size.

sajesuchon サジェスチョン suggestion
- *Kono purojekuto ni kanshite nanika sajesuchon wa arimasen ka?*
  Do you have any suggestions about this project?

sāji サージ serge
- *sāji no gakusei fuku*
  a serge school uniform

sākasu サーカス circus
- *Kare wa sākasu de kūchū buranko o yarimasu.*
  He performs on the flying trapeze in a circus.

sakisofon サキソフォン saxophone *see* **sakkusu**
sakisohon サキソホン *see* **sakkusu**
sakkarin サッカリン saccharine
- *Satō no kawari ni jinkō kanmiryō no sakkarin o*

tsukaimasu.
I substitute saccharine, an artificial sweetener, for sugar.

sakku サック sack, case, fingerstall
  • *megane no sakku*
    a case for glasses
  • *Kanojo wa yubi ni sakku o hamete imasu.*
    She is wearing a fingerstall.

sakkusu サックス sax, saxophone
  • *Kare wa naitokurabu de sakkusu o fuite imasu.*
    He plays a saxophone in a nightclub.

sākuru サークル circle, club
  • *kotengeki kenkyū sākuru*
    a classical drama club
  • *Kare wa kyūshii sākuru katsudō ni bottō shite imasu.*
    He is immersed in quality control circle activities.

sakusesu sutōrii サクセスストーリー success story
  • *Kore wa mazushii imin ga hyakuman-chōja ni natta to iu Amerika no sakusesu sutōrii desu.*
    This is an American success story about a poor immigrant who became a millionaire.

sakusofon サクソフォン *see* **sakkusu**

samā hausu サマーハウス summer house
  • *Samā hausu de o-kyaku o motenashimashita.*
    We entertained some guests at our summer house.

samarii サマリー summary
  • *Kare no ronbun no samarii o yomimashita.*
    I read the summary of his thesis.

samā sukūru サマースクール summer school
  • *Samā sukūru de yon tan'i torimashita.*
    I got four credits at summer school.

samātaimu サマータイム summertime, daylight saving time
  • *Amerika de wa shigatsu no owari ni samātaimu ni narimasu.*

In America, they change to daylight saving time at the end of April.

samitto サミット summit (conference)
- *Kakkoku no riidā ga samitto ni shusseki shimashita.*
The leaders of each country attended the summit.

sāmon サーモン salmon
- *kunsei ni shita sāmon = sumōku sāmon*
smoked salmon

sanatoriumu サナトリウム sanitarium
- *Sanatoriumu no niwa ni kosumosu ga sakimidarete imasu.*
Cosmos are blooming all over the sanitarium garden.

sandaru サンダル sandal
- *Sandaru o haite sunahama o arukimashita.*
I walked on the sandy beach in sandals.

san dekki サンデッキ sun deck
- *Fune no san dekki ni wa hitokko hitori hitokage ga miemasen.*
Not a soul can be seen on the sun deck of the ship.

Sandē sukūru サンデースクール Sunday school
- *Sandē sukūru de naratta koto wa ima de mo oboete imasu.*
I still remember what I learned in Sunday school.

sandoitchi サンドイッチ sandwich
- *Ranchi ni sandoitchi o motte ikimasu.*
I take sandwiches for lunch.

sangurasu サングラス sunglasses
- *Kanojo wa itsumo ōkina sangurasu o kakete imasu.*
She is always wearing big sunglasses.

sanpuru サンプル sample
- *Sanpuru o hitotsu okutte kudasai.*
Please send me a sample.
- *Shin-seihin no sanpuru shukka wa itsu hajimarimasu ka?*
When does the shipping of the new product samples start?

san rūmu サンルーム sun room, sun parlor

- *Sofu wa san rūmu no hachiue ni mizu o yatte imasu.*
  My grandfather is watering the potted plants in the sun room.

Santa-kurōsu サンタクロース Santa Claus
- *Kare wa mainen Santa-kurōsu ni narimasu.*
  Every year he plays Santa Claus.

sapōtā サポーター supporter
- *Kare wa itameta hiza ni sapōtā o atete imasu.*
  He has a supporter on his injured knee.

sapōto サポート support; **~suru** する to support
- *Rihabiri ni wa kazoku no sapōto ga fukaketsu desu.*
  Family support is essential during rehabilitation.
- *Kare no shuchō o sapōto shimasu.*
  I support his claim.

sapuraiyā サプライヤー supplier
- *Ano kaisha wa denki seihin no sapuraiyā desu.*
  That company is a supplier of electric appliances.

saraburreddo サラブレッド thoroughbred
- *Saraburreddo dake atte, kono uma wa jitsu ni rippa desu ne.*
  This horse is as fine as you would expect from a thoroughbred, isn't it?
- *Kare wa seikai no saraburreddo desu.*
  He is a thoroughbred in the political world.

sarada サラダ salad
- *Kanojo wa shokuji ni kakasazu sarada o tabete imasu.*
  She never has a meal without a salad.

sararii サラリー salary
- *Kare wa takai sararii o moratte imasu.*
  He receives a high salary.

sarariiman サラリーマン [Japanese Usage: salary man]
salaried businessman
- *Kare wa sarariiman seikatsu kara ashi o aratte sushiya o*

hajimemashita.

He quit being a nine-to-five businessman and opened a sushi shop.

sarii サリー sari
- *sarii o matotta Indo no josei*

an Indian woman in a sari

saron サロン salon, reception room, reception held by a socialite
- *Pari de nadakai kifujin no saron e shuzai ni ikimashita.*

I went to the famous lady's salon in Paris to get the story.

sarubēji サルベージ salvage
- *Sono nanpasen no sarubēji sagyō wa mada tsuzuite imasu.*

The salvage work on the wrecked ship is still going on.

sasupensu サスペンス suspense
- *sasupensu ni michita sutōrii*

a suspense story

saundo サウンド sound, kind of music
- *Kono sutereo wa ii saundo desu ne.*

This stereo has good sound, doesn't it?
- *Kono saundo wa chūnen-sō ni wa ukemasen.*

This kind of music does not appeal to middle-aged people.

sēbu suru セーブする to save, cut down
- *Kono dēta o sēbu shite kudasai.*

Please save this data.
- *Keihi o sēbu shinakereba narimasen.*

We must cut down our expenses.

sēfu セーフ safe
- *Bōru wa sādo ni nageraremashita ga, rannā wa suberikonde sēfu!*

The ball is thrown to third, but the runner slides and is safe!

sekandohando セカンドハンド *see* **sekohan**

sekando ran セカンドラン second run
- *Sono eiga wa ima sekando ran no eigakan de jōei shite*

imasu.

That movie is being shown at a second-run theater now.

sekkusu セックス sex; **~suru** する to have sex, make love

- *sekkusu no jiyū*

sexual freedom

- *Kōkishin kara sekkusu suru tiinējā ga ōi sō desu.*

I hear that many teenagers have sex out of curiosity.

sekkusu apiiru セックスアピール sex appeal

- *Kanojo wa ōi ni sekkusu apiiru ga arimasu.*

She has lots of sex appeal.

sekohan セコハン secondhand

- *Kono kamera wa sekohan desu ga shinpin dōyō desu.*

This camera is secondhand but it's as good as new.

sekondohando セコンドハンド *see* **sekohan**

sekuhara セクハラ [Japanese Usage: sex(ual) hara(ssment)]

sexual harassment

- *Sekuhara ga shokuba de sawagarete imasu.*

Sexual harassment has become an issue in the workplace.

sekushii セクシー sexy

- *Kanojo wa sekushii na koe o shite imasu.*

She has a sexy voice.

- *Kanojo wa sekushii ni utaimasu.*

She sings in a sexy manner.

sekushon セクション section

- *Kare wa hoka no sekushon ni idō shimashita.*

He moved to another section.

sekushonarizumu セクショナリズム sectionalism

- *Sekushonarizumu wa yamete o-tagai ni kyōryoku*
  shimashō.

Let's put aside sectionalism and cooperate with each other.

sekushuaru harasumento セクシュアル・ハラスメント

see **sekuhara**

sekuto セクト sect

- *Shin-sayoku no aida de wa sekuto no arasoi ga taemasen.*
  There is no end to sectarian strife in the new left wing politics.

sekyuritii セキュリティー security

- *Sono biru ni wa sekyuritii no tame gādoman ga jōchū shite imasu.*
  For security, there is always a guard on duty in that building.

semento セメント cement

- *Kōen no yūhodō ni semento o nutte imasu.*
  They are covering the walkway in the park with cement.

semifainaru セミファイナル semifinal

- *Waga chiimu wa semifainaru de yaburemashita.*
  Our team was defeated in the semifinals.

semikoron セミコロン semicolon

- *Koko ni semikoron o utsu no o wasuremashita.*
  I forgot to put a semicolon here.

seminā セミナー seminar

- *Sono kabushiki tōshi no seminā wa shōkengaisha no shusai desu.*
  The seminar on stock investment is sponsored by a securities firm.

semipuro セミプロ semiprofessional

- *Kanojo wa semipuro no gaka desu.*
  She is a semiprofessional painter.
- *Puro iri wa akiramete semipuro de yakyū o yatte imasu.*
  I gave up the idea of the majors and am playing baseball semiprofessionally.

senchi センチ *see* **senchimētoru, senchimentaru**

senchimentarizumu センチメンタリズム sentimentalism

- *Sono sakuhin no senchimentarizumu o kirau dokusha mo imasu.*
  The sentimentalism in that work turns some readers off.

senchimentaru センチメンタル sentimental
- *senchimentaru na rabu sutōrii*
  a sentimental love story
- *Kanojo wa rabu songu o senchimentaru ni utaimasu.*
  She sings love songs sentimentally.

senchimentaru jānii センチメンタル・ジャーニー sentimental journey
- *Kanojo wa hitori de senchimentaru jānii ni dekakete mada modorimasen.*
  She set off alone on a sentimental journey and hasn't come back yet.

senchimētoru センチメートル [French: *centimetre*] centimeter
- *Ichi mētoru wa hyaku senchimētoru desu.*
  One meter is one hundred centimeters.

sensēshon センセーション sensation
- *Sono denki wa shuppan to dōji ni sensēshon o makiokoshimashita.*
  The biography created a sensation the moment it was out in print.

sensēshonaru センセーショナル sensational
- *sensēshonaru na kiji*
  a sensational article
- *Sono yūkai jiken wa shinbun de sensēshonaru ni toriageraremashita.*
  The kidnapping case was treated sensationally by the newspapers.

senshitibu センシティブ sensitive
- *Kanojo wa atsusa ni taishite senshitibu desu.*
  She is sensitive to heat.
- *Kore wa senshitibu na kotogara desu kara, kuregure mo shinchō ni atsukatte kudasai.*
  Since this is a sensitive matter, please deal with it carefully.

senshuaru センシュアル sensual
- *Kono e wa hito no senshuaru na yokubō o mitashite kuremasu.*
  This picture satisfies people's sensual desires.

sensu センス sense, taste
- *Kanojo wa fukusō no sensu ga ii desu.*
  She has good taste in clothes.

sentā センター center
- *Kare wa gan sentā de chiryōchū desu.*
  He is being treated at the cancer center.

sentā rain センターライン center line
- *Kuruma ga sentā rain o koete hantai-shasen kara kuru torakku to shōtotsu shimashita.*
  A car crossed the center line and collided with an on-coming truck.

sentensu センテンス sentence
- *Ii sentensu wa kanketsu de yō o ete imasu.*
  Good sentences are short and to the point.

sento セント cent
- *Kore wa ni-doru gojussento desu.*
  This costs $2.50.

sentoraru hiitingu セントラルヒーティング central heating
- *Furui biru wa sentoraru hiitingu no setsubi ga arimasen.*
  Old buildings have no central heating systems.

seorii セオリー theory
- *Sono seorii wa mada kagakuteki ni kakuritsu sarete imasen.*
  That theory has not been established scientifically yet.
- *Supōtsu no shiai de wa nakanaka seorii dōri ni wa ikazu, rinki-ōhen ni senjutsu o umidasu hitsuyō ga arimasu.*
  You don't need to follow any theory when playing sports; you need to initiate tactics depending on the moment-to-

moment situation.

sepādo セパード [Japanese Usage: shepherd] German
shepherd
- *Sepādo wa keisatsu ken ni tsukawarete imasu.*
German shepherds are used as police dogs.

separēto セパレート *see* **separētsu**

separētsu セパレーツ separates
- *Kanojo wa separētsu o jōzu ni kumiawasete kimasu.*
She is good at choosing separate pieces that match well.

sepia セピア sepia
- *shitate no yoi sepia iro no sūtsu*
a well-tailored sepia suit

serekushon セレクション selection
- *Sono hon no shashin no serekushon ga okonawarete
imasu.*
The selection of photos for the book is taking place.

seremonii セレモニー ceremony
- *ogosoka na sokui no seremonii*
the solemn enthronement ceremony

serenāde セレナーデ [German: *Serenade*] serenade
- *Sono serenāde ga isshun no aida watashi-tachi o seishun
jidai ni tsuremodoshimashita.*
The serenade momentarily brought us back to our youth.

serofan セロファン cellophane
- *serofan ni tsutsunda kozutsumi*
a package wrapped in cellophane

serohan セロハン *see* **serofan**

sēru セール sale, bargain sale
- *Nigatsu ni fuyumono no sēru ga arimasu.*
They have a sale of winter clothing in February.

serufu-sābisu セルフサービス self-service
- *Kono mise wa serufu-sābisu desu.*
This is a self-service store.

serufu-taimā セルフタイマー self-timer
- *serufu-taimā no aru kamera*
  a camera with a self-timer

sērusu セールス sales
- *Kanojo wa keshōhin no sērusu o yatte imasu.*
  She is selling cosmetics.

sērusu pointo セールスポイント selling point
- *Sora no tabi no daiichi no sērusu pointo wa supiido desu.*
  The prime selling point for air travel is its speed.

sētā セーター sweater
- *Natsu na noni sētā ga irimasu.*
  Although it is summer, I need a sweater.

setto セット set; **~suru** する to set
- *Shōrūmu ni iroiro na dinā setto ga chinretsu sarete imasu.*
  Various kinds of dinner sets are displayed in the showroom.
- *Mezamashidokei o setto suru no o wasuremashita.*
  I forgot to set the alarm clock.

shaberu シャベル shovel, spade
- *Kodomo ga shaberu de ana o hotte imasu.*
  A child is digging a hole with a shovel.

shābetto シャーベット sherbet
- *Ano mise no toropikaru shābetto wa ichiban desu.*
  That store's tropical fruit sherbet is the best.

shai シャイ shy
- *Kanojo wa shai na seikaku na node sono shigoto ni wa mukanai deshō.*
  She wouldn't be suitable for the job because she has a shy personality.

shanpū シャンプー shampoo
- *Asa shanpū o tsukau kare wa seiketsu na nioi ga shimasu.*
  He shampoos in the morning and always smells clean.
- *Shanpū ga nai node kami o arau no wa akiramemashita.*
  I ran out of shampoo so I didn't wash my hair.

shanson シャンソン [French: *chanson*] chanson, French
   song
   • *Furansu e itte honba no shanson o enjoi shimashita.*
   I enjoyed authentic French songs in France.
shāpu シャープ sharp, keen
   • *shāpu na hihyō*
   a sharp criticism
   • *Kanojo wa ongaku ni taishite shāpu na mimi o shite
   imasu.*
   She has a keen ear for music.
shatoru basu シャトルバス shuttle bus
   • *Ōkii kūkō de wa shatoru basu no sābisu ga arimasu.*
   At large airports, shuttle bus service is provided.
shatsu シャツ shirt, undershirt
   • *Wakamono ga shatsu no suso o soto ni tarashite aruite
   imasu.*
   Young men are walking with their shirttails hanging out.
   • *Fuyu ni wa ūru no shatsu o kimasu.*
   I wear a woolen undershirt in winter.
shattā シャッター shutter (for camera, door)
   • *Kono shattā o oshite itadakemasen ka?*
   Would you mind taking a photo for us?
   • *Rokuji ni mise no shattā o oroshimasu.*
   We pull down the store's shutter at six o'clock.
shattoauto シャットアウト shutout; **~suru** する to shut
   out
   • *Sono chiimu wa kinō no shiai de shattoauto make o
   kuraimashita.*
   The team got shut out in yesterday's game.
   • *Kare wa dōgyōsha kara shattoauto saremashita.*
   He was shut out by his fellow traders.
shawā シャワー shower
   • *Maiasa shawā o abimasu.*

I take a shower every morning.

shea シェア share

- *Kono burando no shea wa shijō no sanjuppāsento o koete imasu.*
  This brand has more than a 30% share of the market.

sheā シェアー *see* **shea**

shēdo シェード shade

- *Ressha no mado wa shēdo de ōwarete imasu.*
  The train's windows are covered with shades.
- *Denki sutando no shēdo ga hokori darake desu.*
  The desk lamp's shade is dusty.

sheipu suru シェイプする to shape, tighten

- *Kono kōto wa uesuto o beruto de sheipu shite kimasu.*
  I wear this coat by tightening the waist with a belt.

sheipuappu suru シェイプアップする to shape up

- *Kare wa karada o sheipuappu suru tame ni undō o shite imasu.*
  He exercises in order to shape up his body.

shēkā シェーカー shaker

- *Bātendā ga tejinashi no yō ni shēkā o futte imasu.*
  The bartender is throwing that shaker around like a juggler.

shepādo シェパード *see* **sepādo**

shēpu suru シェープする *see* **sheipu suru**

shēpuappu suru シェープアップする *see* **sheipuappu suru**

sherii シェリー sherry

- *Wain gurasu ni sherii ga haitte imasu.*
  The wine glasses are filled with sherry.

shibia シビア severe

- *Kare no shinkansho wa arayuru hōmen kara shibia na hihyō o ukemashita.*
  His new book received severe criticism from all directions.

shibiā シビアー *see* **shibia**

shibirian シビリアン civilian
- *Kare wa taieki shite shibirian raifu ni modorimashita.*
  He retired from military service and returned to civilian life.
- *Sengo wa shibirian kontorōru ga urusaku iwaremasu.*
  People still strongly advocate control by civilians since the end of the war.

shichū シチュー stew
- *Samui kara konban wa shichū ni shimashō.*
  It's cold, so let's have stew tonight.

shifuto シフト shift; **~suru** する to shift
- *Kare wa yakan no shifuto de hataraite imasu.*
  He works the night shift.
- *Sono kuni wa gunju-sangyō kara heiwa-sangyō ni shifuto shiyō to shite imasu.*
  That country is trying to shift from military to civilian industry.

shigā シガー cigar
- *Bā no naibu wa shigā no kemuri de mōmō to shite imasu.*
  The inside of the bar is thick with cigar smoke.

shigaretto シガレット cigarette
- *Kanojo wa shigaretto ni hi o tsukemashita.*
  She lit a cigarette.

shigunaru シグナル signal, sign
- *Hikōki wa enjin koshō no shigunaru o okurimashita.*
  The airplane signaled that it was having engine trouble.

shii-dii シーディーCD CD, certificate of deposit
- *Kanojo wa tagaku no kane o shii-dii ni shite imasu.*
  She put a large amount of money in a CD.

shii-dii シーディーCD CD, compact disk
- *Katsute atta erupii rekōdo wa shii-dii ni totte kawarare hotondo sugata o keshimashita.*
  CDs have almost entirely replaced LP records.

shii-dii purēyā シーディープレーヤー CDプレーヤー CD

player, compact disc player
* *Shii-dii purēyā o shūri ni motte ikanakereba narimasen.*
I have to take the CD player for repair.

shii-emu シーエム CM [Japanese Usage: CM] commercial message, commercial
* *Aru shii-emu wa ātisutikku ni dekite imasu.*
Some commercials are made artistically.

shiifūdo シーフード seafood
* *Sono resutoran wa shiifūdo ga senmon desu.*
The restaurant specializes in seafood.

shii-ii-ō シーイーオー CEO CEO, chief executive officer
* *Keiken to shuwan o sonaeta jinbutsu ga shii-ii-ō ni shōkaku shimashita.*
The person with both experience and ability was promoted to CEO.

shiimuresu シームレス seamless
* *shiimuresu paipu*
seamless pipes

shiin シーン scene
* *Ano eiga wa uma no hashiru shiin ga ōsugimasu.*
That movie has too many scenes of horses running.

shiiru シール seal
* *Fūtō no ura ni kirei na shiiru ga hatte arimasu.*
A pretty seal has been put on the back of the envelope.

shiisaido シーサイド seaside
* *Sono shiisaido no hoteru kara utsukushii yakei ga miemasu.*
A beautiful night view can be seen from the seaside hotel.

shiisō シーソー seesaw
* *Shiisō ga sakuya no ame de nuremashita.*
The seesaw got wet during last night's rain.

shiisō gēmu シーソーゲーム seesaw game
* *Shiai wa omowanu shiisō gēmu no tenkai ni narimashita.*

Unexpectedly, the match developed into a seesaw game.

shiito シート seat
- *madogiwa no shiito*
  a window seat

shiitsu シーツ sheet
- *Mēdo ga shiitsu o kaete kuremasu.*
  A maid changes the sheets for me.

shiizun シーズン season
- *Ima wa sakura no shiizun desu.*
  Now is the season for cherry blossoms.

shiizun ofu シーズンオフ [Japanese Usage: season off] off-season
- *Ryokō no shiizun ofu de hoteru wa kankodori ga naite imasu.*
  Because it's the off-season for traveling, the hotels are nearly empty.

shikku シック chic, stylish, tasteful
- *shikku na kuro no doresu*
  a chic black dress

shimupojiumu シムポジウム *see* **shinpojiumu**

shinario シナリオ scenario
- *Banji kare no egaita shinario dōri umaku hakobimashita.*
  All has gone well according to the scenario he planned.
- *Kore wa saiaku no shinario desu ne.*
  This is the worst-case scenario for us.

shinario-raitā シナリオライター [Japanese Usage: scenario writer] screenwriter
- *Kanojo wa urekko no shinario-raitā desu.*
  She is a popular screenwriter.

shinboraizu suru シンボライズする to symbolize
- *Eien no heiwa o shinboraizu suru kinenhi ga tateraremashita.*
  A monument symbolizing eternal peace has been erected.

shinboru シンボル symbol
- *Tennō wa Nippon no shinboru desu.*
  The Emperor is the symbol of Japan.

shinfonii シンフォニー symphony
- *Mori no naka ni hairu to kotori-tachi no shinfonii ga tanoshimemasu.*
  You can enjoy the symphony of birds in a forest.

shinfonii ōkesutora シンフォニーオーケストラ symphony orchestra
- *Sono shinfonii ōkesutora wa ima ensō ryokō ni dete imasu.*
  The symphony orchestra is now doing a concert tour.

shingā シンガー singer
- *Kanojo wa hajimete puro no shingā to shite butai ni tachimashita.*
  She made her first appearance on the stage as a professional singer.

shingā-songuraitā シンガー・ソングライター singer-songwriter
- *Sono shingā-songuraitā wa Budōkan de jibun ga sakushi sakkyoku shita uta o utaimasu.*
  The singer-songwriter will sing the songs he composed at the Budokan.

shinguru シングル single
- *Kanojo wa shinguru no seikatsu o tanoshinde imasu.*
  She enjoys her single life.
- *Shinguru no heya o totte arimasu.*
  A single room is reserved.

shingurusu シングルス singles
- *Joshi shingurusu no kesshōsen wa ashita desu.*
  The women's singles championship match is tomorrow.

shinia シニア senior, elderly
- *Gorufu no shinia tsuā ni sanka shimashita.*
  She participated in the golf senior tour.

• *Kare wa igi aru shinia jinsei o okutte imasu.*
He leads a fulfilling life as a senior citizen.

shinikaru シニカル sarcastic, ironic
• *shinikaru na kotoba*
sarcastic words

shinku tanku シンクタンク think tank
• *Shinku tanku to wa arayuru bun'ya no chishiki o teikyō suru kenkyū kikan desu.*
A think tank is a research agency that offers knowledge in all kinds of fields.

shinopushisu シノプシス synopsis
• *Kono hon wa opera no shinopushisu o atsumeta mono desu.*
This book is a collection of opera synopses.

shinpojiumu シンポジウム symposium
• *Sono shinpojiumu de wa chomei na gakusha ga kōen shimashita.*
A noted scholar lectured at the symposium.

shinpuru シンプル simple
• *Sore wa dare de mo dekiru shinpuru na shigoto desu.*
It's a simple job anyone can do.
• *shinpuru na fuku*
simple dress
• *Kono repōto o motto shinpuru ni shite kudasai.*
Please simplify this report.

shiriaru シリアル cereal
• *Shiriaru no shurui ga ōsugite sentaku ni komarimasu.*
With so many kinds of cereal, it's hard to choose one.

shiriasu シリアス serious
• *Motto shiriasu de nai taipu no hito ga suki desu.*
I like a less serious type of person.
• *shiriasu na dorama*
a serious drama

- *Kare wa monogoto o shiriasu ni torimasen.*
  He doesn't take things very seriously.

shiriizu シリーズ series

- *Terebi de atarashii tanteimono no shiriizu ga hajimarimasu.*
  A new series of detective stories will begin on television.

shiroppu シロップ [Dutch: *siroop*] syrup

- *mēpuru shiroppu*
  maple syrup

shirubā シルバー silver

- *Chūshajō ni shirubā no kuruma ga nandai mo arimasu.*
  There are many silver cars in the parking lot.

shirubā eiji シルバーエイジ [Japanese Usage: silver age]
senior citizens

- *shirubā eiji o taishō ni tateta manshon*
  a condominium built for senior citizens

shirubā ēji シルバーエージ *see* **shirubā eiji**

shirubā-gurē シルバーグレー silver-gray

- *Ano shirubā-gurē no sūtsu o kita hito wa dare desu ka?*
  Who is that person wearing a silver-gray suit?

shirubā raifu シルバーライフ [Japanese Usage: silver life]
old age, remaining years

- *Shizuka na shizen no futokoro de shirubā raifu o okuritai mono da to omoimasu.*
  I'd like to spend my old age in the bosom of quiet nature.

shirubā shiito シルバーシート [Japanese Usage: silver seat]
seats for the aged and handicapped

- *Ressha no kaku sharyō ni shirubā shiito ga mōkete arimasu.*
  Each of the train cars has seats for the aged and handicapped.

shiruetto シルエット silhouette, shape

- *utsukushii shiruetto no doresu*

a dress with a beautiful shape

shirukii シルキー silky

- *Kono nunoji wa shirukii na kōtaku ga arimasu.*
  This cloth has a silky gloss.

shiruku シルク silk

- *Kono kiji ni wa shiruku ga majitte imasu ne.*
  This material has some silk mixed in it, doesn't it?

shiruku hatto シルクハット silk hat

- *Majutsushi ga shiruku hatto o kabutte sutēji ni arawaremashita.*
  A magician appeared on the stage wearing a silk hat.

shisutā シスター Catholic nun (sister)

- *Wakai shisutā ga kyōkai nai o annai shite kuremashita.*
  A young nun guided us through the church.

shisutemachikku システマチック systematic

- *shisutemachikku na apurōchi*
  a systematic approach
- *Shisutemachikku ni Nihongo o benkyō shimasu.*
  I study Japanese systematically.

shisutematikku システマティック *see* **shisutemachikku**

shisutemu システム system

- *Furui shisutemu o haishi shimashita.*
  They abolished the old system.

shitii raifu シティーライフ [Japanese Usage: city life] urban life

- *Shitii raifu wa kare ni wa mukimasen.*
  Urban life isn't for him.

shō ショー show

- *Kyō wa fasshon shō, ashita wa charitii shō e ikanakereba narimasen.*
  I must go to a fashion show today and a charity show tomorrow.

shoberu ショベル *see* **shaberu**

shō bijinesu ショービジネス show business
- *Kare wa shō bijinesu ni isshō o kakemashita.*
He staked his life on show business.

shōkēsu ショーケース showcase
- *Kōka na tōjiki ga shōkēsu ni narande imasu.*
Expensive ceramics are in the showcase.

shokkingu ショッキング shocking
- *Shokkingu na uwasa o kikimashita.*
I heard a shocking rumor.

shokku ショック shock
- *Kare no kyūshi ni ichidō ōkina shokku o ukemashita.*
Everybody was greatly shocked at his sudden death.

shōman ショーマン showman
- *Ano kaisha no shachō wa nakanaka no shōman desu.*
The president of that company is quite a showman.

shoppingu ショッピング shopping; **~suru** する to shop
- *shoppingu ni fuben na tokoro*
an inconvenient place for shopping
- *Katarogu de shoppingu shimasu.*
I shop by catalogue.

shoppingu mōru ショッピングモール shopping mall
- *Chikaku no shoppingu mōru ni ikeba hotondo nandemo te ni hairimasu.*
I can get almost everything at the neighborhood shopping mall.

shoppingu puraza ショッピングプラザ shopping plaza
- *Shoppingu puraza ni gyararii ga ōpun shimashita.*
A gallery was opened at the shopping plaza.

shoppingu sentā ショッピングセンター shopping center
- *Shoppingu sentā no eigakan de tokidoki eiga o mimasu.*
Sometimes I go to see movies at the theater in the shopping center.

shōru ショール shawl

• *shiroi shōru o kata ni kaketa fujin*
a woman wearing a white shawl over her shoulders

shorudā baggu ショルダーバッグ shoulder bag
• *Kanojo wa akai shorudā baggu o kakete imasu.*
She is carrying a red shoulder bag.

shōrūmu ショールーム showroom
• *Shōrūmu de denki kigu no atarashii moderu o mimashita.*
I saw the new electric appliance models in the showroom.

shōto katto ショートカット [Japanese Usage: short cut]
short haircut
• *Kanojo wa nagai kami o shōto katto ni shimashita.*
She cut her long hair short.

shōtokēki ショートケーキ shortcake
• *Ichigo no shōtokēki o chūmon shimashita.*
I ordered strawberry shortcake.

shōto shōto ショートショート [Japanese Usage: short
short] very short story
• *Tokiori Eigo no zasshi de omoshiroi shōto shōto o
yomimasu.*
Sometimes I read interesting short stories that are very brief
in English magazines.

shōto suru ショートする to short-circuit, run short
• *Densen ga shōto shita yō desu.*
The electric wire seems to have short-circuited.
• *Shikin ga shōto shite imasu.*
We've run short of funds.

shōto sutōrii ショートストーリー short story
• *Nihon ni wa shōto sutōrii no sakka to shōto shōto no sakka
ga imasu.*
In Japan there are authors of short stories and authors of
very short stories.

shō uindō ショーウインドー [Japanese Usage: show
window] shop window

- *Himatsubushi ni shō uindō o mite mawarimashita.*
  I went around looking at the shop windows to kill time.

shua シュア *see* **shuā**

shuā シュアー sure, skillful

- *shuā na pitchingu*
  masterly pitching
- *Kanojo wa muzukashii yaku o shuā ni konashimashita.*
  She did a difficult task skillfully.

shugā シュガー sugar

- *Kōhii ni wa shugā o irezu ni nomimasu.*
  I drink coffee without sugar.

shureddā シュレッダー shredder

- *Shureddā no juyō ga nobite imasu.*
  The demand for shredders is growing.

Sobieto ソビエト Soviet, former Soviet Union

- *Sobieto no minshuka wa mō yume de wa arimasen.*
  The democratization of the Soviet Union is no longer a dream.

sōda ソーダ soda

- *Sutorō de sōda sui o suimasu.*
  I drink soda water through a straw.

sofā ソファー sofa

- *Sofā de hirune o shimashita.*
  I took a nap on the sofa.

sofuto ソフト soft, software

- *Sofuto na hizashi ga kāten o tōshite heya ni sashikonde kimasu.*
  The soft sunlight streams into the room through the curtains.
- *Saikin kare no taido wa sofuto ni narimashita.*
  His attitude has softened lately.
- *pasokon yō no sofuto*
  software for personal computers

sofutobōru ソフトボール softball
- *Kodomo ga kōen de sofutobōru o yatte imasu.*
  Children are playing softball in the park.

sofutouea ソフトウエア *see* **sofuto**

soketto ソケット socket
- *Denkyū o soketto ni hamemashita.*
  I screwed a light bulb into the socket.

sokkusu ソックス socks
- *Sokkusu o sanzoku kaimashita.*
  I bought three pairs of socks.

somurie ソムリエ [French: *sommelier*] wine steward
- *Sono resutoran de wa somurie ga wain no go-sōdan ni ōjimasu.*
  In that restaurant, a wine steward gives advice about wine.

sonachine ソナチネ [Italian: *sonatine*] sonatina
- *Osanai musume wa kawaii te de sonachine o hiite imasu.*
  My young daughter is playing a sonatina with her tiny hands.

sonata ソナタ sonata
- *Bētōben no sonata no naka de "Gekkō" ga ichiban popyurā deshō.*
  The Moonlight is probably the most popular of Beethoven's sonatas.

sonetto ソネット sonnet
- *Shēkusupia no ririshizumu wa sono sonetto ni kencho ni arawarete imasu.*
  The lyricism in Shakespeare's sonnets is remarkable.

songuraitā ソングライター songwriter
- *Kare wa songuraitā o kokorozashite imasu.*
  He aims to be a songwriter.

sopurano ソプラノ soprano
- *Kanojo wa kōrasu de sopurano desu.*
  She is a soprano in the chorus.

sōrā hausu ソーラーハウス solar house
- *Taiyōnetsu o riyō shita sōrā hausu o tsukuru yotei desu.*
  I'm planning to build a solar house that utilizes the sun's heat.

sorisuto ソリスト [French: *soliste*] soloist
- *Kanojo wa sorisuto to shite ōkesutora de baiorin o hikimashita.*
  She played the violin as a soloist with the orchestra.

soro ソロ solo
- *Kanojo wa soro de utaimashita.*
  She sang a solo.

sōsēji ソーセージ sausage
- *Kare wa chōshoku ni kanarazu hamu ka sōsēji o tabemasu.*
  He always eats ham or sausages for breakfast.

sōsharisuto ソーシャリスト socialist
- *Kare wa binbō na gakusei jidai ni wa sōsharisuto deshita.*
  He was a socialist when he was a poor student.

sōsharizumu ソーシャリズム socialism
- *Kanojo wa sōsharizumu o shinpō suru seijika desu.*
  She is a politician who believes in socialism.

sōsharu dansu ソーシャルダンス ballroom dancing
- *Kanojo wa shisei o yoku suru tame ni sōsharu dansu o naratte imasu.*
  She is studying ballroom dancing to improve her posture.

sōsharu wākā ソーシャルワーカー social worker
- *Ano byōin de wakai sōsharu wākā ga sūnin hataraite imasu.*
  Several young social workers are working in that hospital.

sōsu ソース sauce
- *Sūpā de iroiro na sōsu o binzume de utte imasu.*
  They sell various kinds of bottled sauce at supermarkets.

sōsu ソース source

- *Kono jōhō no sōsu o chekku shite kudasai.*
  Please check the source of this information.

sotē ソテー [French: *sauter*] sauté
  - *Yūbe no dinā wa sakana no sotē deshita.*
    Last night's dinner was fish sauté.

souru ソウル soul music
  - *Kokujin kashu wa mukashi kono naitokurabu de souru o utatte imashita.*
    Long ago black singers sang soul music in this nightclub.

souru myūjikku ソウルミュージック *see* **souru**

suchiimu スチーム steam
  - *Kono heya wa suchiimu de atatamemasu.*
    This room is heated by steam.

suchiimu airon スチームアイロン steam iron
  - *Kono suchiimu airon wa hoka no yori yoku kakarimasu.*
    This steam iron does a better job than the others.

suchiiru スチール steel
  - *suchiiru no kyabinetto*
    a steel cabinet

suchiiru スチール still
  - *Suchiiru wa senden yō no shashin desu.*
    The still is a photo for promotional purposes.

suchuwādesu スチュワーデス flight attendant, stewardess
  - *Suchuwādesu no kanojo wa sekaijū o tobimawatte imasu.*
    As she is a stewardess, she flies all over the world.

suiito スイート sweet
  - *Kono wain no suiito na aji ga suki desu.*
    I like this wine's sweet taste.

suimingu スイミング swimming
  - *Yatte iru uchi ni suimingu ga dandan omoshiroku natte kimashita.*
    Now that I'm practicing, swimming has gradually become fun.

suimingu kurabu スイミングクラブ swimming club
- *Mainichi suimingu kurabu de oyogimasu.*
  I swim at the swim club every day.

suingu suru スイングする to swing
- *Regē no rizumu ni notte wakamono no karada ga suingu shite imasu.*
  The young people are moving their bodies to the rhythm of reggae.

Suisu スイス [French: *Suisse*] Switzerland, Swiss
- *utsukushii Suisu no sangaku fūkeiga*
  a beautiful Swiss mountain-scape

suitchi スイッチ switch; **~suru** する to switch
- *Suihanki no suitchi o iremashita.*
  I turned on the switch on the rice cooker.
- *Pitchā o suitchi shimashita.*
  They switched pitchers.

sukāfu スカーフ scarf
- *Kanojo wa sukāfu o akusesarii ni tsukau no ga jōzu desu.*
  She's good at using scarves as accessories.

sukai-daibingu スカイダイビング skydiving
- *Sukai-daibingu de chakuchi ni shippai shimashita.*
  I made a poor landing when skydiving.

sukairain スカイライン skyline, mountain highway
- *Yūran basu ga sukairain o yukkuri nobotte ikimasu.*
  A sightseeing bus is slowly going up the mountain highway.

sukarashippu スカラシップ *see* **sukarāshippu**

sukarāshippu スカラーシップ scholarship
- *Kare wa sukarāshippu o ukete Hābādo de benkyō shite imasu.*
  He is studying at Harvard University on a scholarship.

sukāto スカート skirt
- *Sukāto o sukoshi mijikaku shimasu.*
  I'll make my skirts a little shorter.

sukauto スカウト scout; **~suru** する to scout
- *Kare no sokkyū no pitchingu ga sukauto no me ni tomarimashita.*
  His fastball attracted the attention of a scout.
- *Yūnō na enjinia o sannin sukauto shimashita.*
  I scouted for three capable engineers.

sukejūru スケジュール schedule
- *Ryokō no sukejūru o tatete imasu.*
  I am making a schedule for the trip.

sukēru スケール scale
- *Kare wa sukēru no ōkina shigoto o shitagatte imasu.*
  He wants to do large-scale work.

suketchi スケッチ sketch, short piece; **~suru** する to sketch
- *Kore wa sono shijin no shōgai no suketchi desu.*
  This is a short piece about the poet's life.
- *Niwa no hana o suketchi shimashita.*
  I sketched the flowers in the garden.

suketchibukku スケッチブック sketchbook
- *Suketchibukku o motte tabi ni demasu.*
  I'm going to bring my sketchbook on my trip.

sukēto スケート skate
- *Sukēto o naraitai desu.*
  I want to learn how to skate.

sukētobōdo スケートボード skateboard
- *Kare wa sukētobōdo ni notte dokoka e o-tsukai ni ikimashita.*
  He went on an errand somewhere by skateboard.

sukēto rinku スケートリンク [Japanese Usage: skate rink] skating rink
- *Sukēto rinku de nando mo subette korobimashita.*
  I slipped and fell many times at the skating rink.

sukii スキー ski

- *Kare wa mainen fuyu ni naru to sukii ni ikimasu.*
  He goes skiing in winter every year.

sukiiyā スキーヤー skier

- *Sukiiyā no tame ni rinji ressha ga dete imasu.*
  Special trains run for skiers.

sukimu miruku スキムミルク skim milk

- *Maiasa sukimu miruku o ippai nomimasu.*
  I drink a glass of skim milk every morning.

sukin daibingu スキンダイビング skin diving

- *Kaisō o toru tame ni sukin daibingu o shimashita.*
  I went skin diving for seaweed.

sukin kea スキンケア skin care

- *Natsu no sukin kea wa toku ni taisetsu desu.*
  Skin care is especially important in summertime.

sukinshippu スキンシップ [Japanese Usage: skinship]
  physical contact

- *Oyako no aijō o hagukumu tame ni wa sukinshippu ga jūyō desu.*
  Physical contact is important to foster love between parents and children.

sukippu suru スキップする to skip

- *Kono chaputā wa sukippu shimashō.*
  Let's skip this chapter.

sukiru スキル skill

- *Kono shigoto ni wa tokushu na sukiru ga hitsuyō desu.*
  This job requires special skills.

sukoa スコア score

- *Roku tai san no sukoa de shiai ni kachimashita.*
  We won the game with a score of 6 to 3.

sukoā スコアー *see* **sukoa**

sukoppu スコップ [Dutch: *schop*] trowel

- *Sukoppu de jimen o hotte tomato no nae o uemashita.*
  I dug in the ground with a trowel and planted tomato

seedlings.

sukōru スコール squall

- *Sono chihō de tabi tabi sukōru ni mimawaremashita.*
  We were often hit by squalls in that district.

Sukotchi スコッチ Scotch whisky, Scotch tweed

- *Kūkō no menzeiten de Sukotchi o kaimashita.*
  I bought a bottle of Scotch at an airport duty-free shop.

sukūpu スクープ scoop, exclusive news; **~suru** する to scoop

- *Sono zasshi wa sukūpu o nosemashita.*
  That magazine ran a scoop.

sukuramu スクラム scrimmage

- *Kare wa sukuramu o kunda toki ni kossetsu shimashita.*
  He broke a bone in a scrimmage.

sukurappu スクラップ scrap, clippings; **~suru** する to cut out

- *Shinbun ya zasshi no sukurappu ga yamazumi ni natte imasu.*
  The clippings from newspapers and magazines are piled in a giant heap.
- *Omoshiroi kiji wa minna sukurappu shimasu.*
  I cut out all the interesting articles.

sukurappu-bukku スクラップブック scrapbook

- *Kono sukurappu-bukku ni wa kyonen no shinbun kiji ga hatte arimasu.*
  This scrapbook contains last year's newspaper articles.

sukuriin スクリーン screen

- *Naganen sukuriin kara tōzakatte ita joyū ga kamubakku shimashita.*
  The actress made a comeback after many years away from the screen.

sukuriiningu スクリーニング screening; **~suru** する to select

- *gan no sukuriiningu tesuto*
  a test to screen for cancer
- *Ōzei no shigansha no naka kara hitori o sukuriiningu shimasu.*
  Out of many candidates, we'll select one person.

sukuriputo スクリプト script
- *Kare-ra wa sukuriputo o te ni geki no shitageiko o shite imasu.*
  They are rehearsing the play with scripts in hand.

sukūru スクール school
- *Tōkyō ni wa kakushu no sukūru ga misshū shite imasu.*
  All kinds of schools are situated in Tokyo.

sukūtā スクーター scooter
- *Sukāto o haita wakai josei ga sukūtā ni notte iru no o yoku mikakemasu.*
  I often see young women in their skirts riding on scooters.

sukyandarasu スキャンダラス scandalous
- *Kanojo wa sukyandarasu na uwasa ni nayamasarete imasu.*
  She is tormented by a scandalous rumor.

sukyandaru スキャンダル scandal
- *Sono sukyandaru ga kare no seiji seimei o ubaimashita.*
  The scandal terminated his political life.

sukyūba daibingu スキューバダイビング scuba diving
- *Kare wa hima sae areba, sukyūba daibingu ni ikimasu.*
  He goes scuba diving whenever he finds time.

sumasshu スマッシュ smash, smashing; **~suru** する to smash
- *Kanojo wa sumasshu ga umai desu.*
  She has a good smash.
- *Kare wa bōru o sumasshu shite ichi pointo torimashita.*
  He smashed the ball and got one point.

sumāto スマート smart, stylish, slim

- *Kare wa sumāto na fukusō de kimashita.*
  He came in a stylish outfit.
- *Kanojo wa se ga takakute sumāto desu.*
  She is tall and slim.
- *Kare wa shanai de sumāto ni tachimawarimasu.*
  He maneuvers well within the company.

sumoggu スモッグ smog
- *sumoggu ni ōwareta sora*
  sky covered with smog

sumōku suru スモークする to smoke
- *Sake o sumōku shimashita.*
  I smoked a salmon.

sumūsu スムース *see* **sumūzu**

sumūzu スムーズ smooth
- *sumūzu na kōkai*
  a smooth sailing
- *Hikōki wa sumūzu ni ririku shimashita.*
  The airplane took off smoothly.

sunakku スナック [Japanese Usage: snack] bar, snack bar
- *Kinō no yoru jōshi ni sunakku ni tsurete ikarete kyō wa hidoi futsukayoi desu.*
  My boss took me to a bar last night and today I have a terrible hangover.
- *Kondo machikado ni dekita sunakku ni wa kawaii ko ga iru no de chūshoku wa kakasazu soko de torimasu.*
  There's a cute waitress in the snack bar that just opened on the corner, so I have my lunch there without fail.

sunappu スナップ snap, snapshot
- *Pitchā wa sunappu o kikasete bōru o nagemashita.*
  The pitcher threw the ball with a snap of his wrist.
- *Kore wa Kanada de totta sunappu desu.*
  These are the snapshots I took in Canada.

sunappu shotto スナップショット *see* **sunappu**

sūpā スーパー [Japanese Usage] supermarket
- *Sūpā ga dekita tame chikaku no kojin keiei no mise wa tsuburete shimaimashita.*
  Because a supermarket opened, the privately-owned stores nearby have gone out of business.

supagetti スパゲッティ spaghetti
- *Itaria de honba no supagetti o tabemashita.*
  I ate authentic spaghetti in Italy.

supai スパイ spy
- *Kare wa supai no kengi de taiho saremashita.*
  He was arrested on suspicion of being a spy.

supaiku スパイク spike; **~suru** する to spike (volleyball)
- *supaiku o utta kutsu*
  spiked shoes
- *Kare wa janpu shite bōru o supaiku shimashita.*
  He jumped up and spiked the ball.

supaishii スパイシー spicy
- *Supaishii na ryōri wa amari suki ja arimasen.*
  I don't like spicy food very much.

supaisu スパイス spice
- *Daidokoro no tana ni supaisu no bin ga zurari to narande imasu.*
  There is an array of spice bottles on the shelf in the kitchen.

supāku スパーク spark; **~suru** する to spark
- *Kurayami ni supāku ga chirimashita.*
  Sparks shot up in the darkness.
- *Kikai no mōtā ga supāku shite imasu.*
  The machine's motor is sparking.

sūpā māketto スーパーマーケット *see* **sūpā**

sūpāman スーパーマン superman
- *Sūpāman de mo kono shigoto wa hitotsuki de wa konasemasen.*
  Even a superman couldn't do this job in a month.

Suparuta スパルタ Sparta
- *Kare wa katei de Suparuta kyōiku o ukemashita.*
  He received a Spartan education at home.

sūpāsutā スーパースター superstar
- *Mazushii shōjo ga ginmaku no sūpāsutā ni natta no desu.*
  A poor girl has become a superstar of the silver screen.

supea スペア spare
- *Kanojo wa itsumo handobaggu ni kuchibeni no supea o irete imasu.*
  She always has a spare lipstick in her handbag.

supeā スペアー *see* **supea**

Supein スペイン Spain
- *Supein de tōgyū o mimashita.*
  I saw a bullfight in Spain.

supekutakuru スペクタクル spectacle
- *Sono eiga wa masa ni ichidai supekutakuru o tenkai shimashita.*
  The movie certainly portrayed a great spectacle.

superingu スペリング spelling *see* **superu**
- *Kono tango no superingu wa tadashii desu ka?*
  Is the spelling of this word correct?

superu スペル spell
- *Kono pēji ni wa superu no misu ga ōi desu.*
  There are many spelling mistakes on this page.

supesharisuto スペシャリスト specialist
- *Kare wa kokusaihō no supesharisuto desu.*
  He is a specialist in international law.

supesharu スペシャル special
- *Watashi wa tanjōbi ni supesharu dinā o gochisō shite moraimashita ga, sore wa otto no isshūkan bun no kyūryō ni sōtō shimasu.*
  I had a special dinner for my birthday, but it cost my husband a week's pay.

- *Ano ryōtei de supesharu sābisu o ukemashita.*
  We received special service at that Japanese restaurant.

supēsu スペース space, room
- *Kono heya ni wa mō hitotsu tsukue o oku supēsu wa arimasen.*
  There is not enough space to put another desk in this room.

supēsu shatoru スペースシャトル space shuttle
- *Supēsu shatoru wa ninmu o hatashite buji kikan shimashita.*
  The space shuttle returned safely after having accomplished its mission.

supiichi スピーチ speech
- *Sono Amerika-jin no gesuto wa Nihongo de supiichi o shimashita.*
  The American guest made a speech in Japanese.

supiidii スピーディー speedy
- *supiidii na haitatsu*
  a speedy delivery
- *Supiidii ni shigoto o katazukemashita.*
  I finished the work quickly.

supiido スピード speed
- *Kuruma wa kābu de supiido o otoshimashita.*
  The car slowed down around the curve.

supiidoappu スピードアップ speedup; **~suru** する to speed up
- *Dōro kōji no supiidoappu ga tōgi sarete imasu.*
  The speedup of the road construction is being discussed.
- *Kōgyō seisan ga supiidoappu saremashita.*
  Industrial production has been speeded up.

supiikā スピーカー speaker
- *Kono sutereo wa katahō no supiikā ga kowarete iru yō desu.*
  One of the stereo speakers seems to be broken.

supirichuaru スピリチュアル spiritual
- *supirichuaru na seikatsu*
  a spiritual life

supiritto スピリット spirit
- *Kare-ra wa dokuritsu no supiritto ni moete imasu.*
  They are burning with the spirit of independence.

supoiru suru スポイルする to spoil
- *Ano ko wa supoiru sarete imasu.*
  That child is spoiled.
- *Kanojo no negatibu na kangae ga arayuru koto o supoiru shimasu.*
  Her negative thinking spoils everything.

supōkusuman スポークスマン spokesman
- *Kare wa gaimushō no supōkusuman desu.*
  He is a spokesman for the Ministry of Foreign Affairs.

suponji スポンジ sponge
- *Suponji de yuka no yogore o torimasu.*
  I wipe up dirt from the floor with a sponge.

suponsā スポンサー sponsor
- *Kono bangumi ni wa shikkari shita suponsā ga tsuite imasu.*
  This program has a reliable sponsor.

supōti スポーティ sporty
- *supōti na burausu*
  a sporty blouse

supōtii スポーティー *see* **supōti**

supōtsu スポーツ sports
- *Natsu no supōtsu mo fuyu no supōtsu mo suki desu.*
  I like both summer and winter sports.

supōtsuman スポーツマン sportsman
- *Kare wa Amerika no idai na supōtsuman no hitori desu.*
  He is one of the greatest sportsmen in America.

supōtsuman-shippu スポーツマンシップ sportsmanship

- *Kare-ra wa sono shiai de supōtsuman-shippu o jūbun ni hakki shimashita.*
  They fully demonstrated their sportsmanship in the game.

supotto スポット spot

- *Kono hantō ni wa pikunikku ni ii supotto ga takusan arimasu.*
  There are many good spots for picnics on this peninsula.

supottoraito スポットライト spotlight

- *Kanojo wa hinoki butai de supottoraito o abite baiorin o hikimashita.*
  She played the violin in the spotlight on a first-class stage.

sūpu スープ soup

- *Todana ni sūpu no kanzume ga gisshiri tsumatte imasu.*
  The cupboard is tightly packed with canned soup.

supūn スプーン spoon

- *Kodomo-tachi ga purasuchikku no supūn de aisu kuriimu o tabete imasu.*
  Children are eating ice cream with plastic spoons.

supurē スプレー spray

- *Satchūzai o supurē de makimashita.*
  I sprayed with insecticide.

supuringu スプリング spring

- *supuringu no haitta mattoresu*
  a spring mattress

supuringu kōto スプリングコート [Japanese Usage: spring coat] topcoat

- *Kare wa shinchō no supuringu kōto o kite shutchō ni dekakemashita.*
  He set out on a business trip wearing a brand-new topcoat.

supurinkurā スプリンクラー sprinkler

- *Supurinkurā de shibafu ni mizu o makimasu.*
  A sprinkler is used to water the lawn.

suraido スライド slide; **~suru** する to slide

- *Kare wa karā suraido o misenagara setsumei shimashita.*
  He gave an explanation as he showed the color slides.
- *Bukka ni suraido shite chingin ga agarimasu.*
  Wages are rising in line with prices.

suraisu スライス slice; **~suru** する to slice

- *remon no suraisu*
  a slice of lemon
- *Gyūniku o usuku suraisu shimashita.*
  I sliced the beef thin.

surakkusu スラックス slacks

- *Kanojo wa surakkusu o haite niwa shigoto o shite imasu.*
  She is working in the garden wearing slacks.

suramu スラム slum

- *Kare wa repōto o kaku tame ni Nyū-yōku no suramu de seikatsu shimashita.*
  He lived in a New York slum in order to write the report.

surangu スラング slang

- *Kono shōsetsu wa surangu ga ōkute wakarinikui desu.*
  This novel has a lot of slang and is difficult to understand.

suranpu スランプ slump

- *Kanojo wa nagai suranpu kara yatto nukedashimashita.*
  At last she came out of her long slump.

surendā スレンダー slender

- *Wakai josei ni surendā na shiruetto ga konomaremasu.*
  A slender figure is what young women want.

surēto スレート slate

- *surēto no yane*
  a slate roof

surimu スリム slim

- *Kanojo wa surimu na karada o iji suru tame ni biyō taisō o shite imasu.*
  She does calisthenics in order to keep her slim figure.

surimu sukāto スリムスカート slim skirt

- *Surimu sukāto o haku to shōjo wa otonappoku miemasu.*
  The young girl wearing a slim skirt looks like an adult.

surippa スリッパ slippers
- *Kinai de wa surippa ni hakikaemasu.*
  I change into slippers on the airplane.

surippu スリップ slip, underslip; ~**suru** する to slip, skid
- *iroiro na iro no nairon surippu*
  nylon slips in various colors
- *Nureta romen de kuruma ga surippu shimashita.*
  The car slipped on the wet road.

surirā スリラー thriller
- *Osoroshii surirā o mita no de yoru osoku made nemuru koto ga dekimasen deshita.*
  The horrible thriller kept me awake until late at night.

suriringu スリリング thrilling
- *suriringu na bōken*
  a thrilling adventure
- *Suriringu na sono shiai no moyō ga hōsō saremashita.*
  The progress of the thrilling game was broadcast.

suriru スリル thrill
- *Suriru no nai jinsei wa omoshiroku arimasen.*
  Life without thrills isn't fun.

surō スロー slow
- *surō na tenpo*
  slow tempo
- *Kare wa atama no kaiten ga surō desu.*
  He is slow-witted.

surōgan スローガン slogan
- *Kare-ra wa rentai to iu surōgan o kakagete kōshin shimashita.*
  They marched under the slogan of solidarity.

surō mōshon スローモーション slow motion
- *Sono shiin wa surō mōshon de mō ichido utsusaremashita.*

The scene was shot once more in slow motion.

surōpu スロープ slope

- *Sono atari wa yuruyaka na surōpu ni natte imasu.*
  That place has a gentle slope.

sutā スター star

- *Kanojo wa wakai nagara tenisu no sutā ni narimashita.*
  As young as she was, she became a tennis star.

sutādamu スターダム stardom

- *Kanojo wa wazuka ichinen de sutādamu ni noshiagarimashita.*
  She shot to stardom in only one year.

sutaffu スタッフ staff

- *Kono byōin wa yūshū na sutaffu ga sorotte imasu.*
  This hospital has a fine staff.

sutairisuto スタイリスト stylist, dandy

- *Kare wa Nihon no wakate sakka no naka de mo mare na sutairisuto desu.*
  He is a rare stylist among the younger generation of Japanese writers.
- *Sutairisuto no kare wa itsumo ryūkō o otte imasu.*
  Being somewhat of a dandy, he always follows the fashion.
- *Sutairisuto no shigoto wa mikake hodo raku de wa arimasen.*
  Working as a stylist isn't as easy as it looks.

sutairu スタイル style

- *Kono kuruma wa sutairu ga furui desu ne.*
  This car's style is old, isn't it?
- *Hito ni yotte seikatsu no sutairu ga chigaimasu.*
  Lifestyles differ from person to person.

sutairubukku スタイルブック stylebook

- *Dezainā shibō no imōto wa tsune ni nansatsu ka no sutairubukku o mite fasshon o kenkyū shite imasu.*
  My younger sister, who wants to be a designer, is always

looking at several stylebooks to study fashion.

sutajiamu スタジアム stadium
- *Sutajiamu wa ōiri desu.*
There is a very large attendance at the stadium.

sutajio スタジオ studio
- *Terebi no sutajio de nama hōsō o kengaku shimashita.*
We watched a live telecast at the TV studio.

sutamina スタミナ stamina
- *Kanojo wa toshi ga wakai kuse ni, sutamina ga arimasen.*
Although she is young, she lacks stamina.

sutan-bai スタンバイ stand-by; **~suru** する to stand by
- *sutan-bai bangumi*
a stand-by program
- *Keikan ga honsho ni sutan-bai shite imasu.*
Policemen are standing by at the main police station.

sutandādo スタンダード standard
- *sutandādo na kata*
standard type
- *Seikatsu no sutandādo ga agarimashita.*
The standard of living went up.

sutando スタンド stand, stands, small lamp
- *Sutando ga keshite arimasu.*
The desk lamp is off.
- *Man'in no sutando de kesshōsen o mimashita.*
We watched the final game in the crowded stands.

sutando-bai スタンドバイ *see* **sutan-bai**

sutando-in スタンドイン stand-in; **~suru** する to stand in
- *Kare wa sutā no sutando-in desu.*
He is a stand-in for the star.
- *Wakai sopurano ga byōki no riido no sutando-in o shimashita.*
A young soprano stood in for the ailing lead.

sutandopurē スタンドプレー [Japanese Usage: stand play]

grandstand play, showing off

- *Kankyaku wa senshu no sutandopurē ni seien o okurimashita.*
  The audience cheered when the players showed off.
- *Kare no sutandopurē ni wa minna hekieki shite imasu.*
  Everybody is fed up with his hot dogging.

sutanpu スタンプ stamp, datemark, postmark

- *Gojukko sutanpu o atsumeru to sen-en no waribiki ga arimasu.*
  If you collect 50 stamps you get a ¥1,000 discount.
- *Kono fūtō no sutanpu wa hakkiri shite imasen.*
  The postmark on this envelope isn't clear.

sutantoman スタントマン stuntman

- *Sono sutantoman wa kakutō no bamen de gake kara ochita no desu.*
  The stuntman fell off the cliff during the fight scene.

sutāto スタート start; **~suru** する to start

- *Kōshō wa sutāto kara kaichō ni susumimashita.*
  The negotiation progressed smoothly from the start.
- *Atarashii karikyuramu wa raigetsu kara sutāto shimasu.*
  The new curriculum will start next month.

sutedii ステディー steady

- *Kono mise wa sutedii na o-kyaku de motte imasu.*
  This store is supported by steady customers.
- *Kare ni wa ima tsukiatte iru sutedii ga iru sō desu.*
  I heard he has a steady girlfriend now.

sutēji ステージ stage

- *Kanojo wa sutēji ni tatsu hi o yumemite imasu.*
  She is dreaming of the day when she performs on the stage.
- *Kōshō wa saishū sutēji ni hairimashita.*
  We entered the final stage of the negotiations.

sutēki ステーキ steak

- *Kono sutēki wa katakute taberaremasen.*

This steak is too tough to eat.

sutekkā ステッカー sticker
- *Kuruma no banpā ni sutekkā ga hatte arimasu.*
 A sticker is pasted on the car's bumper.

sutekki ステッキ stick, cane
- *Rō-shinshi ga sutekki o tsuite aruite imasu.*
 An old gentleman is walking with a cane.

sutendogurasu ステンドグラス stained glass
- *kyōkai no sutendogurasu no mado*
 a stained glass window of a church.

sutenresu ステンレス stainless steel
- *sutenresu no daidokoro yōhin*
 stainless steel kitchen utensils

suteppu ステップ step
- *warutsu no suteppu*
 waltz steps
- *Kaidan no suteppu o fumihazushimashita.*
 I missed a step on the stairs.
- *Kono jiken wa kakumei e no hitotsu no suteppu desu.*
 This incident is one step toward a revolution.

suteppu-appu suru ステップアップする to step up, be promoted
- *Kanojo wa tenchō ni suteppu-appu shimashita.*
 She was promoted to head of the store.

sutereo ステレオ stereo
- *Sutereo de ongaku o kikimasu.*
 I listen to music on a stereo.

sutēshon ステーション station
- *modan na chikatetsu no sutēshon*
 a modern subway station

sutētasu ステータス status
- *Watashi to kare to de wa shakaiteki na sutētasu ga chigaimasu.*

I differ from him in social status.

sutētomento ステートメント statement
- *Daitōryō wa kisha kaiken de sutētomento o happyō shimashita.*
  The President made a statement at the press conference.

sutiimu スティーム *see* **suchiimu**

sutiru スティル *see* **suchiiru** (*still*)

suto スト *see* **sutoraiki**

sutoa ストア store
- *Ano kado no sutoa ni yorimashō.*
  Let's stop by the store on that corner.

sutoā ストアー *see* **sutoa**

sutōbu ストーブ stove, space heater
- *Kono heya de wa denki sutōbu o tsukatte imasu.*
  We use an electric space heater in this room.

sutokkingu ストッキング stockings
- *densen shinai sutokkingu*
  run-proof stockings

sutokku ストック stock, securities
- *Sono seihin wa genzai sutokku ga arimasen.*
  We're out of stock for that product at present.
- *Sutokku wa agarigimi desu.*
  Stocks are going up.

sutoppu ストップ stop; **~suru** する to stop
- *Sono kabu no baibai ni sutoppu ga kakarimashita.*
  The trading of that stock came to a stop.
- *Sono kabu wa sutoppu daka ni narimashita.*
  The stock's price went up to its limit.
- *Kuruma ga genkan no mae de sutoppu shimashita.*
  A car stopped in front of the entrance.

sutoppu-uotchi ストップウオッチ stopwatch
- *Kōchi ga sutoppu-uotchi o oshimashita.*
  The coach started the stopwatch.

sutoppuwotchi ストップウォッチ *see* **sutoppu-uotchi**

sutoraiki ストライキ strike
- *Gozen hachiji ni zen'in ga sutoraiki ni hairimashita.*
  All the workers went on strike at 8:00 A.M.

sutoraiku ストライク strike
- *Ima no wa sutoraiku desu ka bōru desu ka?*
  Was that a strike or a ball?

sutorakuchā ストラクチャー structure
- *Nihon no sangyō sutorakuchā*
  Japan's industrial structure

sutorakuchua ストラクチュア *see* **sutorakuchā**

sutorenjā ストレンジャー stranger
- *Sannen buri ni atta kare wa marude sutorenjā no yō deshita.*
  I hadn't seen him for three years and he seemed like a total stranger.
- *Gaikoku de watashi no shūi wa sutorenjā bakari deshita.*
  Overseas I was surrounded by nothing but strangers.

sutoresu ストレス stress
- *Sutoresu no nai seikatsu ga nozomashii desu.*
  A life without stress is desirable.

sutoretchi ストレッチ stretch
- *sutoretchi sei no aru kiji*
  elastic material
- *Maiasa shokuzen ni sutoretchi taisō o shimasu.*
  Every morning before eating I stretch out.

sutorēto ストレート straight
- *Kare wa itsumo sutorēto ni kotaemasu.*
  He always gives straight answers.
- *Kare wa uisukii o sutorēto de nomimasu.*
  He drinks straight whisky.
- *Kare wa sutorēto de gōkaku shimashita.*
  He passed the examination the first time.

- *Kare wa tenisu tōnamento de sutorēto gachi shimashita.*
  He won the tennis tournament in straight sets.

sutōrii ストーリー story, plot
- *Kanojo wa kodomo muke no sutōrii o kaite imasu.*
  She is writing children's stories.
- *Sono eiga no sutōrii wa totemo shinpuru desu.*
  The movie's plot is very simple.

sutorō ストロー straw
- *Kodomo ga sutorō o omocha ni shinagara jūsu o nonde imasu.*
  A child is drinking juice and playing with the straw.

sutorōku ストローク stroke
- *Sono suiei senshu wa wan sutorōku sa de makemashita.*
  The swimmer lost by one stroke.

sūtsu スーツ suit
- *junpaku no samā sūtsu*
  a pure white summer suit

sūtsu kēsu スーツケース suitcase
- *Ryokō ni wa karui sūtsu kēsu o motteikimasu.*
  I take a light suitcase on trips.

suwiito スウィート *see* **suiito**
suwingu suru スウィングする *see* **suingu suru**
suwitchi スウィッチ *see* **suitchi**

T

T-shatsu Tシャツ see **tii-shatsu**
tāban ターバン turban
- *tāban o maita Indo-jin*
  an Indian wearing a turban
tabū タブー taboo
- *Koko de wa jiinzu wa tabū ni natte imasu.*

Jeans are taboo here.

taburoido タブロイド tabloid

- *Sono shūkanshi wa taburoido ban de dete imasu.*
  The weekly magazine is published in tabloid form.

tafu タフ tough

- *tafu na hito*
  a tough person

tāgetto ターゲット target

- *Kongetsu no uriagedaka wa mada tāgetto ni tasshite imasen.*
  This month's sales haven't reached the target yet.

- *gakusei o tāgetto ni shita zasshi*
  a student-oriented magazine

Tai タイ Thailand

- *Tai ni dono kurai taizai suru yotei desu ka?*
  How long do you plan to stay in Thailand?

tai タイ tie, necktie

- *Junkesshōsen wa tai ni owarimashita.*
  The semifinal game ended in a tie.

- *Kare wa hosoi tai o shimete imasu.*
  He is wearing a narrow tie.

taia タイア *see* **taiya**

tai-appu タイアップ tie-up; **~suru** する to tie up

- *seitō to no tai-appu*
  a tie-up with political parties

- *Gaikoku no kaisha to tai-appu shite kono jigyō o okonaimasu.*
  We'll get together with a foreign firm to carry out this operation.

taimā タイマー timer

- *Suihanki no taimā o irete okimashita.*
  I set the timer on the rice cooker.

taimingu タイミング timing

- *Sono hon no shuppan wa taimingu ga yokatta desu.*
  The publication of the book was well-timed.

taimu タイム time
- *Kare wa marason de besuto taimu o dashimashita.*
  He made his best time in a marathon.

taimu appu タイムアップ time's up
- *Taimu appu de shiai shūryō ni narimashita.*
  Time's up and the game's over.

taimu kādo タイムカード time card
- *Shukkin suru to, taimu kādo o osu koto ni natte imasu.*
  You are required to punch a time card when you come to work.

taimu kapuseru タイムカプセル time capsule
- *Mirai no hito no tame ni taimu kapuseru ni gendai no kiroku o tsumemasu.*
  We put records of the current day in a time capsule for future generations.

taimu mashiin タイムマシーン time machine
- *Taimu mashiin wa kako no sekai e mo mirai no sekai e mo tsurete itte kuremasu.*
  A time machine will take you to the worlds of both the past and future.

taimurii タイムリー timely
- *taimurii na hatsugen*
  a timely remark

taimurii hitto タイムリーヒット timely hit
- *Taimurii hitto de santen iremashita.*
  They scored three runs with a timely hit.

taimu rimitto タイムリミット time limit, deadline
- *Kono genkō no taimu rimitto wa raigetsu no sue desu.*
  The deadline for this manuscript is the end of next month.

taimutēburu タイムテーブル timetable
- *ressha no taimutēburu*

a train timetable

taipisuto タイピスト typist

* *Kanojo wa taipisuto kara konpyūtā no operetā ni shigoto o kaemashita.*
She changed her job from a typist to a computer operator.

taipu タイプ type *see* **taipuraitā**

* *taipu ni utta tegami*
a typed letter
* *Kare wa watashi no suki na taipu de wa arimasen.*
He is not my type.

taipuraitā タイプライター typewriter

* *taipuraitā de kaita repōto*
a typewritten report

taito タイト tight

* *taito sukāto*
a tight skirt
* *Taito na sukejūru de maitte imasu.*
The tight schedule gets to me.

taitoru タイトル title

* *hon no taitoru*
a book title

taitoru matchi タイトルマッチ title match

* *Kare wa taitoru matchi de yaburemashita.*
He was defeated in the title match.

taitsu タイツ tights

* *Taitsu o haite undō o shimasu.*
I exercise in tights.

taiya タイヤ tire

* *Kuruma no taiya ga surihette imasu.*
The car's tires are worn out.

takishiido タキシード tuxedo

* *Takishiido o kita hito ga hoteru no robii o ittari kitari shite imasu.*

Men in tuxedos are coming in and out of the hotel lobby.

takkusu タックス tax
- *Kono shinamono wa takkusu ga kakarimasu.*
  This article is taxed.

takkusu-furii タックスフリー tax-free
- *Ano mise de wa takkusu-furii de kaemasu.*
  You can buy it tax-free at that store.

takushii タクシー taxi
- *Biru no mae de takushii o hiroimashita.*
  I got a taxi in front of the building.

takuto タクト [German: *Takt*] baton, supervision, tempo
- *Ōkesutora wa Ozawa Seiji no takuto de ensō shimashita.*
  The orchestra performed under the baton of Seiji Ozawa.
- *Kare wa sono purojekuto de migoto ni takuto o furuimashita.*
  He directed the project skillfully.

tāminaru ターミナル terminal
- *San'yō Shinkansen wa Hakata ga tāminaru desu.*
  The San'yo bullet train line terminates at Hakata.
- *tāminaru kanja*
  a terminal patient

tān suru ターンする to turn
- *Ano kado de migi ni tān shite kudasai.*
  Please turn right at that corner.

tango タンゴ tango
- *Kare-ra wa jōnetsuteki ni tango o odorimashita.*
  They danced the tango passionately.

tankā タンカー tanker
- *Tankā ga anshō ni noriagete oiru ga umi ni ryūshutsu shimashita.*
  The tanker struck a rock and leaked oil into the ocean.

tanku タンク tank
- *Kōjō no soba ni gasu tanku ga arimasu.*

There is a gas tank near the factory.

taoru タオル towel
- *Pēpā taoru de te o fukimasu.*
  I dry my hands with a paper towel.

tapesutorii タペストリー tapestry
- *kikagaku moyō no tapesutorii*
  a geometrically patterned tapestry

tapisutorii タピストリー *see* **tapesutorii**

tappu dansu タップダンス tap dance
- *Kodomo ga terebi de mita tappu dansu no mane o shimasu.*
  The children are copying the tap dancing they saw on TV.

tarappu タラップ [Dutch: *trap*] ramp
- *Kare wa furasshu o abinagara tarappu o orite kimashita.*
  He came down the ramp in a flood of flashlights.

tarento タレント talent, talented person, TV personality
- *Kare wa saikin sukauto sareta terebi tarento desu.*
  He is a newly discovered TV personality.
- *Kanojo no tarento wa hiroku mitomerarete imasu.*
  Her talent is widely recognized.

tatchi タッチ touch; **~suru** する to touch
- *Sono pianisuto wa sensai na tatchi de shirarete imasu.*
  The pianist is well-known for his delicate touch.
- *Ima wa sono mondai ni tatchi shinai hō ga ii deshō.*
  We'd better not touch that subject now.

taun-uea タウンウエア townwear
- *Sono zasshi no gogatsu-gō ni suteki na taun-uea ga takusan dete imasu.*
  The magazine's May issue carries a lot of stylish townwear.

tawā タワー tower
- *Tōkyō-tawā wa Efferu-tō no kopii desu.*
  Tokyo Tower is a copy of the Eiffel Tower.

tēburu テーブル table

* *Marui tēburu o kakonde kandan shimashita.*
Sitting around the round table, we had a pleasant talk.

tēburu kurosu　テーブルクロス　table cloth
* *aka to shiro no chekku no tēburu kurosu*
a table cloth with a red and white checkered pattern

tēburu manā　テーブルマナー　table manners
* *Pari yuki no jetto-ki no naka de tēburu manā no hon o yomimashita.*
I read a book on table manners on the jet bound for Paris.

tēburu supiichi　テーブルスピーチ　[Japanese Usage: table speech] after-dinner speech
* *Kare wa shachō no tame ni tēburu supiichi o kaite imasu.*
He is writing an after-dinner speech for his company president.

teikuauto　テイクアウト　takeout
* *Ano resutoran wa teikuauto mo dekimasu.*
You can also order takeout from that restaurant.

teisuto　テイスト　*see* **tēsuto**

tekisuto　テキスト　text, textbook
* *Kore wa Honda-kyōju no kōen no tekisuto desu.*
This is the text of Professor Honda's lecture.
* *chūkyū Nihongo no tekisuto*
an intermediate-level Japanese textbook

tekisutobukku　テキストブック　*see* **tekisuto**

tēkuauto　テークアウト　*see* **teikuauto**

tekunikaru　テクニカル　technical
* *tekunikaru na shidō*
technical guidance
* *Tekunikaru na mondai ga mada nokotte imasu.*
Technical problems still remain to be solved.

tekunikaru direkutā　テクニカルディレクター　technical director
* *Atarashii tekunikaru direkutā wa sutaffu to shikkuri itte*

inai yō desu.

The new technical director doesn't seem to get along well with his staff.

tekunikku テクニック technique

- *Sono kikai no sōsa ni wa kōdo na tekunikku ga hitsuyō desu.*

You need good technique to operate that machine.

tekunishan テクニシャン technician

- *Kono kōjō de wa tekunishan ga shinnyū-shain ni atarashii gijutsu o oshiemasu.*

In this factory, technicians teach new skills to the new employees.

- *Kare wa sugureta tekunishan desu ga dokusōsei wa arimasen.*

He is a fine technician but he isn't creative.

tekunorojii テクノロジー technology

- *Konseiki no tekunorojii no hatten wa kyōiteki desu.*

The development of technology in this century is a wonder.

tekusuto テクスト *see* **tekisuto**

tēma テーマ [German: *Thema*] theme, subject matter

- *Sono shōsetsu wa dō iu tēma desu ka?*

What's the theme of the novel?

tēma songu テーマソング [Japanese Usage: G. *Thema* + Eng. song] theme song

- *Orinpikku no tēma songu*

a theme song for the Olympics

tenā テナー tenor

- *Sono tenā wa meisei no zetchō ni tatte imasu.*

The tenor is at the climax of his fame.

- *Kare wa sekai no sandai tenā no hitori desu.*

He is one of the best three tenors in the world.

tenanto テナント tenant

- *Ano biru de wa tenanto o boshū shite imasu.*

They're looking for tenants for that building.

- *Kono biru no chika ni tenanto to shite bā ga kaiten shimasu.*

A bar will open as a new tenant in the basement of this building.

tendāroin テンダーロイン tenderloin

- *Tendāroin nara ha no warui hito de mo taberareru deshō.*

Even those who have bad teeth can eat tenderloin.

tenisu テニス tennis

- *Tenisu wa hajimeta bakari desu.*

I've just started to play tennis.

tenisu kōto テニスコート tennis court

- *Kōen no tenisu kōto de yarimashō.*

Let's play at the tennis court in the park.

tenōru テノール *see* **tenā**

tenpo テンポ [Italian: *tempo*] speed

- *Hayai tempo de bukka ga agatte imasu.*

Prices are going up in quick leaps.

tenshon テンション tension

- *Kokusaikan no tenshon ga sukoshi yurumarimashita.*

International tensions have eased a little.

- *Kare wa tenshon no takai shigoto no tame ni taoreta no desu.*

He collapsed because of work-related tension.

tento テント tent

- *Kyanpu ni iku toki, tento o motte ikimasu.*

We'll take a tent when we go camping.

tēpu テープ tape

- *Tēpu ni jibun no uta o fukikomimasu.*

I put my singing on tape.

- *Sono shikiten de shichō ga tēpukatto o shimashita.*

The mayor cut the tape in the ceremony.

tēpurekōdā テープレコーダー tape recorder

- *Tēpurekōdā de sono kōen o rokuon shimashita.*
  I recorded the lecture on a tape recorder.

terasu テラス terrace
- *Yachō ga terasu ni pan kuzu o tsuibami ni kimasu.*
  Wild birds come to the terrace to pick up crumbs of bread.

terebi テレビ television
- *Sono heya ni nijū inchi terebi ga oite arimasu.*
  There is a TV set with a 20-inch-wide screen in that room.

terebijon テレビジョン *see* **terebi**

terehon kādo テレホンカード telephone card
- *Sono koshū denwa wa terehon kādo ga tsukaemasu ka?*
  Can I use a telephone card in that public phone?

terekkusu テレックス telex
- *Ima Rondon kara terekkusu de kono jōhō ga hairimashita.*
  This information just came in from London by telex.

terepashii テレパシー telepathy
- *Futari wa fushigi na chikara no terepashii de kokoro ga tsūjiatta no desu.*
  Those two communicated telepathically.

teritorii テリトリー territory, jurisdiction, turf
- *Kono mondai wa kagaku no teritorii o koete imasu.*
  This subject goes outside the realm of science.
- *Sono shigoto wa watashi no teritorii de wa arimasen.*
  That job does not fall within my territory.

tero テロ terrorism
- *tero ni yoru shakai-fuan*
  social unrest due to terrorism

terorisuto テロリスト terrorist
- *Sono kōjō no bakuha wa terorisuto no shiwaza desu.*
  The bombing of the plant is an act of terrorists.

terorizumu テロリズム *see* **tero**

tēruraito テールライト taillight, taillamp
- *Mae no kuruma no tēruraito ga yogiri ni kasunde*

miemasu.
The car taillights in front of us look dim in the night fog.
tesuto テスト test; **~suru** する to test, examine
- *Tesuto ni gōkaku shimashita.*
  I passed the test.
- *Wakai joshu ga shiryoku o tesuto shimashita.*
  A young assistant tested my eyesight.
tēsuto テースト taste
- *Kanojo wa interia no tēsuto ga ii desu.*
  She has good taste in interior decoration.
tiin-eijā ティーンエイジャー *see* **tiin-ējā**
tiin-ējā ティーンエージャー teenager
- *tiin-ējā no romansu to nayami no sutōrii*
  a story of a teenager's romance and anguish
tipikaru ティピカル typical
- *tipikaru na jitsurei*
  a typical example
tii-shatsu ティーシャツ or Tシャツ T-shirt
- *Kare wa ryokōsaki de tii-shatsu o kaimashita.*
  He bought T-shirts in the places he traveled to.
tisshu pēpā ティッシュペーパー tissue paper
- *Watashi wa Shibuya de tisshu pēpā o kubaru shigoto o mitsukemashita.*
  I got a job handing out packs of tissue paper in Shibuya.
toire トイレ toilet, restroom
- *Kono depāto no kakukai ni toire ga arimasu.*
  There are restrooms on every floor of this department store.
toiretto トイレット *see* **toire**
tōku トーク talk
- *tōku to uta de moridakusan na bangumi*
  a colorful program with discussion and songs
tōku shō トークショー talk show
- *Sono tōku shō wa totemo shichō ritsu ga takai desu.*

The talk show has a very high audience rating.

tomato トマト tomato
- *Kono tomato wa toritate desu.*

These tomatoes are fresh from the field.

tomato kechappu トマトケチャップ tomato ketchup
- *Hanbāgā ni tomato kechappu o tsukete tabemasu.*

I eat hamburgers with tomato ketchup.

tōn トーン tone, atmosphere
- *Kare-ra wa hisuterikku na tōn de hantai o tonaemashita.*

They made their objections in a hysterical tone.
- *Ryōkoku no kōshō no tōn wa nagoyaka ni narimashita.*

The tone of the negotiations between the two countries has become amiable.

tōndaun suru トーンダウンする to tone down
- *Aite wa saisho no tsuyoi shuchō o tōndaun sasete kimashita.*

They have toned down their initial strong assertion.

tōnamento トーナメント tournament
- *Kanojo wa tenisu tōnamento de yūshō shimashita.*

She took first place in the tennis tournament.

tonneru トンネル tunnel
- *sekai de ichiban nagai kaitei tonneru*

the longest undersea tunnel in the world

topāzu トパーズ topaz
- *burū no topāzu no yubiwa*

a blue topaz ring

topikku トピック topic
- *Kare wa kyū ni topikku o kaemashita.*

He suddenly changed the topic of conversation.

toppu トップ top
- *Suiri shōsetsu sakka de wa izen to shite kare ga toppu desu.*

He is still the top author of mystery novels.

toppu kurasu トップクラス top class, leading
- *Kanojo wa toppu kurasu no fasshon moderu desu.*
  She is a leading fashion model.

toppu manējimento トップマネージメント top management
- *Toppu manējimento ni jinji-idō ga aru to ka kikimashita.*
  I heard that there might be personnel changes in top management.

toppu nyūsu トップニュース top news
- *Sono kaisha no tōsan wa keizai men no toppu nyūsu deshita.*
  The firm's bankruptcy made top news on the financial page.

toppu reberu トップレベル top level
- *Kanojo wa kigyō no toppu reberu de katsuyaku suru josei no hitori desu.*
  She is one of the women who take an active part at the top level of industry.

torabaiyu トラバイユ *see* **torabāyu**

torabāsu suru トラバースする to traverse
- *Sukiiyā ga shiroi shamen o torabāsu shite imasu.*
  Skiers are traversing the white slope.

torabāyu トラバーユ [French: *travail*] change of job;
~suru する to change jobs
- *Kanojo no totsuzen no torabāyu ni odorokimashita.*
  I was surprised at her sudden change of jobs.
- *Kare wa kyōshi kara jānarisuto ni torabāyu shimashita.*
  He gave up teaching to become a journalist.

toraberāzu chekku トラベラーズチェック traveler's check
- *Kaigai-ryokō ni wa toraberāzu chekku ga benri de anzen desu.*
  When traveling abroad, traveler's checks are convenient and safe.

toraberu トラベル travel

- *toraberu yō eikaiwa no hon*
  an English conversation phrasebook for travel

toraberu uotchi トラベルウオッチ [Japanese Usage: travel watch] travel alarm clock
- *Ryokō no toki toraberu uotchi o motte ikimasu.*
  I take a travel alarm clock when traveling.

toraburu トラブル trouble
- *Shanai de toraburu ga taemasen.*
  There is constant trouble in the company.

toraburu-mēkā トラブルメーカー troublemaker
- *Kanojo wa zaishokuchū toraburu-mēkā de tōtte imashita.*
  She was known as a troublemaker in the office.

toraddo トラッド [Japanese Usage or British English: trad] traditional
- *Kanojo wa tsune ni shinpuru de toraddo na mono o kite imasu.*
  She always wears simple, traditional clothes.

toradishonaru トラディショナル traditional
- *toradishonaru na gishiki*
  a traditional ceremony

torai トライ try; **~suru** する to try
- *Sono ragubii no shiai wa torai de tokuten shimashita.*
  They scored a try in the rugby game.
- *Gaikoku no ryōri o iroiro torai shite mimasu.*
  I try many types of foreign dishes.

toraianguru トライアングル triangle
- *toraianguru no katachi*
  a triangular shape
- *Sono kyoku de wa toraianguru ga kōkateki ni tsukawarete imasu.*
  The triangle is used effectively in that music.
- *danjo no toraianguru na kankei o atsukatta eiga*
  a movie about love triangles

torakku トラック track
- *Kare wa torakku kyōgi no sōsha desu.*
  He is a track runner.

torakku トラック truck
- *torakku no untenshu*
  a truck driver

torakuta トラクタ *see* **torakutā**

torakutā トラクター tractor
- *Dono nōka mo torakutā o motte imasu.*
  Every farmstead owns a tractor.

toranjisuta トランジスタ *see* **toranjisutā**

toranjisutā トランジスター transistor
- *Rajio de mo tēpurekōdā de mo nan de mo toranjisutā-ka sarete iru sō desu.*
  It seems radios, tape recorders, and just about everything else are transistorized.

torankiraizā トランキライザー tranquilizer
- *Torankiraizā ga kanojo no shiin datta sō desu.*
  I hear that tranquilizers were the cause of her death.
- *Karui undō ga ii torankiraizā ni narimasu.*
  Light exercise is a good tranquilizer.

toranku トランク trunk
- *ryokō yō no toranku*
  a trunk for traveling
- *Kuruma no toranku ni tenisu shūzu o irete imasu.*
  I keep my tennis shoes in the trunk of my car.

toranku rūmu トランクルーム [Japanese Usage: trunk room] storage room
- *Kazaidōgu o toranku rūmu ni azukemashita.*
  I put my household goods in the storage room.

toranpetto トランペット trumpet
- *Musuko wa gakkō no bando de toranpetto o fuite imasu.*
  My son plays a trumpet in his school band.

toranpu トランプ playing cards
- *Toranpu de katta koto ga arimasen.*
  I have never won at cards.

toranshiibā トランシーバー transceiver
- *Kōjō kara toranshiibā de tsūwa ga dekimasu.*
  You can speak by transceiver from the factory.

toransufā suru トランスファーする to transfer
- *Kono kōza o Tōkyō ten ni toransufā shite kudasai.*
  Please transfer this account to the Tokyo branch.

toransumisshon トランスミッション transmission
- *Kono kuruma no toransumisshon ni toraburu ga arimasu.*
  This car has transmission trouble.

torēdo トレード trade; **~suru** する to trade
- *Yakyū senshu no torēdo wa yoku okonawaremasu.*
  Trading of baseball players is a common practice.
- *Kono kuruma o utte shinsha to torēdo shimasu.*
  I am trading this car in for a new one.

torēdomāku トレードマーク trademark
- *Sono depāto wa torēdomāku o kaemashita.*
  The department store changed its trademark.
- *Ryōte-uchi bakkuhando wa Kurisu Ebāto no torēdomāku deshita.*
  Chris Evert's trademark was a double-handed backhand.

torēnā トレーナー trainer, sweat shirt
- *Kare wa naganen uma no torēnā o yatte imasu.*
  He has been a horse trainer for many years.
- *torēnā sugata no wakai senshu*
  young players in their sweat shirts

torendi トレンディ *see* **torendii**

torendii トレンディー trendy, fashionable, in current vogue
- *torendii na kawa no jaketto*
  a trendy leather jacket
- *Torendii na kankei o egaita rabu sutōrii ga on ea*

saremasu.
A love story that depicts a modern relationship will be televised.

torenchi kōto トレンチコート trench coat
* *Kare wa torenchi kōto o kite sukuriin ni tōjō suru meitantei yaku desu.*
He plays the role of the noted detective who appears in the movies in a trench coat.

torendo トレンド trend
* *Shijō no torendo o mikiwamete tōshi shimasu.*
I check the market trend in investments.

torēningu トレーニング training
* *Shinnyū no kōin wa kōjō de tokubetsu na torēningu o ukete imasu.*
New workers are receiving special training at the plant.

torēningu pantsu トレーニングパンツ *see* **torepan**

torepan トレパン [Japanese Usage] training pants, sweat pants
* *Senshu ga torepan de renshū o shite imasu.*
The players are practicing in their sweat pants.

torērā トレーラー trailer
* *Torērā de nimotsu o unpan shimasu.*
We'll transport the luggage by trailer.

torērā hausu トレーラーハウス [Japanese Usage: trailer house] trailer, mobile home
* *Saikin torērā hausu ga zenkokuteki ni yoku urete imasu.*
Lately trailers homes have been selling well all over the country.

torigā トリガー trigger
* *Kūdetā ga kakumei no torigā ni narimashita.*
The coup d'etat became a trigger for the revolution.

torikku トリック trick
* *Komāsharu ni torikku shashin o tsukaimasu.*

Trick photography is used in commercials.

torio トリオ trio
- *Sono dansei shingā no torio wa kitai-hazure deshita.*
  The male singing trio did not meet my expectations.

torōchi トローチ troche, lozenge
- *Nodo ga itai no de tōrochi o kuchi ni fukunde imasu.*
  I put a lozenge in my mouth because I have a sore throat.

torofii トロフィー trophy
- *Ashita no shiai de wa torofii o morau jishin ga arimasu.*
  I am confident that I will win a trophy in tomorrow's game.

toropikaru karā トロピカルカラー tropical color
- *toropikaru karā de matometa interia*
  an interior harmonized with tropical colors

tosu トス toss, tossing; **~suru** する to toss
- *Kanojo wa barēbōru de umai tosu o agemashita.*
  She made a fine toss in the volleyball game.
- *Koin o tosu shite senkō o kimemasu.*
  We'll toss a coin to decide which team goes first.

tōsutā トースター toaster
- *Kono tōsutā wa mada tsukaemasu yo.*
  This toaster is still working.

tōsuto トースト toast
- *Tōsuto ni jamu o nurimasu.*
  I'll spread jam on the toast.

tōtaru トータル total, whole
- *Tōtaru de ikura desu ka?*
  How much is it in total?
- *tōtaru na mondai*
  an overall problem
- *Tōtaru ni mite kono teian wa amari kinori shimasen.*
  On the whole I'm not very interested in this proposal.
- *Motto tōtaru na mikata o shinai to mondai no honshitsu wa miete kimasen.*

We won't be able to see the essence of the problem without a bigger perspective.

tsuā ツアー tour
- *Kono tsuā wa higaeri desu.*
This is a day's tour.

tsuā kondakutā ツアーコンダクター tour conductor
- *Tsuā kondakutā ga subete o-sewa itashimasu.*
The tour conductor will take care of everything.

tsuin rūmu ツインルーム twin room
- *Sankan no hoteru no hiroi tsuin rūmu de isshūkan sugoshimashita.*
I spent a week in a spacious twin room in a mountain hotel.

tsuisuto ツイスト twist
- *Sanjūnen mae tsuisuto ga ryūkō shimashita.*
The twist was a popular dance thirty years ago.

tsū-piisu ツーピース two-piece
- *Wan-piisu yori tsū-piisu no hō ga suki desu.*
I prefer two-piece to one-piece dresses.

tsūringu ツーリング touring
- *Ano wakai futarizure wa ōtobai ni ainori shite tsūringu ni ikimashita.*
That young couple went touring on a motorcycle together.

tsūrisuto ツーリスト tourist
- *Gaikoku-jin tsūrisuto ga mori no naka de mayoimashita.*
The foreign tourists got lost in the forest.

tsūru ツール tool
- *Denshi techō wa jōhō tsūru desu.*
A pocket electronic diary is an information tool.

tsū-ton ツートン *see* **tsū-ton karā**

tsū-ton karā ツートンカラー [Japanese Usage: two-tone color] two-tone
- *Kondo wa tsū-ton karā no kuruma ga hoshii desu.*
I want a two-tone car next time.

tsū-wē ツーウェー two-way
- *Kore wa beruto o tsukete mo totte mo tsū-wē ni tsukaemasu.*
  You can use this two ways: with or without a belt.

tū-wē トゥーウェー *see* **tsū-wē**

tyūba テューバ tuba
- *Tyūba wa ichiban hikui oto o dasu kinkan gakki desu.*
  The tuba is the brass instrument which produces the lowest sound.

U

U kā Uカー *see* **yū-kā**

U-tān Uターン *see* **yū-tān**

uddo ウッド wood, golf club
- *Gorufu kyō no chichi wa nanbon mo uddo o motte imasu.*
  My father, a golf maniac, owns many woods.

uddo bēsu ウッドベース [Japanese Usage: wood base] acoustic bass
- *Kare wa jazu torio de uddo bēsu o hiite imasu.*
  He plays acoustic bass in a jazz trio.

uea ウエア [Japanese Usage: wear] clothes
- *kagaku sen'i no uea*
  clothing made from synthetic fibers

uēbu ウエーブ wave
- *Kanojo no kami ni wa utsukushii uēbu ga kakatte imasu.*
  She has beautiful waves in her hair.

uedingu ウエディング wedding
- *Kare-ra wa kohan no kyōkai de kossori uedingu o agemashita.*
  They had a quiet wedding in a lakeside church.

uedingu doresu ウエディングドレス wedding dress

- *Uedingu doresu o kita kanojo wa totemo utsukushii desu.*
  She looks very beautiful in her wedding dress.

uehāsu ウエハース wafers
- *Aisu kuriimu ni uehāsu o soete dashimashita.*
  I served ice cream with wafers.

ueito ウエイト *see* **uēto**

uesutan ウエスタン Western (movie, music)
- *Yoru osoku terebi de mukashi no uesutan o mimashita.*
  I watched an old Western late at night.

uesuto ウエスト waist
- *Kanojo wa aikawarazu uesuto ga hossori shite imasu.*
  Her waist is as slim as ever.

Uesuto-kōsuto ウエストコースト West Coast
- *Amerika no Uesuto-kōsuto wa fūkō no bi o motte shirarete imasu.*
  The West Coast of America is noted for its scenic beauty.

uētā ウエーター waiter
- *Kare wa uētā o shinagara resutoran no keiei o manande imasu.*
  He is learning restaurant management while working as a waiter.

uēto ウエート weight, importance
- *Kare wa uēto o herasō to shite imasu.*
  He is trying to reduce his weight.
- *Kare wa kōsai ni ōki na uēto o oite imasu.*
  He attaches great importance to friendship.

uētoresu ウエートレス waitress
- *Kanojo wa kōkō o chūtai shite uētoresu ni narimashita.*
  She dropped out of high school and became a waitress.

uetto ウエット [Japanese Usage: wet] sentimental
- *uetto na hito*
  a sentimental person

uetto sūtsu ウエットスーツ wet suit

- *Sensuifu ga uetto sūtsu o kite imasu.*
  The diver is wearing a wet suit.

uiggu ウイッグ wig
- *Kanojo wa terebi ni deru tabi ni chigatta uiggu o tsukete imasu.*
  Each time she appears on TV, she wears a different wig.

uiikudē ウイークデー weekday
- *Uiikudē wa koko ni chūsha dekimasen.*
  Parking is prohibited here on weekdays.

uiikuendo ウイークエンド weekend
- *Raishū no uiikuendo ni Kyōto de kaigō ga arimasu.*
  We'll have a meeting next weekend in Kyoto.

uiiku pointo ウイークポイント weak point
- *Kare no uiiku pointo wa gaikō ni mikeiken na ten desu.*
  His weak point is his lack of experience in foreign affairs.

uindo ウインド *see* **uindō**

uindō ウインドー window
- *Uindō ni aru akai sētā wa ikura desu ka?*
  How much is the red sweater in the window?

uindō-shoppingu ウインドーショッピング window-shopping
- *Gaikoku no machi de uindō-shoppingu o tanoshimimashita.*
  We enjoyed window-shopping in foreign cities.

uindosāfin ウインドサーフィン windsurfing
- *Wakai dansei ga uindosāfin o shite imasu.*
  Young men are windsurfing.

uingu ウイング wing
- *Nikkō wa dochira no uingu desu ka, minami desu ka, kita desu ka?*
  In which wing is Japan Airlines located—north or south?

uinku suru ウインクする to wink
- *Gaijin ga tōrisugari ni uinku shite ikimashita.*

A foreigner winked at me when passing by.

uintā-supōtsu ウインタースポーツ winter sports
- *Uintā-supōtsu o tanoshimimashō!*
  Let's enjoy winter sports!

uisukii ウイスキー whisky
- *Uisukii de futsukayoi o shimashita.*
  The whisky gave me a hangover.

uitto ウイット wit
- *Kare no hanashi wa itsumo uitto ni tonde imasu.*
  His conversation is always full of wit.

ūman pawā ウーマンパワー [Japanese Usage: woman power] women's strength and ability
- *Ūman pawā o kesshū shite tsugi no senkyo de wa yori ōku no josei giin o Kokkai ni okurimashō.*
  Let's consolidate our female strength and send more women to the Diet in this next election than ever before.
- *Aru bun'ya de wa ūman pawā ga takaku hyōka sarete imasu.*
  In certain fields, women's abilities are highly appreciated.

ūman ribu ウーマンリブ women's liberation, Women's Lib
- *ūman ribu o tēma ni shita ronbun*
  a thesis with women's liberation as its theme

uōkingu ウオーキング walking; **~suru** する to walk
- *Uōkingu wa kenkō ni ichiban ii desu.*
  Walking is the best thing for your health.
- *Mori no naka o uōkingu shinagara, hana o tsumimashita.*
  I picked flowers while walking in the woods.

uokka ウオッカ vodka
- *Kare wa uokka o takusan nonde ita node berobero ni narimashita.*
  He drank lots of vodka and got very drunk.

uōku ウオーク walk
- *kurihiroi no uōku*

a walk for gathering chestnuts

uōmingu appu ウオーミングアップ warming up
- *Senshu ga shiai no mae ni uōmingu appu o shite imasu.*
  Players are warming up before the game.

uōningu ranpu ウオーニングランプ warning lamp
- *Kuruma no keikiban ni akai uōningu ranpu ga tsukimashita.*
  A red warning lamp lit up on the dashboard of the car.

uosshaburu ウオッシャブル washable
- *Uosshaburu na sozai ga benri desu.*
  Washable material is useful.

uōtā ウオーター water
- *Suidō no mizu wa mazui node, sūpā de binzume no mineraru uōtā o kaimasu.*
  I hate the taste of tap water, so I buy bottled mineral water at the supermarket.

uōtā-furonto ウオーターフロント waterfront
- *Uōtā-furonto no chiiki ga don don kaihatsu sarete ikimasu.*
  The waterfront district is being developed rapidly.

uōtā-purūfu ウオータープルーフ waterproof
- *Kono tokei wa uōtā-purūfu desu.*
  This watch is waterproof.

uotoka ウオトカ *see* **uokka**

uotsuka ウオツカ *see* **uokka**

uran ウラン [German: *Uran*] uranium
- *Uran wa genshiro no nenryō ni tsukawaremasu.*
  Uranium is used as fuel for a nuclear reactor.

ūru ウール wool
- *ūru no mafurā*
  a wool scarf

urutora C ウルトラC *see* **urutora shii**

urutora shii ウルトラ・シー ウルトラC [Japanese Usage:

ultra C] feat, genius
- *Kare no urutora shii ga chiisai kikai kōba o sekai no dai kigyō ni shita no desu.*

It was his genius that turned a small machine shop into a giant international company.

V

VIP *see* **bippu**
vaiorin ヴァイオリン *see* **baiorin**
vaitamin ヴァイタミン *see* **bitamin**
vēru ヴェール *see* **bēru**
veteran ヴェテラン *see* **beteran**
vividdo ヴィヴィッド *see* **bibiddo**
vōkaru ヴォーカル *see* **bōkaru**
vokyaburarii ヴォキャブラリー *see* **bokyaburarii**

W

wādo purosessā ワードプロセッサー *see* **wāpuro**
wādorōbu ワードローブ wardrobe closet
- *ki de dekita gōka na wādorōbu*

a gorgeous wardrobe made of wood
waffuru ワッフル waffle
- *Jussai no musume ga waffuru o tsukutte kuremashita.*

My ten-year-old daughter made waffles for me.
wagon ワゴン wagon, car, station wagon
- *Uētā ga ryōri o wagon ni nosete hakonde kimashita.*

A waiter brought the meals out on a cart.

- *Wagon-sha de kodomo-tachi o kyanpu mura made tsurete ikimashita.*
  I took the children to a camping village in a station wagon.

Wai-daburyū-shii-ē ワイ・ダブリュー・シー・エー YWCA
YWCA, Young Women's Christian Association
- *Kanojo wa Wai-daburyū-shii-ē de jimuin o shite imasu.*
  She is working as an office worker at the YWCA.

waido ワイド wide, extra-long
- *shinbun no waido ban*
  a wide edition of a newspaper
- *terebi no waido bangumi*
  an extra-long TV program

waido-renzu ワイドレンズ [Japanese Usage] wide-angle lens
- *Waido-renzu o tsukau to, enkinkan ga hakkiri demasu.*
  If you use a wide-angle lens, the distance appears distinctly.

waido sukuriin ワイドスクリーン wide screen
- *Eiga o waido sukuriin de jōei shimasu.*
  They show movies on a wide screen.

Wai-emu-shii-ē ワイ・エム・シー・エー YMCA YMCA,
Young Men's Christian Association
- *Kare wa Wai-emu-shii-ē no jūdō kurabu de ii tomodachi o tsukurimashita.*
  He made some good friends at the YMCA judo club.

waifu ワイフ wife
- *Shinkon no kare wa waifu no koto bakari hanashite imasu.*
  As he is newly married, he is always talking about his wife.

wain ワイン wine
- *Furansu kara yunyū shita gokujō no wain*
  the finest wine imported from France

wain-gurasu ワイングラス wineglass
- *Wain-gurasu ga tēburu kara ochite yuka de kudakemashita.*

A wineglass fell off the table and smashed on the floor.

waipā ワイパー windshield wiper

- *Waipā no chōshi ga warui kara, mite moraimasu.*
  Something is wrong with the windshield wipers, so I'll have them checked.

wairudo ワイルド wild

- *Ano rokku myūjishan ni wa wairudo na miryoku ga arimasu.*
  That rock musician has a wild appeal.

wairudo pitchi ワイルドピッチ wild pitch

- *Wairudo pitchi de rannā ga sanrui ni susumimashita.*
  A runner advanced to third because of the wild pitch.

waishatsu ワイシャツ or Ｙシャツ [Japanese Usage: white shirt] dress shirt

- *Watashi wa kono guriin no nekutai ni au atarashii waishatsu ga hoshii no desu.*
  I need a new dress shirt that will go with this green tie.
- *Waishatsu sugata de jimu o totte imasu.*
  They are doing office work in their dress shirts.

waiya ワイヤ *see* **waiyā**

waiyā ワイヤー to wire, connect electrically

- *Kono futatsu o waiyā de musunde kudasai.*
  Please wire these two together.

waiyaresu maiku ワイヤレスマイク wireless mike

- *Kisha ga waiyaresu maiku de gaitō rokuon no intabyū o shite imasu.*
  A reporter is conducting a curbside interview with a wireless mike.

wakkusu ワックス wax

- *Kono yuka wa wakkusu o nutta bakari desu node, ki o tsukete kudasai.*
  This floor has just been waxed, so please be careful.

wākā ワーカー worker

- *Ano kōjō ni wa gosen nin no wākā ga imasu.*
  There are five thousand workers at that factory.

wākahorikku ワーカホリック workaholic
- *Nihon no bijinesuman wa wākahorikku da to hinan sarete imasu.*
  Japanese businessmen are criticized for being workaholics.

wākingu ūman ワーキングウーマン working woman *see* **kyaria ūman**
- *Airon no iru sozai wa wākingu ūman ni wa ninki ga arimasen.*
  Fabric that needs ironing is not popular among working women.

wākubukku ワークブック workbook
- *Kono tekisuto ni wa ii wākubukku ga tsuite imasu.*
  This textbook has a good workbook that goes with it.

wakuchin ワクチン [German: *Vakzin*] vaccine
- *Kodomo ni hashika yobō no wakuchin o shimasu.*
  We vaccinate children against measles.

wākushoppu ワークショップ workshop
- *konpyūtā no wākushoppu*
  a computer workshop

wan-man ワンマン one-man, bossy person
- *wan-man basu*
  a one-man-operated bus
- *Wan-man keiei no kaisha wa sakiyuki ga kurai desu.*
  A company with an autocratic president is doomed.
- *Kare wa kaisha de wa feminisuto desu ga uchi de wa wan-man na otto desu.*
  He's nice to women at the office but is a bossy husband at home.

wan-man shō ワンマンショー one-man show
- *Yūbe no amachua engeikai wa bosu no wan-man shō deshita.*

Last night's amateur entertainment was a one-man show by our boss.

wan-piisu ワンピース one-piece (dress)
- *Sono futago no shōjo wa o-soroi no wan-piisu o kite imasu.*

The twin girls are wearing identical one-piece dresses.

wan pointo ワンポイント one point
- *Kono kikaku wa wan pointo ki ni iranai tokoro ga arimasu.*

There is one point in this plan that I don't like.

wan-rūmu manshon ワンルームマンション [Japanese Usage: one-room mansion] one-room apartment
- *Kare no wan-rūmu manshon wa itsumo chirakatte imasu.*

His one-room apartment is always untidy.

wansaido gēmu ワンサイド・ゲーム [Japanese Usage] one-sided game
- *Wansaido gēmu wa tsumaranai desu ne.*

One-sided games aren't fun, are they?
- *Shiai wa wansaido gēmu ni owarimashita.*

A one-sided game ended the match.

wan suteppu ワンステップ one step
- *Kono shigoto wa kare ni totte shōrai e no wan suteppu to shite daiji desu.*

This task is an important step toward his future.

wan uē ワンウエー one way
- *Kono tōri wa wan uē desu.*

This is a one-way street.

wan uei ワンウエイ *see* **wan uē**

wāpuro ワープロ word processor, word processing
- *Wāpuro de genkō o kakimasu.*

I write manuscripts on my word processor.

wārudo rekōdo ワールドレコード world record
- *Kanojo wa suiei de wārudo rekōdo o yaburimashita.*

She broke the world record in swimming.

warutsu ワルツ waltz

• *Chūnen no kappuru ga yūga ni warutsu o odotte imasu.*
A middle-aged couple is waltzing gracefully.

wāsuto ワースト worst

• *Sono shō wa wāsuto bangumi no nanbā wan ni ranku sarete imasu.*
That show is ranked the number one worst program.

watto ワット watt

• *hyaku watto no denkyū*
a 100-watt bulb

wea ウェア *see* **uea**

wēbu ウェーブ *see* **uēbu**

wedingu ウェディング *see* **uedingu**

wedingu doresu ウェディングドレス *see* **uedingu doresu**

weitā ウェイター *see* **uētā**

weito ウェイト *see* **uēto**

weitoresu ウェイトレス *see* **uētoresu**

wesutan ウェスタン *see* **uesutan**

wesuto ウェスト *see* **uesuto**

Wesuto-kōsuto ウェストコースト *see* **Uesuto-kōsuto**

wetto ウェット *see* **uetto**

wiggu ウィッグ *see* **uiggu**

wiikudē ウィークデー *see* **uiikudē**

wiiku pointo ウィークポイント *see* **uiiku pointo**

windō ウィンドー *see* **uindō**

windosāfin ウィンドサーフィン *see* **uindosāfin**

windō shoppingu ウィンドーショッピング *see* **uindō shoppingu**

wingu ウィング *see* **uingu**

winku suru ウィンクする *see* **uinku suru**

wisukii ウィスキー *see* **uisukii**

witto ウィット *see* **uitto**

wōkingu ウォーキング *see* **uōkingu**

wōku ウォーク *see* **uōku**

wōmingu appu ウォーミングアップ *see* **uōmingu appu**

wōningu ranpu ウォーニングランプ *see* **uōningu ranpu**

wosshaburu ウォッシャブル *see* **uosshaburu**

wōtā ウォーター *see* **uōtā**

wōtāfuronto ウォーターフロント *see* **uōtā-furonto**

wōtāpurūfu ウォータープルーフ *see* **uōtā-purūfu**

X

X *see* **ekkusu**

Y

YMCA *see* **Wai-emu-shii-ē**

Y shatsu Ｙシャツ *see* **waishatsu**

YWCA *see* **Wai-daburyū-shii-ē**

yādo ヤード yard
- *Kono kiji wa ichi yādo ikura desu ka?*
  How much is this cloth per yard?

yangu ヤング young
- *Gaisha wa yangu ni wa chotto te ga demasen ne.*
  Owning a foreign car is beyond the reach of most young
  people, isn't it?

yangu adaruto ヤングアダルト young adult
- *Kono shōhin no tāgetto wa yangu adaruto desu.*
  The target consumer for this product is young adults.

Yankii ヤンキー Yankee, American
- *Nōka no hitori musuko ga Yankii musume to kakeochi
  shimashita.*

The farmer's only son eloped with an American girl.

yāru ヤール *see* **yādo**

yesu イェス *see* **iesu**

yesu man イェスマン *see* **iesu man**

yoga ヨガ yoga
- *Seishin shuyō no tame ni yoga o shimasu.*
  I do yoga to cultivate my mind.

yōga ヨーガ *see* **yoga**

yōguruto ヨーグルト yogurt
- *Karushiumu no ōi yōguruto o tabemashita.*
  I ate yogurt, which is high in calcium.

yotto ヨット yacht
- *Mizuumi e yotto ni nori ni ikimasu.*
  We go yachting on the lake.

yotto hābā ヨットハーバー yacht harbor
- *Gaikoku no yotto ga yotto hābā ni hairimashita.*
  A foreign yacht entered the yacht harbor.

Yudaya ユダヤ [Latin: *Judaea*] Judea, Jewish
- *Yudaya kyōkai*
  a synagogue

yū kā ユーカー Uカー [Japanese Usage] used car
- *yū kā no chirashi*
  a flyer for used cars

yūmoa ユーモア humor
- *Kare wa majimesugite yūmoa o kaisanai no desu.*
  He is too serious to have a sense of humor.

yūmorasu ユーモラス humorous
- *yūmorasu na supiichi*
  a humorous speech

yunibāshitii ユニバーシティー university
- *Kare wa Amerika no yunibāshitii kara kita kōkan kyōju desu.*
  He is an exchange professor from an American university.

yunifōmiti ユニフォーミティ *see* **yunifōmitii**

yunifōmitii ユニフォーミティー uniformity
- *Ima wa arayuru hōmen de yunifōmitii ga kyōchō sareru jidai desu.*
  We live in an age when uniformity is emphasized in all fields.

yunifōmu ユニフォーム uniform
- *Yunifōmu o kita uētā ga ryōri o hakonde imasu.*
  Waiters in uniforms are carrying dishes.

yunihōmu ユニホーム *see* **yunifōmu**

yuniiku ユニーク unique
- *Kare no zuihitsu wa yuniiku na sutairu de dokusha o hikitsukemasu.*
  His essays' unique style attracts readers.

yunitto ユニット unit, pre-fabricated
- *yunitto kagu no seizōmoto*
  a manufacturer of pre-fab furniture

yūsu ユース *see* **yūsu hosuteru**

yūsufuru ユースフル useful
- *yūsufuru na adobaisu*
  useful advice

yūsu hosuteru ユースホステル youth hostel
- *Yūsu hosuteru wa zenkoku itaru tokoro ni sanzai shite imasu.*
  Youth hostels are found here and there throughout the country.

yū-tān ユーターン or Uターン U-turn; **~suru** する to make a U-turn, return
- *Kiseikyaku no yū-tān de Tōkyō-eki wa daikonzatsu desu.*
  Tokyo Station is very crowded due to the return of passengers who went home for their holidays.
- *Yū-tan shita totan ni pato-kā ni tsukamarimashita.*
  The moment I made a U-turn, I got stopped by a police car.

yūtopia ユートピア Utopia
- *Kare wa isshō yūtopia o motomete samayoimashita.*
He wandered about searching for Utopia his whole life.

yūzā ユーザー user
- *Yūzā ni shōhin mihon o okurimasu.*
I'll send trade samples to users.

Z

zemi ゼミ *see* **zemināru**

zemināru ゼミナール seminar
- *Ashita Nihon kotengeki no zemināru ga arimasu.*
We'll have a seminar on Japanese classical drama tomorrow.

zenerēshon ゼネレーション *see* **jenerēshon**

zentoruman ゼントルマン *see* **jentoruman**

zerii ゼリー jelly, jello
- *Zerii wa karukute ii dezāto ni narimasu.*
Jello is light and makes a nice dessert.

zero ゼロ zero
- *Zero o daiyaru shimashita.*
I dialed zero.
- *Kanojo no tenmongaku no chishiki wa zero desu.*
Her knowledge of astronomy amounts to zero.

zesuchā ゼスチャー *see* **jesuchā**

zesuchua ゼスチュア *see* **jesuchā**

zubon ズボン [French: *jupon*] trousers, pants
- *Kare wa itsumo airon no kakatte iru zubon o haite imasu.*
He is always wearing pressed trousers.

zukku ズック [Dutch: *doek*] canvas, canvas shoes
- *Kanojo wa zukku no fukuro o sagete imasu.*
She is carrying a canvas bag.

- *Kare wa zukku no kutsu o haite shigoto ni kimasu.*
  He comes to work wearing canvas shoes.

zōn ゾーン zone

- *Sono shi o mittsu no zōn ni bunkatsu shimashita.*
  They divided the city into three zones.

zūmu ズーム zoom lens

- *Zūmu o tsukaeba, shashin wa pinboke ni narimasen.*
  If you use a zoom lens, the picture won't be out of focus.

zūmu renzu ズームレンズ *see* **zūmu**

Place Names

Continents
Afurika アフリカ Africa
Ajia アジア Asia
Kita-amerika 北アメリカ North America
Minami-amerika 南アメリカ South America
Oseania オセアニア Oceania
Yōroppa ヨーロッパ Europe

Countries
Afuganisutan アフガニスタン Afghanistan
Airurando アイルランド Ireland
Aisurando アイスランド Iceland
Amerika アメリカ the United States of America
Angora アンゴラ Angola
Arubania アルバニア Albania
Arujeria アルジェリア Algeria
Arumenia アルメニア Armenia
Aruzenchin アルゼンチン Argentina
Azerubaijan アゼルバイジャン Azerbaijan
Banguradeshu バングラデシュ Bangladesh
Benan ベナン Benin

Benezuera ベネズエラ Venezuela
Berarūshi ベラルーシ Belarus
Berugii ベルギー Belgium
Betonamu ベトナム Vietnam
Boribia ボリビア Bolivia
Burajiru ブラジル Brazil
Burugaria ブルガリア Bulgaria
Burukina-faso ブルキナファソ Burkina Faso
Burunji ブルンジ Burundi
Chado チャド Chad
Cheko チェコ Czech Republic
Chiri チリ Chile
Chunijia チュニジア Tunisia
Denmāku デンマーク Denmark
Doitsu ドイツ Germany
Dominika ドミニカ Dominican Republic
Echiopia エチオピア Ethiopia
Ejiputo エジプト Egypt
Ekuadoru エクアドル Ecuador
Eru-sarubadoru エルサルバドル El Salvador
Finrando フィンランド Finland
Firipin フィリピン the Philippines
Furansu フランス France
Gaiana ガイアナ Guyana
Gāna ガーナ Ghana
Ginia ギニア Guinea
Girisha ギリシャ Greece
Guatemara グアテマラ Guatemala
Haichi ハイチ Haiti
Hangarii ハンガリー Hungary
Honjurasu ホンジュラス Honduras
Iemen イエメン Yemen
Igirisu イギリス United Kingdom, Great Britain, England

Indo インド India
Indoneshia インドネシア Indonesia
Iraku イラク Iraq
Iran イラン Iran
Isuraeru イスラエル Israel
Itaria イタリア Italy
Jamaika ジャマイカ Jamaica
Jinbabue ジンバブエ Zimbabwe
Kamerūn カメルーン Cameroon
Kanada カナダ Canada
Kanbojia カンボジア Cambodia, Kampuchea
Kazafu カザフ Kazakhstan
Kenia ケニア Kenya
Kirugisu キルギス Kyrgyzstan
Kongo コンゴ Congo
Koronbia コロンビア Columbia
Kosuta-rika コスタリカ Costa Rica
Kōto-jiboāru コートジボアール Côte D'Ivoire
Kuroachia クロアチア Croatia
Kuwēto クウェート Kuwait
Kyūba キューバ Cuba
Madagasukaru マダガスカル Madagascar
Maraui マラウイ Malawi
Marēshia マレーシア Malaysia
Mekishiko メキシコ Mexico
Minami-afurika 南アフリカ South Africa
Mongoru モンゴル Mongolia
Mōritania モーリタニア Mauritania
Morokko モロッコ Morocco
Morudoba モルドバ Moldova
Mozanbiiku モザンビーク Mozambique
Myanmā ミャンマー Myanmar
Naijeria ナイジェリア Nigeria

Nepāru ネパール Nepal
Nijēru ニジェール Niger
Nikaragua ニカラグア Nicaragua
Noruwē ノルウェー Norway
Nyū-jiirando ニュージーランド New Zealand
Oranda オランダ Holland, the Netherlands
Ōsutoraria オーストラリア Australia
Ōsutoria オーストリア Austria
Pakisutan パキスタン Pakistan
Panama パナマ Panama
Papua-nyū-ginia パプアニューギニア Papua New Guinea
Paraguai パラグアイ Paraguay
Perū ペルー Peru
Pōrando ポーランド Poland
Porutogaru ポルトガル Portugal
Raosu ラオス Laos
Ratobia ラトビア Latvia
Rebanon レバノン Lebanon
Riberia リベリア Liberia
Ritoania リトアニア Lithuania
Roshia ロシア Russia
Rūmania ルーマニア Romania
Ruwanda ルワンダ Rwanda
Sauji-arabia サウジアラビア Saudi Arabia
Senegaru セネガル Senegal
Shiera-reone シエラレオネ Sierra Leone
Shingapōru シンガポール Singapore
Shiria シリア Syria
Somaria ソマリア Somalia
Sūdan スーダン Sudan
Suisu スイス Switzerland
Supein スペイン Spain
Suri-ranka スリランカ Sri Lanka

Surobakia スロバキア Slovakia
Suwēden スウェーデン Sweden
Tai タイ Thailand
Tajiku タジク Tadzhikistan
Tanzania タンザニア Tanzania
Tōgo トーゴ Togo
Toruko トルコ Turkey
Torukumen トルクメン Turkmenistan
Uganda ウガンダ Uganda
Ukuraina ウクライナ Ukraine
Uruguai ウルグアイ Uruguay
Uzubeku ウズベク Uzbekistan
Yorudan ヨルダン Jordan
Yūgosurabia ユーゴスラビア Yugoslavia
Zaiiru ザイール Zaire
Zanbia ザンビア Zambia

Cities

Ankara アンカラ Ankara
Amusuterudamu アムステルダム Amsterdam
Atene アテネ Athens
Atoranta アトランタ Atlanta
Bagudaddo バグダッド Baghdad
Bankoku バンコク Bangkok
Bankūbā バンクーバー Vancouver
Benechia ベネチア Venice
Benisu ベニス Venice
Beogurādo ベオグラード Belgrade
Berun ベルン Bern
Berurin ベルリン Berlin
Bienchan ビエンチャン Vientiane
Bogota ボゴタ Bogota
Bon ボン Bonn

Bosuton ボストン Boston
Budapesuto ブダペスト Budapest
Buenosu-airesu ブエノスアイレス Buenos Aires
Burajiria ブラジリア Brasilia
Buryusseru ブリュッセル Brussels
Daburin ダブリン Dublin
Denbā デンバー Denver
Detoroito デトロイト Detroit
Erusaremu エルサレム Jerusalem
Furankufuruto フランクフルト Frankfurt
Habana ハバナ Havana
Hanoi ハノイ Hanoi
Herushinki ヘルシンキ Helsinki
Honkon ホンコン Hong Kong
Honoruru ホノルル Honolulu
Isutanbūru イスタンブール Istanbul
Jakaruta ジャカルタ Jakarta
Kairo カイロ Cairo
Kēpu-taun ケープタウン Cape Town
Kopenhāgen コペンハーゲン Copenhagen
Kuara-runpūru クアラルンプール Kuala Lumpur
Kuwēto クウェート Kuwait
Kyanbera キャンベラ Canberra
Madoriido マドリード Madrid
Manira マニラ Manila
Mekishiko-shitii メキシコシティー Mexico City
Meruborun メルボルン Melbourne
Mosukuwa モスクワ Moscow
Myunhen ミュンヘン Munich
Nyū-derii ニューデリー New Delhi
Nyū-yōku ニューヨーク New York
Ōkurando オークランド Auckland
Osuro オスロ Oslo

Otawa オタワ Ottawa
Pari パリ Paris
Pāsu パース Perth
Pekin ペキン 北京 Beijing
Punon-pen プノンペン Phnom Penh
Puraha プラハ Prague
Rangūn ラングーン Rangoon
Rasu-begasu ラスベガス Las Vegas
Reikyabiku レイキャビク Reykjavik
Rima リマ Lima
Rio-de-janeiro リオデジャネイロ Rio de Janeiro
Risubon リスボン Lisbon
Riyado リヤド Riyadh
Rōma ローマ Rome
Rondon ロンドン London
Rosanzerusu ロサンゼルス Los Angeles
San-furanshisuko サンフランシスコ San Francisco
Shiatoru シアトル Seattle
Shidonii シドニー Sydney
Shikago シカゴ Chicago
Shingapōru シンガポール Singapore
Suri-jayawarudenepura スリジャヤワルデネプラ Sri
  Jayewardenepura
Souru ソウル Seoul
Sutokkuhorumu ストックホルム Stockholm
Taipei タイペイ 台北 Taipei
Teheran テヘラン Tehran
Teru-abibu テルアビブ Tel Aviv
Toronto トロント Toronto
Warushawa ワルシャワ Warsaw
Washinton ワシントン Washington
Werinton ウェリントン Wellington
Wiin ウィーン Vienna